THE
GANGBUSTER

THE
GANGBUSTER

PETER BLEKSLEY

TO CATCH A GANGSTER, YOU HAVE TO LIVE LIKE ONE

JOHN BLAKE

Published by John Blake Publishing Ltd,
3 Bramber Court, 2 Bramber Road,
London W14 9PB, England

www.johnblakebooks.com

www.facebook.com/johnblakebooks ▪
www.twitter.com/jblakebooks ▪

First published in paperback in 2002
This edition published in 2017

ISBN: 978 1 78606 248 2

British Library Cataloguing–in–Publication Data:

A catalogue record for this book is available from the British Library.

Design by www.envydesign.co.uk

Printed in Great Britain by CPI Group (UK) Ltd

3 5 7 9 10 8 6 4 2

Papers used by John Blake Publishing are natural, recyclable products made from
wood grown in sustainable forests. The manufacturing processes conform to the
environmental regulations of the country of origin.

Every attempt has been made to contact the relevant copyright–holders,
but some were unobtainable. We would be grateful if the appropriate
people could contact us.

For Sarah, Brad, Jack and Ben. You're my life.

And to the brave men and women working
undercover who continue to tackle terrorism and
serious and organised crime, I salute you.

CONTENTS

ACKNOWLEDGEMENTS

The names of certain serving police officers have been changed throughout this book to protect ongoing investigations.

PREFACE

He was the best undercover cop the police ever had.

In a ten–year career with Scotland Yard's most secretive squad, Peter Bleksley helped nail dozens of crooks and stopped millions of pounds' worth of drugs and counterfeit cash hitting the streets.

He bent the rules but he got results.

A master of disguise, a crack shot with a pistol, his exploits in the dangerous world of criminal subterfuge earned him thirteen commendations for bravery and a reputation that spread throughout Europe and America.

He was the cop's own crook, skilled in the dangerous ways of the underworld. He knew more about cocaine, heroin, cannabis, LSD, ecstasy and amphetamines than any other serving officer. He needed to. His skill in handling drugs, of talking the language of the perilous world of international trafficking, kept him alive.

THE GANGBUSTER

Peter Bleksley adopted the guise of a big-time drug-dealer, gangster, counterfeiter, even hit-man, to combat some of the most powerful and ruthless crooks in the world.

He went deeper undercover than any other detective before him. A maverick by nature, there were times when he crossed the line, taking cocaine and cannabis when necessary to prevent detection by suspicious and sometimes paranoid pushers.

Bleksley was the James Bond of Scotland Yard, slipping effortlessly into countless roles in seedy drug dens or five-star hotel suites. He once made love all night to a cocaine-addicted aerobics instructor as he pursued a leading envoy suspected of smuggling huge amounts of cocaine into Britain in his diplomatic bags.

He faced shotguns, pistols and knives. He faced the wrath of the Mafia and the IRA. So successful did he become in penetrating the inner sanctums of international crime, that the godfathers of organised crime in New York hired a professional hit-man to fly to London to kill him. He'd blown one of their big operations out of the water and they wanted him dead.

Bleksley was regularly hired out to police forces across Britain to carry out dangerous undercover missions that their own men could not, or would not, undertake.

Posing as a swaggering drug-dealer, he regularly set traps for international traffickers and baited them with up to £350,000 of the Metropolitan Police Commissioner's money.

He was at the centre of many spectacular police operations in which armed officers seized some of the world's most dangerous crooks and met violence with violence. The words 'courageous', 'fearless' and 'professional' feature readily in his numerous commendations. The top award, the Commissioner's High Commendation, can only now be made public because any media publicity at the time, in 1990, could have placed his life in even greater danger.

In his recommendation for the honour, Bleksley's boss, Commander Roy Penrose, head of the Yard's SO10 branch wrote, 'All of us who know DC Bleksley, and more especially those of us who have had the pleasure of working with him or observing him at work in an undercover role, have come to accept the high standards of excellence, bravery, and ingenuity he continually displays.

'At the same time, I am sure that none of us fully realises the extent of the danger and few of us would want to change places with him. He is an officer dedicated to his role with the unique ability to think quickly on his feet as the circumstances change. While it is impossible to quantify, it is nonetheless an indisputable fact that DC Bleksley's actions in bringing about the early arrest and successful conviction of so many career criminals have saved this force in particular and the police service in general many thousands of pounds in man hours that would have been necessary to achieve a similar result by more conventional methods.

'DC Bleksley has consistently over a period of years maintained the highest standards of professionalism and integrity in the most difficult and dangerous role of undercover officer, both within and beyond the Metropolitan Police District. Moreover, he has shown a level of bravery far beyond the normal course of his duties and, in my view, is richly deserving of the Commissioner's High Commendation.'

THE GANGBUSTER

Peter Bleksley lived under a multitude of different aliases as he hunted down criminal scum the length and breadth of the country. Many swore revenge. Bleksley, now retired, still keeps a wary eye over his shoulder and is cautious of any unexpected knock at the door.

He could have written this book under the protection of yet another pseudonym. But he has decided to come out of the shadows and tell his remarkable story in his own words and under his own name, with candour, with courage and with humour.

Co-author Mike Fielder was the former Chief Crime Reporter of the *Sun* newspaper. His previous bestsellers include *Killer on the Loose*, the story of the Rachel Nickell murder on Wimbledon Common, and *Alibi at Midnight*, the story of the Barn restaurant murder in Braintree, Essex.

Chapter One

DON'T GO HOME

Four million quid. There it was, inches away from me on a hotel table. Not in conventional currency, but the world's deadliest commodity – heroin. The guy sitting opposite me was there to sell it. I was there to buy it. This was the trap we'd set for one of the biggest fish in international drug trafficking. And we were about to fry him alive.

In smoky room 4136 of the Gatwick Hilton, I carefully weighed and tested thirty 500g bags of the smack. It was a time for steely nerves and a cool composure that belied the ever-tightening knots in my stomach. When I talk about big-time drug-dealing, this was premier league.

It had taken months of careful planning, the help of a high-level informant, and the combined efforts of Scotland Yard's SO10 undercover unit, Customs and Excise, the American Drug Enforcement Agency and the Royal Ulster Constabulary to sow the seeds of this dangerous sting.

THE GANGBUSTER

Ranged against us in Operation Zulu Cricket was the fearsome might of the IRA, the corporate capacity of the Mafia godfathers plus a motley assortment of heroin dealers and money-launderers spread halfway round the world. You didn't get a much more potent combination than that on a drugs bust. It's a cliché to say it was like a plot from a blockbuster novel, but it was. And I was in the thick of it.

I had been dropped into the operation posing as a big-shot heroin dealer after the US-based informant had tipped off the authorities in the USA and in Britain about a gang offering phenomenal quantities of heroin for sale in London. They were talking 20kg a time on a weekly basis. Millions and millions of pounds in cash terms. A lot of misery and death in human terms. And, incidentally, the informant had said if cash wasn't always available to buy the heroin, then they would take guns and ammunition instead. A terrifying scenario.

I moved into room 4136 of the Hilton, nestling beside Gatwick's south terminal and a good cosmopolitan venue for a drugs deal, where people come and go without attracting too much attention, on Monday, 29 June 1992. The technical wizards of Scotland Yard had been in before me to wire the place for sound and insert tiny hidden video cameras. The crack shots of Sussex Police Tactical Firearms unit had discreetly settled themselves into hiding places inside and outside the hotel. Armed back up had been deemed essential after intelligence reports suggested a couple of tooled-up minders might be sent along to watch over the heroin deal.

Alan James Johnston arrived in the hotel reception carrying an obviously heavy holdall. The trade was on. The signal went out to all units: 'Zulu Cricket is go.' He was allocated the room we'd had bugged up. He took the lift up to the fourth floor and rapped on the door.

'Hello, Al,' I said, shaking his hand gingerly.

This was the Al I'd been introduced to a few nights earlier at a four-star London hotel as we baited our trap with a juicy wedge of banknotes held in a West End safety deposit box. The gang had seen our funds. Now it was time for a sight of the smack.

'Hi, Peter, how are you doing?'

'I'm fine.'

The arrangement was that Johnston would phone other members of the syndicate once our transaction had been completed. The cash, close on half a million, would be handed over in central London. Cut and recycled a dozen times, the heroin would more than quadruple in value by the time it hit the streets. I knew there was no way big Al was going to leave room 4136 to make that call and set this consignment of death on its fateful journey.

Formalities exchanged – and formalities do exist even in the mercenary world of drug-dealing – we sat down to the tense business of international trafficking, our £4 million heroin bounty nestling between us. First, I weighed each of the cling film-wrapped packages on my portable scales, part of my dealer's undercover kit I kept with me at all times on covert drug missions. All present and correct in 500g batches. A nod and a smile from Johnston.

Then it was on to testing the biggest pile of Class A narcotics I'd ever seen in my life. It took me nearly four hours to test the powder. My painstaking but infallible method of determining the quality of heroin was to take a tiny sample from each bag and burn it on silver foil over a lighter flame. It was time-consuming but necessary. No dealer worth his salt would walk away with an untested batch of the gear. And, as the hard-nosed buyer, I had to convince Al and his pals that I knew what I was doing and was only going to accept top-grade stuff. So every one of the thirty bags had to be slit, a pinch taken out with the blade of a Stanley knife and the powder gently incinerated in front of us. If it left a heavy blackened residue, it would indicate that it had already been cut with some additive (such as baking powder or talc), substantially reducing its purity and therefore its value. Al's heroin burned well, with barely a scrap of residue left behind. This was top dollar gear.

Being sure not to inhale the pungent fumes was vital. Even accidentally 'chasing the dragon' would have rendered me ineffective for the bust I knew was about to happen. As it was, I had nothing more than a slight headache to concern me as we shook hands again and prepared to go our separate ways, our transaction complete.

'Nice doing business with you,' he said.

And then he walked slap-bang into the awesome power of a police ambush.

'ARMED POLICE, STAY WHERE YOU ARE.'

He was seized by three or four burly cops. To make it look as if I was also being arrested, and preserving my undercover role, the police team grabbed me as well and flung me on the floor beside Johnston, slapping handcuffs on me with such force that I was bruised for days.

We all met up later that evening for a celebration drink,

toasting another triumph for SO10. The secret squad had pulled it off again with what was then the biggest ever land seizure of heroin in the UK. Messages were relayed to law enforcement agencies around the globe that we had picked off a key player in the world's biggest drug ring. More would certainly follow.

Amid the euphoria of that evening, I never dreamed that Operation Zulu Cricket was to blight my life forever.

* * *

It was nine months later and I was motoring towards my local in south-east London on an unexpected early evening break from SO10. It was a warm spring evening, the radio was playing golden oldies and I was only minutes from a decent pint. My mobile rang. It was Detective Chief Inspector Neil Germaine calling from the squad office at Scotland Yard. 'Whatever happens,' he said urgently, 'don't go home tonight.'

'What's up, Guv?'

'Can't say over the mobile, but the wheel's come off big time.'

I slowed the Porsche almost to a standstill, anxious for more details.

'Who do you live with, Blex?' he asked, using the nickname familiar to my colleagues on SO10.

An odd question, I thought, because he was the officer in charge of the welfare of the covert officers in Special Operations, the man with our files available at the push of a computer button.

'My girlfriend, Elaine,' I said.

'Right, Blex, get on the phone to her right away. Tell her to go and pack an overnight bag for the pair of you, then vanish. Book yourself into a hotel, then see me at 9.00am sharp tomorrow in my office and I'll tell you what it's all about.'

End of message.

My mind was racing. There was a touch of panic in the DCI's voice. Not like him at all. He was normally Mr Cool. There was obviously trouble brewing big time. I rang Elaine, repeated Germaine's mysterious message and arranged to see her in the pub for a much-needed drink. She was as puzzled as me.

'We've just got to do what the man says,' I told her. 'Could be anything.'

We headed for a decent hotel a few miles away from home and booked in for the night under false names, using the phoney documentation and credit cards I always carried as part of my undercover kit. Not credit cards that were going to bounce and leave the hotel out of pocket. These were creations of SO10's own M department, complete and valid in every detail, down to bank accounts in place to settle the finances. All part of the meticulous planning and attention to detail that went into the lifestyle of an undercover cop. These were the sort of contingencies we were trained for, suddenly having to switch into undercover mode at a minute's notice. But never quite like this before.

We talked through a dozen possibilities for this sudden panic. You didn't earn Mr Popular medals in my game. It could be anything. There was only one thing to do in the circumstances – we hit the mini-bar with a vengeance. I'd planned a night of passion with Elaine to alleviate the niggling worries of tomorrow but the booze took its toll and I crashed into a fitful half-sleep until dawn.

I was at the Yard at 8.00am, a good hour before my appointment with Germaine, feeling both apprehensive and hungover. I was the first in at the undercover unit's office, the Crime Operations Group, nerve centre of some of the most important ongoing police investigations here and abroad. Minutes later, a very near and dear pal of mine, who must remain nameless, sidled up to me and said, 'Do you know what this shit is about, Blex?'

'Haven't a clue,' I replied. He looked cautiously around to ensure no one else had arrived, then ushered me towards the photocopying room. He locked the door and pulled a bundle of papers from his pocket. It was a six-page report headed 'Operation Zulu Cricket'. Now it was ringing bells. The Gatwick Hilton bust.

'This is what's causing the stir,' said my pal. 'Read it and be prepared for a shock. Then put it in your pocket and take it with you. You might just need it.'

Shocked I certainly was. The mob behind the Gatwick job had put out a contract on me and was touting in the US for a hit-man to fly to Britain and take me out. It was all there, in chilling detail. But what was worse – much, much worse – was that a copy of this highly confidential document had gone missing, stolen from a police officer's car while he was out shopping. It could now be in enemy hands. And it had my *real* name in it. If the Mafia and IRA thugs behind the heroin racket had only been looking for 'Peter', the guy who'd set them up at Gatwick, they would have had a near impossible task to find me for a hit. If they now had my full name, and Bleksley is not that common, I might as well stick a target on my back. 'Bang – you're dead, Peter Bleksley.'

It took me a good ten to fifteen minutes to digest the report.

THE GANGBUSTER

I knew the job was big from the start, with international links in half a dozen different countries, from briefings I attended before the Gatwick arrest of Alan Johnston. I had been a small but crucial cog in the detention of the gang's top courier. I had become a threat to this vast criminal enterprise. I had double-crossed the Mob. And I was now very dispensable. Other top members of the gang were still at large. They had the power, the money and the resolution to exact a dreadful revenge.

The message that my part in the Gatwick bust was highly suspect got back to the drug barons when Johnston appeared in court the next day and there was no 'Peter' the drug buyer beside him in the dock. His suspicions were relayed back to the US via a network of go-betweens. They had found out I was a cop. Then the FBI picked up confirmation of a potential hit against me in bugged phone calls to an Irish bar in Boston, Massachusetts.

So here I was, thirty-five years old, in the prime of life and reading about a death sentence on me passed by aggrieved gangsters 3,000 miles away. And wondering how a copy of such a highly confidential report could ever have been 'lost' by a member of the most security-conscious unit at Scotland Yard. How could such a sensitive report, with so many ramifications around the world, come to have been pinched with such ease from a copper's car? The answer, I'm afraid, came down to thoughtlessness and lack of concentration. The officer who had compiled the report, at the request of a Deputy Assistant Commissioner who needed an urgent update, had it in a briefcase in his car when he pulled into a supermarket car park to do some shopping. He was only gone a few minutes, but this was time enough for a thief to break into the vehicle and snatch what he could. Probably an opportunist looking for cash or valuables. It happens every two minutes. But could this be more sinister? Could the report now be in the wrong hands, the people who wanted me dead and now knew exactly who I was and where I worked?

Surveillance on the drugs gang had profiled the kind of hard-case villains we were up against. The main suspect, an Irish Catholic we knew as Joe, and Alan Johnston, a known contraband smuggler from Ulster, had been seen at meetings with known middle-ranking IRA members discussing the funding of heroin shipments into the UK for onward transfer to the USA. The suggestion that guns would be acceptable as payment in lieu of cash clearly implied that the weapons could end up in terrorist hands.

The report said starkly that the gang bosses knew that 'Peter' was a policeman and not the heroin dealer they thought, and 'did not intend to let the matter rest'. Irish Joe, whose surname I can't disclose for legal reasons, told another undercover operator, this time from Customs, who had also infiltrated the gang, that they were planning to 'put a team on Peter to do the hit'. They had actively been seeking a professional hit-man to do the job and discussing locations in London where it could be successfully carried out. Irish Joe had been so confident of terminating me that he had talked to our informant about resuming the heroin deals once I had been taken out. The hit-man was to be referred to as 'the Doctor' during his mission to London and his gun was to be called 'the Doctor's bag' in all conversations among the crooks. It was chilling stuff, straight from the pages of *The Godfather*.

The Drugs Enforcement Agency in America had relayed

details of the assassination plot against me to the British Customs investigation branch on 18 July 1992, just nineteen days after the arrest of Johnston. A detective inspector at Scotland Yard was alerted by phone, followed by the DEA fax. Yet amazingly the first I knew about it was *nine months* later when my pal whisked me into the photocopying room and shoved the report under my nose. It had also been a full two weeks since the dossier had vanished from Detective Sergeant Sam Davies' car. And nobody had bothered to tell me. Every hour of every day had left me exposed. Such was the detail about the death plot, the source, the places involved, the people involved, that I knew we weren't dealing with empty threats. I'd been threatened many times. It goes with the territory. Now I was dealing with serious honchos on both sides of the Atlantic. I was potential target practice for some of the most dangerous and violent hoodlums on the planet.

What to do now? I went in to see DCI Germaine as arranged. I was now armed with vital information about my intended murder that had somehow failed to come my way until the Zulu Cricket report had gone missing. Germaine was with two of the Yard's most experienced and respected senior officers, Deputy Assistant Commissioner Roy Ramm and Detective Chief Inspector James Read of the Witness Protection Programme, which was now under the SO10 umbrella and used more for looking after frightened witnesses and informants rather than their own men.

Their mood was grim. They obviously wanted to know my feelings given the deeply ominous revelations of an hour ago in the photocopying room. I expressed my fears forcibly. Why hadn't I been told about the hit? That was serious enough. How on earth had the report been stolen from a copper's car? That made things a thousand times worse. I told them I wanted out, meaning out of my home address for good. They had turfed me out without notice the night before and it would surely be madness to return now. DCI Read's response puzzled me.

'What, out of the police?' he asked.

I said, 'No, out of my house permanently. I will need a completely new ID and address. They might be onto me already.' We agreed that the only sensible precaution at that point in time was for me to keep my head down, look for new accommodation and pray that the missing report hadn't fallen into the wrong hands.

I took my filched copy of the Zulu Cricket dossier back to the hotel and went through it line by line, with a worried Elaine at my side. I just couldn't believe that my name was in it, bold as brass. Even in internal communications, all undercover operators were supposed to be referred to by their covert aliases or by a registered number. Over the years, I had worked with so many false names I sometimes had to do a double-take at Tesco's checkout before remembering who I was supposed to be that day and making sure I proffered the right credit card. The whole Zulu Cricket cock-up made a nonsense of our squad's supposedly skilled undercover techniques devised to protect each and every operator out there in the field on frequently dangerous assignments. This looked very much like a flagrant breach of procedure which had resulted in me now facing the most serious threat of my career.

The report, referred to officially in police terms as a Briefing

Note, had been written by Detective Sergeant Davies in response to a request from the DAC in charge of Special Operations to bring him up to speed on the complexities of Zulu Cricket. So many different law enforcement agencies were involved that conflicts of interest had arisen between them, with allegations of informant-poaching and double-dealing, and a few egos had got bruised along the way. The DAC had become so concerned at the bad feeling creeping into such an important investigation that he had called a meeting with the head of the Customs Investigation branch in London in a bid to iron out the problems. The targets were just too big to risk the chances of petty in-fighting jeopardising a successful conclusion to the operation.

This highly detailed report, which also named the Customs undercover officer involved with the gang at top level, but retained the secrecy of the informant, had been left by Sam Davies in his car in a central London car park as he stopped off to do some shopping either on his way to work or on the way home. The exact details were never made clear to me.

OK, it happens. Car crime is a big, big problem. It can happen to anybody. But a dynamite report like this, left sitting in an unattended car? And by a highly trained detective. Why take it home in the first place? The inner sanctum of Scotland Yard is where material like that belongs.

I didn't know what to think. But I knew I was angry. Common sense and experience told me that some opportunist kid had snatched it looking for easy drugs money. But on the other hand ... I mean crooks have contacts all the way up the criminal ladder. If someone realised the value of the information they could have sold it on for a tasty sum. We had to consider the very serious possibility that the once-anonymous 'Peter', the pony-tailed drug-dealer, was now known to the Mafioso and the IRA as Peter Bleksley, Detective Constable, New Scotland Yard. In short it might already have put me 'in the frame' big time. We weren't talking some scrote drug-dealer from a South London sink estate. We were talking about having two of the world's most ruthless criminal organisations on my trail.

My first priority was to get myself and Elaine right away from my old address. I was struck off normal duties while I looked for a suitable, but safer, place to live. The Yard's witness protection people were on the case through their internal property purchase section. We decided to move from our pricey hotel, away from the temptation of the well-stocked mini-bar, and take a room in a lower-grade hotel a few miles away. It was a time for restraint and reflection. The Yard came up with three properties which might suit, all unoccupied police houses. Although it didn't seem awfully bright on the surface using ex-police homes as safe houses, I was assured they had all been empty long enough for them not to be traceable back to the police. They laughed at my joke about the blue light outside being a dead giveaway. Realistically, we had no choice but to take one of them and we set off on a weekend viewing trip.

We ruled out the first one instantly. It overlooked a hospital where Elaine's father had been treated for alcoholism. Too many bad memories. The next had no garage. When you've collected the baggage of life that I had, you needed a garage. And I reckoned it would be safer if I could lock the car away at night if the boyos were looking to place a bit of Semtex under it.

It was third time lucky, or so we thought. Number 4 Glendale

Mews, Beckenham, seemed a decent house in a pleasant street and was in an area I knew well and liked. But when we walked through the door, our hearts sank. It was a complete shit-house. How a police officer and his family had lived there, no matter how long ago, was unbelievable. There was total squalor everywhere. It was filthy from top to bottom. Maybe squatters had messed it up, I don't know, but one thing was sure, this was totally unacceptable. Even in the perilous situation I found myself, a Mafia bullet almost seemed more preferable.

I drove back up to the Yard to tell them, 'No deal, not in that condition, thank you very much.'

To their credit, they gave us virtually free rein to bring it up to standard at their expense. It took about a month, with help from willing friends in the building trade, to make it habitable.

No Jacuzzi and no gold taps. Just pleasantly liveable. Although I was still mightily aggrieved at my life being turned upside-down, I realised there was no mileage in upsetting the Yard with extortionate refurbishing costs. We were shipshape for £11,000. We moved in without any of the excitement that a new home usually engendered. To date it had been all stress and worry. This was a hideout, not a home.

I kept in touch with colleagues working on the Zulu Cricket investigation and the internal inquiry into the missing dossier. I asked for the courtesy of letting me know of any breaking developments which might affect me. I remained perturbed at aspects of Zulu Cricket which had been talked through at the highest level at a series of meetings in Providence, Rhode Island, attended by the DEA and the British police, including a DCI and Sergeant Davies. Should they authorise the American informant to release agreed details about me with a view to getting enough evidence to charge two of the IRA-linked crime bosses over here with conspiracy to murder me? Dangerous and slippery territory, particularly as the option had been discussed without me knowing a thing about it. I was relieved to find the idea had been dropped, even though I knew that in the event of such a plan I would have been given protection second to none to ensure my safety.

All I had to worry about now was that the mobsters might find me of their own volition. I didn't draw much consolation either from discovering I wasn't alone on the drug gang's hit list of '92.

The informant, a key man in the whole operation and known by the alias Miguel, had received an urgent coded message from one of the main players in the UK. He rang back almost immediately. It was an Irish bar in Boston, Massachusetts. A man with a heavy Irish accent answered.

'Michael, you're fucking dead.' The line went dead.

Miguel knew his head was on the block as well.

Then there was a woman in the Irish Republic who had contacted police with so much detailed background on Irish Joe and his activities, particularly his links with Irish police officers and money-laundering activities on behalf of the IRA, that detectives believed she must be in the law enforcement or security business. There was no way, she said, that she was going to identify herself because she, too, was scared of an assassin's bullet. Then, sinisterly, her calls stopped. It was more evidence, if any were needed, that the very highest echelons of a powerful criminal world were at work.

THE GANGBUSTER

I finally moved into the new house with my new identity and all the false documentation I needed for the gas man, the council tax, the phone people and what have you. I yearned for a respite from the constant threat of an early grave and the niggling hassles with the Yard. A chance to recharge the batteries and prepare as best I could for whatever tomorrow might bring. Mr and Mrs Peter Charles became the new occupants of a spruced-up 4 Glendale Mews. Unimaginative, I know, using my first two Christian names, but what the hell. We were, as far as the neighbours were concerned, a nice ordinary couple who kept themselves to themselves, enjoyed the occasional drink and went for an Indian curry at weekends. Certainly, Mr Charles, now minus his pony tail, didn't look the sort of chap who might go off buying £4 million worth of heroin on behalf of the police or might just find himself on the wrong end of a bullet as he walked out of his front door one morning. Elaine, though living as my wife, didn't change her name. It was different from mine and anyone checking financial databases looking for a P. Bleksley wouldn't identify her with me. It looked safe enough for the time being. One neighbour who saw me making a routine bomb check under my motor looked a bit apprehensive. 'It's just the exhaust,' I said, 'got a bit of a rattle.'

A couple of months down the line, I decided I would like to buy the property for the long-term security of home ownership. I didn't want to be off the property ladder too long. My own place was up for sale, but not attracting much interest. We'd hit a slump in the property market. The only offer I received left me £12,000 in negative equity. As the entire move was not my fault, and I was being asked to stump up twelve grand I hadn't got to clear the mortgage, it was time to go back up the Yard for more delicate negotiations. It was as I expected: 'Sorry, old chap, we've got every sympathy with you but we can't make a decision like that. You'll have to take it higher.'

I went right to the top. Not quite rapping on the Commissioner's door but very nearly. It paid off. Somebody – and to this day I don't know who – authorised that my negative equity shortfall would be paid by the police. The relief was tangible as the sale was completed and another problem shelved.

We sped ahead with finalising the purchase of the new house. And straight away we hit another unexpected and probably unique snag. Strictly speaking, the person buying the property, Peter Charles, did not exist. He was a figment of my imagination along with my other spurious identities. To whom, then, would the property be left if I should suddenly die? And given the circumstances that was not such a remote possibility. It occupied my waking moments more than the average man. We had encountered a situation that the Metropolitan Police had not faced before and had set their legal eagles a conundrum they weren't equipped to handle. So a former police colleague, now a financial adviser, used his contacts and expertise to go to a building society that was prepared to lend me the money for the house in a moody name. He, too, had to go to the top to persuade them to finance a man who didn't really exist. The solution in the end was for me to supply the society with a legal document verifying who I really was, that Peter Charles was really Peter Charles Bleksley, police officer. The building society, for their part, swore never to divulge a word about the transaction to a living soul.

THE GANGBUSTER

With my home life settled, in a fashion, it was back to work as normal at SO10 – if undercover work can ever be described as normal. For 'normal', read subversive, secretive, dirty, dangerous work in the sewers of society. Welcome to my world.

Chapter Two

NOTHING VENTURED

Life in the undercover unit was life as the Great Pretender – pretending to be a drug-dealer, a hit-man, a counterfeiter, a fraudster, a gunrunner. Pretending, in fact, to be the very opposite of what I was. I was the cop playing the villain in all the disparate venues of gangland, from swish hotels to grimy back-street pubs. And I learned very quickly that if I was to stay alive in this dangerous and murky world of make-believe, I had to be good. Fucking good. When I went out as a drug-dealer, I became a drug-dealer. I knew the language, I knew the gear, I knew the risks. And I knew just one mistake could be fatal. You don't get a second chance in the front line. A bullet in the brain is the quick solution to sorting the bastard cop who has infiltrated your scam.

It was never what I had envisaged when I walked out through the gates of Hendon Training College in north-west London in

1978, as fresh-faced, proud-as-punch PC Bleksley. In fact, I'd never imagined being in the police force at all, let alone the most elite squad at Scotland Yard. It was dear old Mum I had to thank. Like many teenagers with a lot of time on their hands and little ambition, I'd run into a spot of bother with Mr Plod and Mum had received a couple of home visits from a friendly neighbourhood bobby. I think she took the view, 'If you can't beat 'em, join 'em,' and the next thing I knew a Scotland Yard recruitment officer was round helping me fill in an application form.

Up to that point, my only qualifications towards a career in crime-fighting were my skills as a schoolboy shoplifter and my lucky streak as an under-age gambler. Born on 11 December 1959 at Barnehurst in Kent before it became swallowed up in the great suburban sprawl it is today, I'd had a miserable life as a kid after the old man had left Mum, and I was a dismal failure academically even though, by some miracle, I'd managed to pass the entrance exam for Erith Grammar. I remember the assistant headmaster Mr Mason telling me on my last day, 'Bleksley, you came to this school with nothing, you are leaving with next to nothing, you are nothing, you will become a nothing. Get out of my school.' I suppose I wasn't the greatest advert for Erith's educational structure at the time. I remember that we'd been over the pub that lunchtime, were a bit pissed and had ink and flour all over a torn uniform.

My final farewell. The classroom had always been an alien place to me so it was no problem leaving it behind.

The real fun had started when the grammar was swallowed up by a comprehensive and we had turf wars to contend with.

NOTHING VENTURED

The comprehensive kids seemed to think that us ex-grammar boys were posh tossers. I spent most of my days proving the opposite. I bunked off, took sickies, played the classroom clown, and was generally a pain in the arse. Then I discovered that I had a natural talent for shoplifting. Didn't take any time-consuming study, just a mac with some long baggy sleeves.

When my parents divorced, and it was good riddance to my father, we moved to Bexleyheath. On my way home from school, I used to go into Hides, the old-style department store, and slip long, thin geometry kits up the sleeves of my mac, one in each arm. They were much in demand among the brainier kids at school and I built up a nice little trade supplying them at discount prices. It was 'sod school dinners' after that; it was doughnuts, pasties and ice creams from the shops. Hence I became pretty rotund as a kid. My shoplifting prowess moved me on to dinky toys and other assorted items it was easy to sell on the playground black market.

I'd also started what was to be a lifelong love affair with gambling. I suppose it's the risk factor that hooks you. Anyway, I was pretty successful, but strictly under age to be punting. I'd change out of my school uniform into something nicely anonymous and slip into the local William Hill to lay bets known as 'patents' – three horses backed in combinations, three singles, three doubles and a treble. And Bingo! They kept on romping in. Even at 25p stakes it mounted up. At one stage, I was picking up so much in winnings I had to stick it under the floorboards of Mum's flat in case she started asking awkward questions.

I suppose it was these nefarious activities which ultimately set me on course for the duplicitous life of an undercover cop, if you use the time-honoured maxim 'It takes a thief to catch a thief.' I was out of school at sixteen and signed up for the Metropolitan Police. Mum thought it was a nice, safe job pinching a few motorists for parking, giving crime prevention talks to kiddies.

I headed apprehensively for Hendon College, and found I loved it. All of a sudden, instead of a bunch of toss-pot teachers, I was confronted by hard-nosed ex-marine training instructors. You knew if you stepped out of line you'd get a hiding. It really concentrated the mind. They were massive on sport and physical exercise, so the bulky trappings of a porky teenager fell away and for the first time in my life I became 100 per cent fit and mentally alert. They knocked you into shape on the drill square – a flabby cop is a bad cop – and knocked any lurking criminal inclinations out of you in the lecture rooms. This, at last, was where I wanted to be. I was hard, lean and ready to go. I adopted the view, 'I'm in the Old Bill now, and I'll act like Old Bill.' The year at Hendon totally shaped my life and I was just about the proudest guy in Britain when I walked out of those gates, top of my class, winner of the book prize, to begin my career as PC Peter Bleksley in the then seething cauldron that was south-east London.

I saw racial tension boiling. I saw Brixton burning. But I never dreamed that the next twenty years would see my life become such a roller-coaster of conflicting emotions.

Chapter Three

POSEIDON MISADVENTURE

A force nine gale was sending waves crashing over the two vessels as they nudged closer together in the Atlantic, 600 miles off Portugal, to offload a massive £25 million cargo of cannabis resin. The navigational skills of the two skippers couldn't prevent the terrifying clash of metal on metal as they were finally thrown together. The crews were undeterred by the danger, for those in peril on the sea had chosen to be there as part of the world's biggest cannabis smuggling ring – except two. They were undercover detectives, and probably the bravest men I've ever worked with.

We were involved in one of the most amazing undercover operations of all time, on land and sea, pitted against a drugs gang whose army of traffickers would have required a dozen stickers on a world map, from Britain to Croatia, to Holland, to Canada, Venezuela, France, Spain and beyond. This was Operation Dash, a combined venture by law enforcement agencies triggered off by a South East Regional Crime Squad surveillance on an old-time villain looking to pull off one last big job before he retired.

It all went wrong for Bobby Mills and his cronies when the entire haul of 6.5 tons of high-grade hash was snatched from under their noses in a combined operation by the police in six countries, Customs, and Royal Navy. It was the first time, in fact, that British Naval vessels had been used to round up drug smugglers on the high seas.

I was on secondment from SO10 to the SERCS office in Tottenham Court Road in 1993 when we received an underworld tip-off that Bobby Mills was 'at it' again. I say again because Mills was already in prison serving ten years for exactly the same crime, smuggling puff in huge quantities into the UK. He'd been a good boy inside and had been transferred towards the end of his sentence to HMP Latchmere House, on Ham Common, near Richmond, Surrey, as part of a resettlement programme. He was allowed out on a daily basis to 'reintegrate' into society and get used to returning to the routine of work. Or that was the idea. Mills had managed to get a friend of his, as most of them do, to say that he was going to be offered employment when he left jail. The authorities allowed him out in the morning and back at night. But Bobby Mills was never intending to work. He was busy sorting out a major league cannabis importation that he reckoned would set him up financially for the rest of his life. Mills became our number-one target. He was the key to bigger things. We were discreetly watching him as he toddled off daily to his non-existent job.

We discovered he was working in cahoots with a world-renowned international drug-dealer called Marc Feviet, a Frenchman, and a Sicilian Mafia figure called Locatelli who was known to be involved with Colombian-organised crime gangs. Our surveillance work stretched from weeks into months. The unmistakable message was simple: something really big was on the go. Finally our intelligence network picked up the information we needed; the job was to be the biggest-ever shipment of cannabis into a South of England port. It was to be picked up in the Atlantic from a 'mother ship' operated by an international drugs cartel. The 1,000–ton vessel, called *Poseidon*, was fitted with state-of-the-art navigational systems and satellite communications. In effect, it was a floating warehouse from which the world's drugdealers could buy their supplies. That is, if they liked a sea trip and had the bottle to brave the Atlantic ocean at its most unpredictable. *Poseidon* operated solely in international waters. No cosy handovers in the calm of coastal waters. She returned to port only to re-stock with more drugs, normally in Morocco. The gang were dealing in tons of the stuff on a wholesale basis. Ganja galore; Spliffs 'R' Us.

Our intelligence network gained a major breakthrough when we discovered Mills and his associates were looking to hire a boat, plus crew, to make a trip out to *Poseidon* to pick up 6.5 tons of hash for distribution to UK dealers. The boat would sail out to meet the *Poseidon* at a given point off the Portuguese coast and ferry its valuable cargo back to a British port under cover of darkness. A chance, at last, to infiltrate the very heart of this huge cannabis conglomerate. Step aboard SO10. Undercover operators required.

I was up for it but had to admit I hadn't the best sea legs and would throw up on a cross-channel booze cruise let alone hack it against an Atlantic storm. My guv'nor decided I wasn't crew material, not through a queasy tummy but because I'd been involved in the protracted surveillance operation watching suspects in bars and hotels and my face might trigger alarm bells. We couldn't risk it. Although I'd never spoken to any of them and had worked in various disguises, my face might have registered with one of them thinking, I know that bloke from somewhere. Maybe I'd moved up close in a bar trying to hear a conversation or followed someone into the gents to see if a meet was going on. It was decided the undercovers on the boat would need to be guys who'd had no contact at all with the suspects. I was disappointed in a way because I knew we were hitting big-time operators and the drug haul was going to be massive. But professionally, it made sense for me to stay with the land-based team.

We had two blokes among the SO10 ranks who were suitably qualified for the maritime mission on the pick-up vessel. As part of their training schedule they had been sent on specialist courses to acquire nautical skills. One had a skipper's licence, the other seagoing skills which would equip him to handle pretty well any crisis, all part of SO10's rigorous training programme paid for by Scotland Yard in the ever-expanding and diverse battle against crime. We had people trained in anything from armaments to accounting ready to swing into action at a moment's notice. Even against the mighty Atlantic. Once we knew the gangsters were looking for a boat and a crew we were able to effect the introduction of our undercovers, two of the bravest cops I've ever met. Mick, whose surname must stay secret, was the potential skipper. He was a guy I had the utmost respect for, personally and professionally. His skill and courage were unquestioned. Hard as nails, dedicated to the job. Through the contacts we had made with unsuspecting gang members, we arranged the hire of a British-registered fishing trawler for the Atlantic voyage. I can't say where or how this was done because they still use the same methods against drug smugglers. But one thing was for sure about our little boat. This would be its biggest catch.

The surveillance and intelligence-gathering had by now gone on for over eight painstaking months. Tension mounted as we neared the time for Operation Dash to be launched in the hope of smashing the world's biggest drugs syndicate right out of the water. We followed the suspects, we photographed them, we logged our evidence in mounting dossiers. Our units were fed information by international police units on the movements of the two big players, Feviet and Locatelli. These were master international criminals with a lifestyle to match, flying in and out of Britain and half a dozen other countries – Canada, France, Italy, Spain, you name it – they had contacts there as part of their crooked enterprises. They lived high on the hog in the process with only the best hotels and restaurants good enough for their lavish tastes.

By now the three key members – Mills, Locatelli and Feviet – were having regular meetings in London. We watched them having dinner one evening at a five-star hotel in Mayfair and with a hastily acquired search warrant decided to give their room a spin. Feviet had booked in and the other two had joined him there – it was a perfect opportunity to look for incriminating evidence. We desperately needed pointers to exactly where the big drugs trade was due to take place. We had undercover guys in the restaurant watching the suspects stuff their faces, appearing to be casual diners as well, but in secret radio communication, watching every move the drug barons made, ready to warn the search teams if they looked in danger of returning suddenly to the room, or even if they just stood up and walked out for a piss.

The search squad hit the room running, knowing it was a race against time to get in and get away. First in was the Polaroid Man. It was his job to move round the room taking instant stills of everything that was likely to be rummaged. Vital because we had to make sure that every single item was replaced exactly as the suspects had left it, not even a millimetre out. This was the sort of detail that made SO10 the best in the world at this kind of thing. After the Polaroid Man had taken his snaps, the gloved-up search teams swung into action. Drawers, cupboards, desks, cases, clothing – we searched every inch. Then we found the shipping charts. Great evidence which told us where the Atlantic exchange would take place. Plane tickets told us where they had been flying to and from, hoping it would point to the source nation for the cannabis. We found fantastic first-class evidence which reinforced our belief that we were dealing with the foremost cannabis gang in the world.

With the maritime charts, we were now able to play our ace card – the trip out to *Poseidon*. The Royal Navy were put on standby, with ministerial consent, to shadow the entire operation and seize the *Poseidon*. Every scrap of evidence we found was photographed on conventional film for the evidence file. Then we put everything back where it was when we started, using the Polaroid shots to ensure 100 per cent accuracy. 'Move that curtain to the left a bit, the suitcase to the right a bit. Yes, that's it, spot on.' All the time, we had our covert earpieces tuned in to the guys downstairs in the restaurant watching the suspects. At one point, Feviet got up from the table to go to the bog. Fucking panic stations upstairs. Shit, was he coming up to the room? Heart-stopping stuff. No, just a piss.

Just in case of a potential disaster, we also had undercover guys in hotel livery ready to delay the lifts with baggage trolleys to give us space to get out. Seconds could be vital. But no problems, thank God. Our teams were in and out like ghosts without Feviet and Co ever knowing we'd been there.

It was nearing D-Day for *Poseidon* and our little fishing trawler. Mick, and another SO10 stalwart, Paul, had been accepted as skipper and crewman for the harrowing trip into the wild Atlantic. A couple of equally courageous Customs investigators had also managed to get aboard as deckies. The rest of the crew were UK drug-dealers off on a shopping trip to a floating cannabis supermarket.

The trawler left a south coast port on a cold and blustery day in early November 1993 for its rendezvous with *Poseidon*, which was sitting in a huge Atlantic swell off Portugal. She had been bought by the drugs cartel specifically for the purpose of large-scale drug-trafficking, registered under a flag of convenience in the British Virgin Islands, and fitted out with no expense having been spared on equipment and comfort. A considerable upgrade in some respects on her previous life as a somewhat battered remnant of the German Navy.

By the time our boat had battled its way out to the mother ship, on precise compass bearings given by the master of the *Poseidon*, gales had churned the sea into a terrifying turbulence that was going to make the transfer of the cannabis bales from one ship to another – known as coopering – a hazardous and frightening job. The game plan had been to transfer the entire cargo, packed into dozens of multi-coloured, polythene-wrapped bales, onto the trawler and sail straight back to Littlehampton. But because the sea was now so rough, the hired crane on the *Poseidon* had broken and the crews were left with no alternative but to haul the bales manually from one ship to the other. They started by using a rigid inflatable boat called a rib, which was part of *Poseidon*'s equipment, to transfer it load by load across a 20-yard expanse of raging ocean. But it began filling up with water as waves crashed over it and the manoeuvre was deemed too dangerous to continue, for both men and cargo. Crewmen were needed on board the rib to guide it to the pitching trawler and back. Lives could be lost. Cannabis could be lost.

A hurried decision was made to abandon the seaborne transfer after a couple of largely abortive runs and to move on to plan B, the even riskier option of moving the two vessels side by side and physically hauling the cannabis bales from the *Poseidon*'s deck over the side onto the trawler's deck. Despite the stomach-churning crunches as the two boats smashed together under the pressure of the waves, they managed to offload 2.7 tons of hash. The vessels repeatedly banged together, with the bigger *Poseidon* in serious danger of sinking the smaller fishing boat with, potentially, a dreadful loss of life, including two undercover coppers and two Customs men. Their very presence was bravery of the highest order and the drama still sends as much of a chill down my spine today as it did when those guys first told me about it at the debriefing in 1993. Under the circumstances, there was no alternative but to abandon phase two as well. Less than half the cargo had been shifted. The weather was worsening and it was time to head home. The trawler set a course for quiet Littlehampton in Sussex – the port designated by Bobby Mills – and battled against boiling seas for three or four days before it reached safety. It was shadowed throughout by a Customs cutter sitting discreetly out of sight on its tail.

The *Poseidon*, meanwhile, with the remaining 3.8 tons of cannabis still on board, was being watched by two Royal Naval vessels, equally invisible out there in the vast Atlantic. It was, I believe, the first time the Navy had sanctioned the use of such powerful ships against drug smugglers in international waters. Their job was to keep tabs on the *Poseidon* until after our reception committee in Littlehampton had surprised the drug-runners with a quayside ambush. Then they would move in for the kill.

We'd prepared quite a homecoming. We'd identified the yard on the River Arun where the cannabis would be unloaded. We'd also identified several UK drug-dealers who were planning to be there to pick up their share of the dope. I'd been delegated by DI Chris Jameson to lead a team of four blokes to spearhead the ambush. It was a fantastic operation.

We did a recce a few days before and saw a stretch of wasteland we could cross unnoticed under cover of darkness and get up close to the dockside with only a few feet between us and the point where the smuggled drugs would be brought ashore. On the big night, we got geared up in black from top to bottom, balaclavas with eyeholes, torches, guns at the ready. We'd planned a pincer movement with other teams once the drugs were ashore. Customs had a team in position; Scotland Yard's SO11 intelligence boys were dotted round the plot.

The UK drug-dealers waiting for the booty had a fleet of refrigerated vans waiting all dolled up in the fake livery of some wholesale fishmonger's company. They hoped to move out the cannabis under the guise of cod and herring and deliver it to various destinations across the country.

We decided that the hit must be done on the quayside. We couldn't risk one of the vans getting out with drugs on board. We weren't in the business of bringing cannabis in free of charge for drug-traffickers. With the meeters and greeters assembled in front of us at the quay, it was just a question of waiting for our sturdy little boat to come chugging up the river.

Me and my fellow men in black were so close to the suspects we could hear every word they were saying as the boat finally docked and they started piling the bales on the quay. We were right under their noses but they couldn't see a thing as we lay in the dark behind a fence and small wall, under some bushes. Spirits were high among the smugglers and their greeters as they stacked the bales. They obviously thought the worst was over and the good times were about to come. We sat waiting and listening. All the time, the guv'nor was on the radio to me through my neatly concealed earpiece.

'Can you see the crew?'

I gave three clicks for 'Yes' on the talk button.

'Have they unloaded it all yet?'

Two clicks for 'No'. We are communicating within feet of the bad guys but no one is talking.

Finally, the trawler was unloaded and its contraband cargo neatly stacked on the edge of the quay. Our undercover boat weighed anchor and sailed a little way up the Arun, turned down a creek and disappeared from view. We didn't want the ship, the skipper and crewmen on site when we got the order to strike. We had a bit of time to play with. The meeters and greeters still had to lug the 2.7 tons of cannabis up the quay and into their vehicles before they could move off. They were in the middle of loading, huffing and puffing, when Chris Jameson called up on my earpiece.

'Everything OK?' Three clicks.

'Can you put the hit in?'

Three clicks.

'As soon as you're ready, do it.'

We crept out of our hiding places, put on our Kangol hats with the chequered band, pulled out our fluorescent torches and moved in over the small wall. There was so much clanking and chattering going on as they humped the heavy bales into the vans that no one was listening for us. We were right on top of them before they realised what was happening.

'ARMED POLICE, STAY WHERE YOU ARE.'

Torches straight in their faces. You've never seen shock like it. They could not believe it. By then a van full of hairy-arsed Old Bill had crashed through the main gates of the yard and screeched to a halt by the bales. The driver said, 'Oh shit, I thought we were going to get a piece of the action ... but you've got 'em all lined up on the floor like dummies doing everything you tell them.'

I think they were all hoping for a bit of a dust-up to brighten a long night. We were delighted with the result. We'd taken out some big names on the British drug scene. There were other people waiting at the local railway station who were crooks and we nicked them too. There was a string of simultaneous arrests right across the south-east of England wiping out a big chunk of the British cannabis distribution network.

Bobby Mills was arrested as he celebrated prematurely in a London restaurant. Feviet and Locatelli, either by luck or design, had already left the country. They weren't going to hang around to dirty their hands. But what they hadn't realised was that for months we'd built up a dossier on them that could put them behind bars for twenty years.

Meanwhile, out in the stormy Atlantic, the Royal Navy had moved in for its own nautical assault on *Poseidon*. Under special authority from the Ministry of Defence, a team from the Special Boat Section – forerunners of the SAS and every bit as tough – were lowered by helicopter to seize the swaying vessel. It was the first time since World War II that the Navy had put a 'prize crew' aboard a vessel in international waters, effectively an act of piracy on the high seas. The SBS took control of *Poseidon*. Then she was sailed back towards the UK by the Navy, its remaining cargo of hash impounded by Customs and eventually destroyed. The ship was sold for £1million and the money put into public funds to help offset the huge cost of Operation Dash.

Nobody aboard *Poseidon* had offered physical resistance to the hard bastards of the SBS as they swung aboard down the helicopter winches. No one, that is, except a former French paratrooper called Gilbert Astesan, who had grabbed the helm from Dutch skipper Peter Seggermahn as the Navy attacked.

Astesan fancied he was smart enough to outrun the British Navy. He zig-zagged through the Atlantic at maximum knots trying to prevent the SBS chopper squad from boarding. But there was no way a drug-dealing freighter was going to outrun Her Majesty's Navy. The Navy stormtroopers boarded her in appalling conditions and detained the entire crew, which included the skipper's wife. They were winched off to a fleet auxiliary vessel to be transported back to Britain to face arrest.

The SBS lads had saved a little surprise for the swashbuckling Astesan. He was the last to be winched from the *Poseidon*'s deck. And his adventure of a lifetime was about to begin. He was fitted with a rescue harness, winched to 100ft then taken on a gut-churning, vomit-inducing whirlwind spin over the roaring Atlantic waves in pitch darkness to teach him a lesson. Don't mess with the Navy. It must have petrified the poor sod. It's a funny thing, but after Astesan was brought back to England with his cronies, he had acquired the utmost respect for the Navy and the SBS.

It was one of the most incredible operations I had ever been associated with. I can only say I was as proud as punch to have been involved, and awash with pride at the heroism of those undercover guys, police and Customs, who went out into the Atlantic to bust this gang. I think about those heaving decks and 20ft waves and wonder if I would have acquitted myself with such honour. I hope so, for the sake of SO10.

One memory of the operation still seared on my mind is that of our man Paul frantically trying to offload the bales of cannabis in nightmare conditions and trying, at the same time, to get recorded evidence for the prosecution case. He was fitted with a tiny hidden tape recorder for blow by blow commentaries. At one point, he talked breathlessly about the desperate attempts to offload the cannabis from *Poseidon* onto the slippery deck of our trawler. Then he can clearly be heard throwing up over the side. 'Urrrghh,' breakfast overboard. Poor sod.

Bobby Mills' case was dealt with by me and seasoned detective Freddy Bateman, former Flying Squad, former Regional Crime Squad, and as sound as a pound. Mills was an absolute gent to deal with, one of the old school of villains. He realised just how much in the shit he was. He was nearing the end of one ten-year sentence and was now nicked for another big 'un, having been identified as the British agent for the top drug-smuggling cartel around. He was walking back into another ten-year stretch and knew it. He'd almost cracked it, almost completed his porridge; why on earth had he risked it all again? Well, he would have come out to thousands of pounds if all had gone well; I suppose that's reason enough.

He didn't try for deals. He told me and Freddy, 'I'm not going to talk to you, I'm not going to tell you a fucking thing about it. But I'll save you work and plead guilty in court.' Being a man of his word, he duly did so. But no way in the world was he going to grass anyone up to get a lesser sentence. He could have told us a lot. He was in his mid-fifties, his criminal career was over and he was looking at prison walls for many years to come. But he retained that old underworld code you rarely see now and we had a grudging respect for his values. You could say his life had totally gone to pot.

The rest of the gang were brought back to the UK on a British destroyer, held captive in specially equipped secure cabins for the three-day journey and minded by a Customs team who'd sailed with the Navy. We were all standing on the quay at Portsmouth Naval base when they arrived. The SBS guys came off first, all cloak and dagger. No cameras, no fuss, no celebration drink. I think they probably went for a bit of private R and R of their own as they slipped away with kitbags over their shoulders. We all went aboard then with the Customs officers and arrested the *Poseidon* mob, a real United Nations bagful, an international crime corporation. They were read their rights, told what they were being arrested for, and taken off to various police stations in the South of England where they were charged with drugs offences and sent to remand prisons to await their trials.

Although Feviet and Locatelli, effectively the company chairman and managing director of this gigantic offshore venture, appeared to have slipped the net, we had enough evidence to issue an international arrest warrant. We'd managed to get photographic evidence of both men meeting up with Mills, including at Heathrow Airport, during the run-up to the *Poseidon* seizure. We had damning evidence from the surveillance teams. Locatelli was arrested a few weeks later at Madrid Airport for the *Poseidon* drugs shipment and a range of other drug-related offences. He was in the company of an Italian criminal court judge. I make no comment. Feviet was arrested later in connection with *Poseidon*, pleaded guilty in court and received what appeared to be a paltry four-year sentence. Then it emerged that *Poseidon* was just the tip of the iceberg. He was wanted in Canada for the illegal importation of 6 tons of cocaine. In cash terms, that dwarfed the 6.5 tons of puff we had seized. The value of the coke would have gone off the Richter scale in drug-trafficking terms – hundreds of millions. The *Poseidon*, it appeared, had also been used in that smuggling operation. It illustrated just what a top villain Feviet was and why it was so vital to hunt him down. He was duly extradited to Canada and is now serving a substantial prison sentence there. Having had his boat confiscated, his drugs seized and burned, hopefully Feviet will never reap the rewards of his criminal activities.

A total of eighteen people were arrested over *Poseidon*, and all but three were convicted and jailed in a series of trials lasting through until June 1995. A huge and sophisticated foreign drug cartel, with the UK as its principal target, had been taken out in what was hailed as one of the most successful joint operations ever between police and Customs, a combination, I must say, that did not always sing from the same hymn sheet. With the unique involvement of the Royal Navy and SBS, it was a fantastic example of courage and co-operation in the face of the gravest danger.

The trial judge at Croydon Crown Court, His Honour Judge Devonshire, was unstinting in his praise of the undercover officers, Customs and police, who had risked their lives in that petrifying drama on the high seas. He said the rivalry between police and Customs had often been commented on but, in Operation Dash, 'It was uplifting to see the co-operation evident in this case.' I'd certainly had some unfortunate run-ins with the Cuzzies over the years, and I was grateful to see a new era of collaboration.

Customs boss Dick Browne was equally fulsome in his plaudits to Mick and Paul and the courageous roles they played. And in a letter to Commander Roy Clark of the South East Regional

Crime Squad, he noted how much humour our Team 12 had shown during the long months of surveillance leading up to the quayside ambush.

'I would like to single out DI Chris Jameson,' he wrote. 'His enthusiasm and professionalism greatly impressed all of us here and we have come to regard him as a credit to SERCS and to the police service in general.'

Mr Browne had heard that we'd never had a dull moment on the job. I won't argue with that. And it still went on after the bad guys had been rounded up.

We'd all suffered a bit from the sharp tongue and acid wit of Freddy Bateman and we decided collectively to get our own back on him once the dust had settled. We hatched a little plot. One of the guys on the team knew Freddy's family quite well and said he had a daughter who was game for a laugh. So we sent Freddy down to the south coast on some spurious inquiry to get him out of the way. Then a team of us went round to his house with a video camera and filmed a Loyd Grossman–style *Through the Keyhole*. Who would live in a house like this? Well, Freddy did and he was in for a shock. Camera on. One of the girls on the team went into the bathroom, ran a foamy bath and got into it, posing seductively. I got into Freddy's marital bed, put a QPR poster above it, then his daughter clambered in beside me. 'Let's go into the bedroom for more clues...' Up from under the duvet popped Bleksley and his daughter with big cheesy grins on our faces.

At the conclusion of the job, we all sat down for a final debriefing. Chris Jameson stood up and said, 'Before we start, we've got a brief instructional video for you all to watch.' The video film rolled. All eyes were on Freddy. Cut to Chris at the front door of a nice semi saying, 'I wonder whose house this is?' Freddy sat bolt upright.

'That's my house, you bastards.'

His face was a picture as he watched the guided tour, the beauty in the bath then Blex and his daughter romping in bed. To cap it all, we'd filmed the family's pet hamster scurrying round inside the microwave (off, of course). 'Now, who would keep a hamster in a microwave like this?' Revenge was sweet.

Chapter Four

GUN LAW SW5

The gun was 2in from my face. The business end of a sawn-off, double-barrelled, up-and-over shotgun with enough firepower to splatter my brains over half of West London. And the eyes at the other end were cold, hard and desperate.

This was the moment I came face to face with one of Britain's most wanted criminals, on the run from jail after the brutal murder of a bar manager and now holed up on my patch. Vicious James Baigrie was sleeping rough in the back of a white van in a select street in Earl's Court, where I was then based in the local Kensington CID office and determined to make my mark as a good detective.

In the few seconds I was peering into the gaping twin holes of that shotgun barrel, I thought my mark was going to be my epitaph. Then instinct and training took over. I had taken Baigrie by surprise, but I was equally as shocked. I had expected the van to be empty when I checked it out in Philbeach Gardens as part of a dawn search for the fugitive Scotsman. I had played a hunch. The police knew Baigrie had fled from Scotland to London, was living in the Kensington area, and was probably working as a builder. A check at a suspected hideout address had proved futile.

My team had been discussing the important issue of the day – where to have breakfast – when I spotted the white Transit van parked across the road. That, I thought, was the classic jobbing builder's motor and was worth a quick spin. I peered through the windows. Too mucky to see much except some typical builder's kit – paint pots, bucket, tools, some sand, that sort of thing. I pulled at the rear door handle, out of inquisitiveness really, and – lo and behold – the fucking thing opened. I thought, OK, let's have a nose around: pulled the door open and stuck my head inside. With that, I saw a slight movement and, all of a sudden, this balaclava-clad head popped up from beneath a blanket. I was totally taken aback because I hadn't dreamed anyone would be kipping in there. I blurted out the first thing that came into my head which happened to be, 'Good morning.' That caused a few laughs later. Anyway my police training kicked in straight afterwards. I yelled at him, 'I am an armed police officer.' And no way was I bluffing. I was carrying a gun and I'd undergone intensive firearms training at the Metropolitan Police training centre at Lippitts Hill in Essex – I'd qualified with flying colours – I'd got a 007-style Smith and Wesson .38 six-shot revolver in my shoulder holster and I was ready to use it.

As I spoke Baigrie ducked down and, wallop, had grabbed

something. In a flash he had pulled out the double-barrelled shotgun. It was obvious from the steely glint in his eyes that he was prepared to shoot me if needs must. We were in a 'quickest on the draw' shootout situation. Except this wasn't the Wild West, just West London. I had been caught unawares, I knew, and this convicted killer had the edge on me. The dark glowering holes of the Winchester barrels hovered close to my temples. I was fumbling under my coat and into my shoulder holster to reach for my gun. I thought, shit, he's beaten me to it. I'm going to die. I was staring death in the face in the back of a Transit van. I only had one option. I ducked out of his line of fire and legged it up the road as fast as I could, shouting and screaming at my colleagues, 'Look out, he's got a fucking gun, leg it.' They were close behind me and could be in the line of fire. They scattered for cover as well. They knew from my tone and the way I was running like a fucking maniac that this wasn't one of my jokes. I dashed about twenty-five yards then dived under a car for cover. I got my gun out and shouted at Baigrie, 'You are surrounded by armed police.' That wasn't strictly true because some of the team, notably my mucker with the other firearm, had already gone off for their bacon and eggs before I opened the Transit door.

It was now about 7.00am and Earl's Court was just coming to life. We'd got an armed murderer trapped in a van in a busy street not far from Earl's Court tube station, one of the busiest in London. What do we do now to ensure public safety? To make his getaway in the van he's going to have to come out of the back door and get round the front to the driver's seat. Will he come out all barrels blazing? I made a decision there and then. If he comes out I'm going to shoot him, whether I see his gun or not. I'm going to put a bullet in him. If he crosses the line, he's dead. I've got to stop him getting away and possibly shooting someone else. All these things were racing through my mind as I made my way towards the front of the Transit, out of the line of fire, from where I'd first been facing the rear. He'd got to come out of the van if he was going to start shooting and that gave me an even chance.

I dived down under another car and was quickly joined by my police colleague who by now, amid the action, had for some reason lost a shoe. One had come off as he scrambled to a safe position and was lying in the middle of the road. As more police units raced to the scene for what was rapidly becoming a major incident, there was no movement from the gunman. It was obvious that he believed my warning about being surrounded by armed cops. Now we had a tense and dangerous siege situation which was to last for the next forty-four hours.

I could see Baigrie moving about in the van. I saw him close the back door. I didn't know what his next move might be. Should I reposition myself again to get a line of sight through the back doors? But I knew the might of Scotland Yard would soon be descending on Philbeach Gardens to seal it off. I thought, bollocks, I'll stay where I am. I didn't know where he might go, so I remained prone on the ground with as much of me tucked round a parked car as possible and just my head, hands and gun out for exposure. I wanted to present him with as small a target as possible if he did come out shooting.

By now, all hell had broken loose. People had heard that something big was going on and, human nature being what it is, had come to have a look. That's the last thing I wanted. I'd got a maniac killer with a sawn-off shotgun in a van in a busy street and members of the public could be in danger. One young woman, I think she was Asian or Mediterranean, had started walking towards me, oblivious to what was happening. I'd hidden myself away as much as possible because I wanted her to get past me and out of the line of fire. She was right between him and me. That's not where I wanted anyone to be, I wanted them behind me.

I whispered to my colleague to keep quiet and let her walk up, walk up, walk up until she was safely past us. Suddenly, she looked down and saw me on the ground with a gun and she froze, absolutely froze rigid. I said, 'Move, move quickly, I'm a policeman.'

She still stood there frozen solid. In the end I just levelled my gun at her and yelled, 'Just fucking move, will you?' At which point she did and legged it off down the road at a rate of knots. She looked petrified but it was for her own good.

As other people came out to see what was happening, I was shouting at them, 'Stay indoors, stay inside, there's a siege going on.' I lay in the middle of the road behind the car for about an hour and a half, keeping my gun trained on the Transit and its dangerous occupant. It was March, early morning and it was cold, so I had to keep changing my gun from one hand to the other because it was freezing cold and I'd got to keep my trigger finger warm. Fortunately I can shoot reasonably proficiently with both hands but I had to keep blowing on them one at a time to keep some movement just in case the situation blew up and I had to take a shot. An hour and a half is a long time in one position in this crisis situation and my gun began to feel like a ton weight. It was as much as I could do to keep it levelled towards White Van Man. I was mightily relieved when armed officers from Scotland Yard's SO19 firearms unit eventually made their way through the rush-hour traffic and took over from me and my colleague. I went off to brief senior officers who had arrived to take charge of the siege along with trained negotiators who would try and talk Baigrie out of doing anything rash.

We first knew about Baigrie when police in Scotland phoned to ask us to check an address in Philbeach Gardens and had warned us then, 'He's top of our wanted list. Watch out, he's very, very dangerous.' He was a 37-year-old hard case who had escaped from Saughton Prison near Edinburgh in October 1983 while serving a life sentence for blasting a pub manager to death with a sawn-off shotgun. He'd also got a lot of form for armed robbery, so he was a tasty villain by any standards.

He'd made a fantastic escape from prison, which was as maximum security as you could imagine, by removing a plaster cast from a broken arm, using it to smash a window without making any noise, and going over the wall. He'd been on his toes for well over eighteen months and nobody had got a sighting of him. Officers in Scotland searched the address of Baigrie's best friend and went through it with a fine-tooth comb for clues to his whereabouts. They accounted for every item of correspondence, every article, except for one telephone number, a London number.

The Scottish detectives did a subscriber check on it and traced it to a flat in Philbeach Gardens. It was just an unaccounted-for telephone number at that stage, nothing particularly significant.

It might have been an old mate or ex-girlfriend, but they wanted it checked out. A colleague of mine traced it to a house which had been divided into flats which had all been rented out. He asked me what I thought we should do. The phone checked out to a man called Fred Robertson so we weren't all that confident it was connected to Baigrie. As it happened, it was a moody name he was using.

We arranged a search of the flat the following morning in one of the Yard's famous 'dawn raids'. Two of us would be armed – myself and DS Jim Clarkson – and we were to exercise the utmost caution in view of Baigrie's past history of violence. I'd always wanted to be a firearms officer and had worked hard on my course to be as good as possible. I was confident I would have no qualms about shooting someone dead if the circumstances merited it. I was a qualified marksman and proud of it.

We steamed into the flat at the crack of dawn the next day, smashing down the door, and went in with guns drawn. It was a twin-bedded room, one of which was occupied by a young guy in his late teens and the other was empty. We got the terrified lad out of bed at gunpoint and started to search the flat. He told us he shared the room with a 'lovely bloke' who was a builder, who had gone out the previous night, pulled a bird and hadn't come home. He gave the name of Baigrie's suspected alias, Fred Robertson. But there was still no firm evidence that this really was our man. So I nicked an old photograph of 'Robertson' I found in a drawer with a view to sending it to Scotland to see if the lads up there could identify it as Baigrie. That's as far as we could take it at that moment, and with such an early start to the day breakfast became a more pressing objective. That's when I spotted the Transit van over the road. And James Baigrie suddenly loomed very large in my life.

The siege went on for two days with our negotiators setting up a telephone link with Baigrie inside the van in a bid to talk him into surrender. But Baigrie did not respond positively, saying he was going to 'shoot his head', to use his own expression, rather than surrender. In an attempt to break the stalemate, the police decided to whack a couple of Ferrett CS gas canisters through the rear windows of the van to force him out. But only seconds later, there was a muffled bang from inside and Baigrie had left his brains dripping off the roof of the Transit. Baigrie had ended the siege the way he had predicted. I wasn't surprised. All he'd got to look forward to was going back to prison for the rest of his life and he must have reckoned this was the best option. He'd enjoyed himself since his escape. He'd re-established his lifestyle, got a new ID, and had a good time – crumpet, booze, earning a few quid as a builder. His options were very limited.

I'd been long gone from the scene when the shooting happened. In fact, I was at a black-tie CID function at a big hotel in Kensington and was chatting to some pals when a uniformed police officer came in. I thought, what's a helmet doing here? He tapped me on the shoulder and said he wanted a word outside.

'It's all over at Philbeach Gardens,' he said. 'Your man has just topped himself.'

I was told later that the trained psychologist at the scene had become increasingly concerned that Baigrie was going to kill himself, and our lot had only decided to go for the CS gas option in an attempt to save Baigrie from himself. It was the first time that CS gas had been fired by the police on mainland Britain. Baigrie had put both barrels of the gun to his head and pulled both triggers. They asked me if I wanted to go to the scene afterwards for a look but I knew what it would probably be like so I declined their generous invitation.

I suppose it could easily have been my brains splattered over Philbeach Gardens. When they examined Baigrie's gun, they found the firing pin had only discharged one cartridge. The pin had hit the other cartridge but had failed to fire it. One superintendent had the theory that the first trigger could have been fired when Baigrie pulled out the gun and pointed it at me in the van. I don't know to this day whether that was a possibility but I count it as another of my nine lives taken care of.

It transpired that Baigrie was only in the van because the landlord of his bedsit had tipped him off. We'd spoken to him the previous day and he thought it was a load of rubbish because his tenant was such a lovely, hard-working bloke who always paid his rent on time. The Old Bill had got it all wrong, he reckoned. He told Baigrie – or Fred as he knew him – that we'd been in looking for him and Baigrie had decided to level with his young roommate about his dodgy background over a few pints before clearing off in the Transit. They went out and got absolutely arseholed. Baigrie went out and got in the back of his van expecting the cold to wake him up at the crack of dawn, and he'd hoped to be long gone before we arrived. But he obviously got so pissed he overslept and his alarm clock turned out to be me coming in through the back doors at first light.

There were quite a lot of people, like the civil liberties lot, who thought the police might get a bit of a kicking over it, what with using CS gas and ripping off the van doors with grappling hooks fitted to a Land Rover. I was mightily relieved when the coroner who heard the inquest into Baigrie's death said the police had done everything right to try to get Baigrie out alive. He said I hadn't done anything to prompt the siege and had acted in the best traditions of Scotland Yard in everything I did. What he was saying was that I could have started letting off bullets, trying to take him out without giving the geezer a chance. At the end of the day, I'm glad it was his gun that killed him, not mine, though I would have had no qualms about it if it had come down to a 'him or me' shoot-out.

The letter of congratulations I received later from my divisional commander, Detective Chief Superintendent Basil Haddrell, did my prospects at the Yard no harm at all. This was real police work and I couldn't get enough of it. I woke up each day waiting for the next job, never mind the risks, never mind the hassle. I was pumping.

It was the first time I had been forced to draw my gun in earnest and it wasn't the last. I'd learnt the hard way that you don't mess with firearms. During my training at Lippitts Hill, I had been taken 'hostage' by two of the instructors in an exercise, right nasty bastards who weren't known to us, who had been recruited from the Army as a sort of test of our self-control and discipline. I was handcuffed, made really uncomfortable, and these guys were really pissing me off. Real sadistic bastards, I thought. You get so into the role, like you do working undercover, that your survival instincts start coming to the surface. They served me up a dinner with only a metal fork to eat it with and I was still handcuffed. One geezer was sitting to my right scratching his arse and really irritating me. The gun that they had was left unattended across the room.

I was so seriously, seriously into the role that I thought while he wasn't looking I could stick the fork in his eye, incapacitating him for long enough to grab the gun and shoot both geezers. Afterwards, I told them I was that close to stabbing him in the eye, one more push and I'd have gone for it. I know now that if I had reacted like that, they would never have let me loose with a gun in a million years. Severe character flaw, Bleksley. End of career.

I told the two blokes afterwards, 'You want to be careful who you choose as a hostage. If it's anybody with a short fuse like me, you could have been in trouble. I was ready to do you both.' They just smiled.

* * *

On the subject of sadists, I can honestly say I've met some wacky women in my time but I think Margi Dunbar, the torture queen, just about takes the cake. She was a lesbian prostitute who ran a sadomasochistic sex parlour in Queensgate, South Kensington, catering for that weird breed of pervert who likes to be whipped, beaten and humiliated. Margi lived with an equally oddball partner called Christine Offord, effectively as man and wife, and had even gone to the lengths of having a baby by artificial insemination.

Unfortunately, it had all gone wrong and Christine had ended up dead in the bath with her neck crushed and broken with an iron bar. I was on the murder squad formed to investigate her death. Margi had to be among our prime suspects.

I couldn't believe my eyes when I went into their brothel.

There were leather harnesses, rubber suits, chains, handcuffs, gags, torture equipment of all sorts. Scrawled on the walls were sick messages for the clients like 'Lick My Boots, Dog!' 'Worthless Slave!' and 'Your life is nothing, your death is nothing.'

These two women made a fortune dishing out pain and punishment to their punters. Christine, the dominant one of the partnership, had persuaded Margi to have a baby by inseminating her with the sperm of a young medical student, and they pretended to lead a 'normal' life at a plush home in Hounslow, Middlesex, thirty miles away from their sordid vice world in Kensington. Margi operated a similar sex-for-sale racket to Offord from a flat in nearby Cornwall Gardens, Kensington, advertising her services as Miss Whiplash and charging wealthy clients £100 an hour to be tortured on a rack until they bled or strung up against a wall and thrashed with a leather whip.

I have to say, Margi did take a shine to me, even though she was a lesbian. She used to sit with her legs apart showing her crotch or even playing with herself in front of me and saying, 'Come on, Blex, when are you going to fuck me?' No chance of that. I wouldn't have put my dick near Margi Dunbar if she were the last woman on earth.

For some bizarre reason, two detective inspectors were allocated to this murder, which was very unusual and was to be very destructive to the course of the investigation. It meant each DI had their own agenda, each having their own ideas as to who had done it. It was a divisive squad right from the start, causing problems we could have well done without. I was assigned to one DI, with some friends of mine, and the other one was a bit of an old sweat who'd been around a bit and had all his old hands on his team.

I suspected right from the start they were barking up the wrong tree, but I sure as hell wasn't going to tell them. They had decided to go off on a tangent and investigate some people who, as it transpired, had fuck all to do with the murder.

Christine Offord's throat had been crushed against a wall with the iron bar causing excruciating pain and a horrible violent death. Then she had been tied up and put in the bath. Pretty horrendous all round. I decided the only sensible place to start my investigations was at the beginning and work systematically through every scrap of evidence we could dig up.

So who was the last person to see Christine alive? Margi Dunbar pretty soon became a key suspect and was arrested for questioning. She really was as weird as they come. She was in possession of some drugs which might have been partly responsible for her condition. But she was definitely not of this planet. The two DIs tried to get some sense out of her, some clues or a confession, but with little or no success. As I was at the heart of the inquiry, I was asked to go in to question her. I didn't get very far either. Margi was right off the wall! But the interview served to reaffirm my suspicions that she had something to do with Christine's death. We had to release her after we'd held her in custody for the maximum amount of time and we took her back home.

Margi used to talk filth all the time, just for the sake of it. She was obsessed with sex. When I'd got her back to the house, she started to come on really strong, flashing her fanny and asking me to lick it and saying things like, 'Come on, you dirty copper, come and stick it up here, you know you want it.' Then she would start playing with herself.

We were once in her garage when she started picking up things and using them as sex toys, dildos. I couldn't believe my eyes or ears. I thought, what is going on here? Lesbians, prostitutes, nymphos ... what's it all about? This was London's vice world at its seediest.

We had come to a bit of a standstill in the investigation so I decided to spend a long time interviewing Margi's 'maid', who showed punters in and out of her torture chamber. I use the term 'maid' advisedly – 'minder' would have been more appropriate.

She was in fact a he, a huge man called Tony. He was a man mountain but he was gay and a bit of a teddy bear, as soft as you can come across, which was just as well seeing the size of him. He could move some furniture. I found out from him that there were two people unaccounted for in our enquiries so far, two blokes who had been on the premises on the last occasion before Christine had been found dead. I was deeply interested in finding out more about them.

I'd managed to get snippets of information from Tony. One was that he'd heard the word 'Littlehampton' mentioned. All the time you are looking for a trigger word that might fire the investigation down the right path. Tony said these two characters were enraptured by Margi, who did have a sort of intoxicating personality if you are into that sort of thing. He only knew their Christian names – Barry and Bob. So that gave me three trigger words – Littlehampton, Barry and Bob. It had taken days to elicit this information but I knew I had something important to work on. Two people never mentioned by anyone else, who appeared to have been deliberately left out of the scene. I felt very excited at the development, and I felt at last we were getting somewhere. I then rang Littlehampton Police Station on a long shot, and this is how fate or luck can help you out. I spoke to a detective there and told him I was fishing in the dark but had two names, Bob and Barry, and did he know of any pair of oiks who hung around together who fitted the names? He said he wasn't sure.

I told him this was a major murder inquiry with sexual links, deviancy and so on.

He said, 'Fuck me, I've got a geezer called Barry on bail for allegedly interfering with a 13-year-old boy. Is that any use to you?'

I thought, Bingo. This is it.

My next move was to go down to Littlehampton and, with the help of the local CID boys, I identified the two mystery suspects – Robert Causabon-Vincent, aged forty-one, and Barry Parsons, forty-five, two partners in crime who fitted the bill exactly as the men who had been in Christine's flat the night she'd been murdered. We staked out their houses for a night then went in and arrested them the next morning.

They were eventually convicted at the Old Bailey and jailed for life. Margi was found guilty of manslaughter and given seven years after the court heard that she had hired the two men to kill her lesbian lover. But she was later cleared on appeal as a result of the trial judge's misdirection to the jury and freed from her sentence.

The Old Bailey jury sat through the most bizarre evidence and you could see that some of them were really uncomfortable with all the details about stormy lesbian passions, torture chambers and Margi's beautiful baby being born into the middle of it all.

It seemed that the two of them had lived together for about seven or eight years with Offord being the older of the two and acting as 'husband' in the weird partnership. Offord, a posh sort who was educated at a leading girls' school and divorced from her businessman husband, had persuaded Margi to have the baby to cement the affair. But it only brought a load of grief with Christine objecting to Margi taking the little boy to her basement torture chamber while she worked. The two killers were petty crooks who carried out burglaries in London and on the south coast. Causabon-Vincent had visited Margi as a client, presumably for a good thrashing or something, and had become sexually obsessed with her. He introduced her to his pal, Parsons, a one-time builder who was nicknamed Psychopathic Barry after he told her he had killed more than fifty people. It was a load of bollocks, of course, but it led to them becoming involved in killing Christine and putting her naked in the bath to make it look as if it had been just a sex game that had gone wrong and not a deliberate killing. They might easily have got away with it if I hadn't had a lucky break.

Throughout all this, Margi, who was from the back streets of Liverpool with a pretty poor education, had denied any involvement in her lover's death and said all along that she had adored her and hadn't wanted any harm to come to her. She said Chrissie treated her better than most men treat their wives and their lifestyle certainly suggested that, with Chrissie heaping expensive presents like jewellery and clothes on Margi like a proud husband. Then she wanted Margi to have the baby to make things complete, and this was arranged through some sort of artificial insemination agency, with Christine present at the birth like a proud dad.

Apparently, it all got stranger and stranger with Christine becoming more and more butch, wearing men's clothes when she was off-duty from her business and even buying men's Y-fronts from Marks & Spencer. At the same time, she demanded that Margi wear more feminine sexy clothes: see-through nighties, stockings and suspenders. But it wasn't what she really wanted. Margi told me she was a gay girl and wanted to make love to another woman, not a make-believe man. The last straw came, apparently, when Christine said she wanted to go the whole hog and have a sex change.

I was pleased with the outcome of the case. Right at the start, one senior officer came into the office and said, 'Just do enough to keep the relatives happy.' Now that really pissed me off. She might have been a prostitute, she might have been a lesbian, but she didn't deserve any more than anyone else did to end up murdered. So we did a little more than keep the relatives happy. We put the men who killed her behind bars for a long, long time.

I still shudder at the depravity of those two women. If I live to be a hundred, I'll never understand how anybody could pay good money to have electric nipple clips fitted to their bodies, their testicles beaten or thrashed over a whipping stool, bound by their hands and ankles. Apparently, Christine once had a punter in for slave treatment and set him polishing her floor. Then she went out for the rest of the day and came home at night to find him still hard at work and in possession of just about the shiniest floor in London. He loved it.

Chapter Five

SLEEPING WITH THE ENEMY

I suppose it should have been 'Not tonight, Josephine' or even 'Not any night, Josephine'. But this particular Josephine was irresistible. A slim, super-fit, gorgeous aerobics instructor. Great figure, great personality. The trouble was, she was up to her beautiful armpits in the drug scene, not so much a dealer but a go-between for jet-setters looking to buy recreational drugs. And she was heavily hooked on cocaine herself.

She came on to the scene when a reliable informant of the undercover unit told us he could arrange a meet with a woman who was actively touting for business involving large amounts of cocaine. The snout said she was claiming to be in a position to introduce would-be buyers to a big-league dealer who could supply substantial quantities of good quality coke, or 'Charlie' as she called it. It looked like a tasty lead. Senior officers approved a covert operation and I was briefed to go in as a potential buyer.

THE GANGBUSTER

I was introduced a few days later to Josephine in a pub in Fulham, the normal sort of 'neutral' territory favoured by undercover detectives in this sort of operation. I would always nominate pubs, hotel bars, hotel rooms, clubs, restaurants, some public place or other, partly for security reasons and partly for the right atmosphere, where all parties would feel comfortable dealing with the business in hand.

There was an immediate spark between us. She was a good-looking woman, intelligent, witty and really toned-up from working at the top health studios in central London. She was a little older than me, but you would have been hard pushed to tell if we stood side by side. We got on well at our first meeting. As far as she was concerned, I was an up-and-coming dealer looking for some coke; she clearly had contacts who could supply it. 'I've got a friend who has plenty,' she said.

We talked it over in general terms, nothing heavy to start with. She made it clear that she was a go-between and would have to introduce me to the man who controlled the operation, Fernando Perez, who lived in Kensington in a plush apartment and worked for the Peruvian Embassy.

'You'll like him,' she smiled coyly.

Right away, I thought he had got to be bringing the stuff in from South America in diplomatic bags. It looked like a classy operation.

The meeting went well. Josie and I agreed to go ahead and buy some stuff. She said she'd set it up right away. We parted with a kiss on the cheek. The signals were go.

I went back to the Yard and reported the situation to my superior officers. I told them this woman and I were hitting it off so well that, to enhance my credibility as a drug buyer, I'd like to take her out socially after our next business meeting. It was a logical step as we'd really hit it off, and it might make her reveal more than she would about her connections on the drug scene. And, by the by, there was more than half a chance of a serious leg-over. Only I didn't tell my bosses that. She was a suspect under investigation and I was a copper. A dangerous liaison that had to be treated with the utmost caution. Should I cross that line with the lovely Josephine?

A couple of meetings later and I finally met Perez, the main mover and shaker of this particular cocaine network. Once again, it went well. We got on famously. He was impressed with my phoney gangland credentials – a dealer heading for the top, money to burn. Both Josephine and Perez had liked me, apparently, and Perez was happy to do the business. One thing led to another and I set a dinner date with Jo to get to know each other better. She was fun. A lot better to be dealing with than most of the lowlifes I have met on the drug scene.

It soon became obvious that she was very seriously hooked on cocaine. She was taking a lot by any standards. At her home in Fulham, she was habitually smoking it as crack, reducing cocaine to rocks by mixing it with baking powder and cooking it. But doing her brains on crack every day just didn't seem to gel with her fitness lifestyle. She was obviously in the supply business to fund her habit. But I still couldn't help liking her.

The extent of her addiction was fully revealed after our meal out at Brown's Hotel. I'd spared no expense wining and dining her. By the time we were going home, the dinner, the drink, the whole ambience meant we were only going back to her place for one thing – sex. It was the seal on our relationship and I didn't know anything in the police manuals which prohibited a good shag with a tasty bird. Or perhaps I did in the back of my mind but chose to ignore it. We arrived back at her place both up for it, fired by some good wines and liqueurs. The aphrodisiac for her seemed to be danger. To her I was an up-and-coming gangster taking the drug scene by storm. Pony tail, flash car, big talk, shares in a couple of snooker halls. We went into the kitchen and Jo started pouring us a couple more drinks. We brushed against each other and there was electricity. Then it was into a passionate clinch and we were tearing at each other's clothes. I couldn't believe my luck, this was work, I was being paid for making love to a beautiful woman.

We stumbled from the kitchen, leaving our drinks untouched, into the bedroom and fell onto the bed virtually naked. She caressed and kissed every part of my body. It was the most incredible night of passion I can remember. She was insatiable. We'd have sex then she'd be on the bedside pipe, a toot of crack then back to bed for more, rarin' to go again. This went on all night long. Nothing was out of bounds. She kept going back for another puff on the pipe then leaping back for more sex. She even supplied the condoms, slipping them on skilfully and sensually. She'd done that before! I did a couple of lines of powdered coke. I could hardly have refused, as it could have blown my cover.

I stayed all night, and I must say it was one of the most amazing of my life. Although it wasn't strictly planned, we both knew it was going to happen. As we'd left the restaurant earlier, I made a coded telephone call to allow the surveillance team backing me up to stand down and go home. I wasn't going to keep them up all night watching a flat while I was inside enjoying myself. And they might get nosey with their video cameras.

The pillow talk suggested she was warming to me a bit too much, a bit worrying as I knew she was eventually going to get busted. I put it to the back of my mind. She beckoned me back to bed for a final session before breakfast. Forget the cornflakes! Obviously, I didn't have time to go home to shave or change and headed straight off to the Yard to update my bosses ... or tell them as much as I thought they should know.

I dragged myself into the squad office bleary-eyed and bedraggled, completely shagged out. They would have panicked if I hadn't been there first thing so it was important to put in an appearance whatever my condition. I went into the guv'nor's office clutching my receipt from the restaurant, one of the best in town, and started the debrief, if you'll pardon the expression, about how the meeting had gone.

I told them the drug deal was progressing well. It was likely to go off pretty soon. Then came the burning question, which from my appearance they knew the answer to already: 'Well, did you take her out after the meet?'

I said, 'Yes, it was good.'

'Did you give her something to eat?'

'Yes, Guv.'

'Plenty of drinks?'

'Oh yes, Guv, plenty.'

'You don't look as if you've been home.'

'No, I haven't.'

'So you stayed then?'

'Er, yes Guv.'

They knew by the smile on my face that they needn't ask much more. But there was only so much I was prepared to tell them, a lot was personal now. I didn't feel they needed to know we'd been at it all night in more positions than the *Kama Sutra* or that she had kept herself fuelled up on crack. Our secrets and lies.

Then came the tricky business of the bill. It was close on two hundred pounds and I knew the Yard could be difficult with some expenses. My boss took it from me and said straight away, 'Oh that's not too bad, Blex.' I looked at him a bit surprised, then looked at where his finger was ... right by the VAT figure. I said, 'No, sorry Guv'nor, you're looking at the wrong line ... that's just the VAT.' He just went, 'Fucking hell.' So I said with a big grin on my face, 'It was worth it.'

We planned to do the cocaine deal on a Saturday morning and I'd persuaded Perez to use his basement flat, in Abingdon Road, W8. I'd done a close recce and knew it was a flat that the police could access easily, it wasn't a Fort Knox. The whole geography of the area suited me and my knowledge of this type of operation. Jo and I agreed that after we had done the trade we were going to Brighton for the weekend to celebrate our first successful deal of many, a new Bonnie and Clyde partnership. Poor cow. She turned up on the day, although she wasn't strictly a part of the deal, and was scooped up in the raid along with Perez. It was a good nick, a foreign envoy using diplomatic channels to smuggle in cocaine and flogging it all over London. Quite a capture. He was later jailed for possession of a kilo of cocaine with intent to supply.

As Jo was being nicked, I'd legged it off down the road to

make it look like I had escaped, hoping she wouldn't put two and two together and know that it was me who had stitched her up. Guilty conscience, I suppose. My colleagues searched the weekend bag she had packed for going away with me and found a nice batch of freshly-baked hash cookies and two wraps of cocaine. When the team met up later for a drink, it was, 'Oh, you really were going to have a good weekend away, weren't you?'

Jo was charged with possessing the drugs intended for our weekend treat but not with the main cocaine conspiracy in order to protect our undercover operation. She got fined for it, and not jailed thankfully. I don't know whether she ever realised that it was me who had betrayed her. Our paths never crossed again ... but she's a girl I'll never forget. Betrayal is the name of the game in the world of undercover policing. Sometimes it leaves a bitter taste.

There were times when I was in situations where I genuinely got to like the people I was investigating, like Jo. I felt a real affinity. In different circumstances, perhaps, we could have been real friends. It happens now and again, that you end up liking the people you are setting up. They might be on the other side of the fence, but they can still be likeable people. And at the end of the day, if you are an undercover copper I don't even know whether you are given the freedom to have a judgement; you only have one choice – you have the angel on one shoulder and the devil on the other. There can be only one loyalty, to the police service and the public, your paymasters.

You are always walking a tightrope between good and bad to some degree or other, whatever crimes you are investigating. It goes with the territory. But there are no demarcation lines when it comes to murder. And an informant in the Midlands had tipped off the police there that a murder was in the offing, a murder that could only be stopped by the intervention of undercover officers. It was a murder that would have devastating repercussions if we failed to halt it.

I had just been posted back to Carter Street Police Station in Walworth, South London, after a highly successful series of undercover operations with Scotland Yard's Central Drugs Squad. Under the police rules of tenure, brought in to help prevent pockets of corruption building up after the scandal of the Obscene Publications Squad in the seventies, detectives weren't allowed to stay in one squad or at one station for more than three years. I had no choice but to fall in line with this policy though I and many fellow officers thought it was ludicrous, especially in the highly specialised area of undercover work. We would be living this very secretive life under various aliases, only going out to meet people undercover, never letting our real identities be known, building up contacts in the underworld and so on, and then suddenly you were put back to being a public domain detective at a local nick dealing with day-to-day burglaries and muggings. By then, I'd had a lot of success with covert operations and our argument against being transferred back to normal duties was quite simply that it placed us in danger. We envisaged a situation where we would be called out to an inquiry, going off to meet someone, saying, 'Hello, I'm DC Peter Bleksley,' and them taking one look at me and realising that last time we'd met I'd been a fucking drug-dealer. You're blown out, the informant's blown out and a job which might have been running for months is blown out.

Sometimes, an undercover job doesn't come to a successful conclusion and you just withdraw gracefully. They won't deal with you, they can't deal with you, they choose not to deal with you – there were myriad reasons why a job might collapse. You pull out and let them carry on in the hope that you might get another crack at it another time. Then back on conventional CID duties you could potentially meet a suspect from a previous undercover job and be sussed out.

However, the management at the Yard were unyielding in these matters, as they largely are to this day, so it was back to Carter Street for me near where I had started my police career pounding the beat in a pointy hat years earlier. I was told, however, that it wouldn't be too long before I was back with SO10.

I hadn't been at Carter Street more than a few days when there was a call from HQ.

'Blex, are you available?'

I told them, 'Yes, I'd like to think I am, but I'll need to square it with the bosses here.'

I walked up to the DCI's office, a very old-style detective called Hughie Parker. He was out, it was lunchtime. I rang SO10 back and said I couldn't get permission to get away.

'We need you,' they said. 'There can't be any ifs, buts or maybes. We need you straight away. Who's your Chief Super?'

At that time it was Bill Griffiths. So they went right over Hughie Parker's head to the Chief Super and told him, 'There's a sensitive operation coming up and we need his experience. Now.'

Griffiths asked what it was about but the Yard boys wouldn't tell him. Then I got a call from Griffiths upstairs saying, 'OK, you can go.' When Hughie Parker got back, he went ballistic because I'd vanished without his say so.

It was very quickly apparent that this job was something special. They said I'd be away for some time and to go home and pack some bags and get up to the Yard as soon as possible. And don't say anything to anybody.

I went home, packed a holdall and reported in to the Yard. I met the fellow officer who was to be my partner on the operation, DC Andy Nicholau. This pleased me, he was someone I knew well and had the utmost admiration for. He was more experienced than me, had more service than me and had been one of the trailblazers and innovative thinkers in the setting up of the Yard's undercover squad. I was happy to be working with him, even though at this stage neither of us had a clue what we were heading for.

The only briefing we had at the Yard was that we were being dispatched to Birmingham, headquarters of the West Midlands police force on an important undercover assignment. We would meet local officers there who would tell us what this secret mission was all about. We were given the confidential number of a senior police officer to ring as we approached Birmingham on the M1. Then we'd go to an appointed place named by him for the meeting. We were told to book into a particular hotel, leave there, find a secure land-line phone, ring in the details of the hotel and our West Midlands police contacts would come and pick us up. It was the type of cloak-and-dagger stuff I revelled in. We knew the job had to be big.

Within minutes of phoning in, two senior West Midlands detectives came to pick us up – DCS Ron Canter and DI Alex

Davidson. They sat down in our hotel room and for the first time told us of the enormity of the job we had been asked to undertake.

They had evidence that one of their own detectives, Sergeant Michael Ambizas, was trying to hire a hit-man to kill his lover's husband. They had clearly dug deep into the background of Ambizas before calling in SO10. He was, they said, a bit of a flash character who liked the high life – casinos, top restaurants, designer suits and beautiful women. He swanned around town in a top-of-the-range motor, a playboy with charm, guile, and not a little style. Suspicious West Midlands police chiefs had recently transferred him from regular CID duties to their training establishment where he taught young officers the art of detection. Our operation was to come as a salutary lesson in detection for him at the end of the day.

Ambizas, at thirty-four unmarried but with a string of affairs behind him including a Page Three pin-up, had approached an underworld figure in an illegal gambling casino and asked if he could put him in touch with a professional hit-man from London. The target was to be his girlfriend Anona Murphy's husband. He was offering £20,000 for a successful hit on Shaun Murphy, a convicted crook and a domestic thug.

Now, there's all sorts of police corruption, but conspiring to kill someone ... it doesn't get much worse than that. It focused our minds on the profound importance of the task at hand, for all concerned.

The West Midlands police force was, at that time, a beleaguered and much pilloried organisation following a series of scandals, notably the Serious Crime Squad being disbanded and some of its officers standing trial. They'd become the whipping boys of the national press. We knew, and the West Midlands force knew, that we could not afford to fuck this up.

We began meticulously planning our tactics and decided what roles we would play. My colleague, Andy, was going to be the main negotiator of the contract killing and I was going to be his trusted henchman who would help set up the murder. We were the double act up from the Smoke, hired hit-men with no qualms and no conscience.

Andy first contacted Ambizas by phone.

'I believe you've got some business for us to attend to.'

'Yes, but I can't talk on the phone.'

They arranged to meet at the Holiday Inn. Ambizas and his girlfriend arrived right on time and took the lift to the second floor. Andy met them as they got out, put a finger over his lips to indicate silence, then got them into another lift and went up to the fourth floor where I was waiting in our room, hidden tape recorders on. Then it was down to the business of murder.

Would-be victim Shaun Murphy was a well-known 'face' in the West Midlands with a penchant for guns and a nasty addiction to wife-beating. Ambizas wanted Murphy dead because he was having a passionate affair with Anona and intended to set up home with her. He was prepared to hire us for twenty grand to get Murphy out of the way. Anona would get a hefty insurance pay-out plus an inheritance which would be hers once Shaun was six feet under.

Murphy had accumulated a spurious fortune. He was a classic wheeler-dealer, entrepreneur, company director, call it what you like, and had done a bit of porridge along the way. No Sunday school teacher, but he didn't deserve to die, and certainly not at the instigation of a serving police officer.

Ambizas seemed convinced from the start we were a genuine hit team. We came up with an elaborate scam to lure Murphy into a position where he could be assassinated in the driveway of his house. His business address would be fire-bombed, he would be phoned, and we would shoot him as he rushed from his home to deal with it.

'Sounds good,' Ambizas enthused.

We would supply the rifle for the job. We'd arranged for a Heckler and Koch semi-automatic to be available from a firearms unit if we needed to show it. We got Ambizas and Anona to supply photographs, maps, car numbers, descriptions, known movements, everything a hit team would need to know. We went out and recce'd the property as they would have expected and found a perfect spot from which we could deliver a clean hit. There was a sturdy tree we could perch up overlooking the front drive, no obstructions in the line of fire. I was a lot more athletic in those days so it wouldn't be a problem.

The two of them were hooked. They never doubted our credentials. We were the professional hardened killers they had anticipated. We gave them a 'shopping list' of what we wanted in preparation for the hit. They had provided some items, but we needed to buy a bit of time to report back to our bosses at the Yard.

'We'll be back when you get the rest of the stuff,' we said.

We needed to leave them to sweat for a couple of weeks, to see if they really did want us to go ahead. If they'd come back and said, 'We've changed our minds and we don't want him killed after all,' our case wouldn't stand up in court. Intent was all important. And we had to be careful not to incite or encourage the crime – that would be entrapment. We needed to be very precise with our evidence. We were, after all, dealing with one of the West Midlands' serving detective sergeants who knew the law. And we wanted to leave the pair no legal loopholes to escape through.

A phone call from Ambizas. They had decided to go ahead with the hit. Andy and I returned up the M1 to Birmingham as hired assassins. Throughout the dealings, I'd been in the background as Martin Scott, the suitably sinister minder, the muscle. Doesn't need to know all that's going on. I wore the hat of being thick – some unkind folk may say rather too well – but it was an act I could switch on or off. It often allayed suspicions if you didn't seem too bright, and weren't present at all the conversations. But I was listening all right, thanks to the hidden electronic bugs in our hotel room.

As the hit was set, Ambizas and Anona produced the first half of the £20,000 contract cash. I was asked to count the £10,000 in a hotel room at the Metropole Hotel in Birmingham. They had apparently struggled to cobble the money together. Ambizas had cleaned out his building society account and Anona had flogged off jewellery. But they were still £200 short. Ambizas offered Andy a cheque for the balance. He turned round and said, 'You must be fucking joking.' Ambizas had to rush out and get it from a bank cash till to make up the shortfall ... brand-spanking-new notes in numbered sequences. Perfect evidence. The £10,000 was kept in a brown envelope which Anona had stuffed up her jumper. There was surprisingly little emotion as we sat talking murder for money.

I pretended that I wasn't happy with crisp cash point notes and told them in my best 'thicko' voice they could be identified and used in evidence if the job went bottoms up and we were all nicked. I told them, 'I only take used notes.' It was all bluff because we knew then that the trap was ready to be sprung and armed police would be coming through the door of room 5032 in thirty seconds flat. The game was up for the Casanova cop and his lady. The sting went off on schedule and as the cops crashed through the door Anona gasped, 'Oh no,' and nearly fainted. Ambizas was visibly shocked. He said, 'Someone has jumped the gun, lads,' and claimed *he* was setting *us* up for being contract killers.

It was a textbook case for the undercover unit. I was pleased for West Midlands police because they had been mullered over the Serious Crime Squad business and the guy we were working for, Ron Canter, was one of those officers who'd had his name dragged through the mire for no reason other than that he was in the West Midlands police force. We found him to be one of life's lovely people. And Alex Davidson, a short, stocky, rugby-playing Scotsman was tough and feisty but a lovely man with it. They were excellent to work with. They didn't have the experience of undercover operations that we'd had at the Yard and were led by us throughout. They were happy to be guided by our expertise and knowledge and the result was a highly successful joint operation. Rank never came into it, there was never any necessity to remind anyone of who was in charge; we were respectful of their rank, they were respectful of our skills.

Sadly, that wasn't always the case. You'd sometimes encounter a rank-obsessed prick who made life awkward for everyone and turned a difficult job into a nightmare. We'd been in and out of Birmingham like ghosts. No one except Ron and Alex knew we were there. Ambizas had a lot of connections in the job and they feared one leak could have blown the whole operation. And nobody knew when we had gone. Just the way we liked it.

Ambizas stood trial at Nottingham Crown Court in September 1990 charged with conspiracy to murder and was jailed for six years. He was convicted after we had given evidence to the jury from behind screens so that our faces would not be seen by anyone apart from the judge, jury and lawyers.

Anona delivered a slap in the face to Ambizas by pleading guilty to the charge, then giving evidence against her former lover. The jury was told about terrible violence in the Murphy household which had nurtured the murder plot. It seemed that Shaun, even though he no longer lived with Anona in their Tamworth home, often went back and subjected her to both physical and sexual abuse. He had shot their young daughter's Rottweiler dog and ill-treated a pony and a kitten. The full extent of her abuse never came out because she said she was just too frightened to disclose all the dreadful details. Shaun Murphy sounded an all-round nasty bastard and you could begin to see what a desperate state she had been in when she and Ambizas began planning his murder.

But there was no love lost between them when they finally parted company. They didn't even exchange glances in court as he was taken off to prison. Anona was set free with a one-year suspended prison sentence after the judge said she had been driven beyond all reasonable limits by her husband's reign of terror in their home. It transpired that Ambizas had fallen for Anona while he was on the rebound from an affair with a glamorous police cadet-turned-model called Gina Waddoups. She fell hook, line and sinker for his Mediterranean good looks and they had a torrid fling for nearly five years. She reckoned he looked like Omar Sharif and she and her three sisters thought he was a real charmer.

Gina, a Page Three girl and a right stunner, had been engaged to Ambizas but their romance hit the rocks when she left the police and moved to London to do topless modelling. The threats Ambizas made to her and her new boyfriend were apparently frightening enough for them to report it to the police. She said she knew he was trained in firearms use, kept guns under the bed and she was terrified he might try to take his revenge on her.

Some people thought Ambizas and Anona had got off pretty lightly in court but we often felt in undercover cases that the judiciary were a bit sceptical of our techniques despite the good results we were getting. The attitude of some judges in the late eighties and early nineties – and possibly still even now – was that undercover operations 'just aren't cricket, you know'. There is something about it that unsettles them. I think perhaps they think they are losing their control over part of the legal process. The police are running off doing things for which the courts haven't got a great weight of judicial precedence to rely on. They think, perhaps, that the police are becoming too inventive and doing things not legislated for and they don't particularly like that.

Sometimes you'd find that, having given evidence after an undercover operation, the sentences were less than if a conviction had been achieved through conventional police work, like steaming in with a sledgehammer, waving your warrant card and yelling, 'I'm a police officer.' Methods have changed because times have changed. Today's villains are smarter bastards and we've got to keep pace with investigative techniques. At the end of the day, my job wasn't about getting people massive sentences. I was the great pretender in order to clean the streets of as many villains as I could by the methods I knew best.

Chapter Six

SCUM OF THE EARTH

David Norris sounded pretty chipper when I spoke to him in his local pub to fix a business meeting for the following morning.

'Take care, Blex,' he said as he rang off.

Half an hour later, he was lying dead on the pavement near his South London home, pumped full of bullets from point-blank range. For David Norris's 'business' was the most dangerous in the world – police informant.

Call them what you like – squealer, grass, snitch, nark, snout – it's a fact of life that the police can't do without them. They are the bread and butter, the inescapable mainstay of the undercover work I was involved in. We couldn't function without them. The squad's ability to operate, its results, its success or failure invariably mirrored the quality of its informants and the way they were handled. They are a necessary evil in the battle against crime. At the same time, I have no hesitation in describing them as the utter, total, pits of the earth. And I reckon I'm more qualified than anyone to say that because I've worked with hundreds, most of them utter scum.

I'd known Dave Norris as an informant for a couple of years. As grasses go, he was in the big league. It came as no surprise to me at all that he became the victim of a carefully planned and ruthlessly executed hit. He'd grassed on dozens of fellow villains; he'd got cocky, too many people had got to know what he was about. It was only a matter of time before someone took him out.

I'd phoned him at his local, the Fox in Belvedere, South London, on a Sunday evening in April 1991 to fix up a meeting for 8.00am the following day when he was going to give us some information on yet another firm of villains involved in drug-dealing. He'd made thousands of pounds grassing up his cronies for years. This was another potential earner for him. I was driving to the meet the next day with a colleague when I heard on the radio that a man had been gunned down in Belvedere. Before I heard the name, I knew it was going to be Norris. Sure enough, it was, blasted to death when he stepped out of his car near his home as he returned from the pub. A two-man hit team on a powerful motorbike took him out with merciless efficiency. He'd begged for his life after the first bullet sent him crashing to the ground. He offered the killers money to spare him – to no avail. His frantic wife, Debbie, ran out screaming for mercy for her dying husband, but they were clinical professionals and finished him off with a volley of shots to the head before roaring off on a powerful 500cc Honda motorbike. It was a classic gangland hit. And one of my best informants was the victim.

I couldn't feel anything when I heard it on the radio. At the end of the day, informers are playing a dangerous game for money. Getting yourself splattered over the pavement is an occupational hazard. I've worked with some of the most successful informants the police have ever had and got to know what slippery bastards most of them were. I always tried to have an air of detachment from them. You sometimes had to purport to like them, pretending to want to work with them to get the best out of them. But deep down I was always thinking, 'Thank fuck you're not a mate of mine.' They are grasses and they would sell their grandmother for money.

These people are totally unprincipled, callous bastards. They earn from crime for years then change sides when they want to eliminate the opposition, or when they find themselves in the shit, or when they want revenge for some matter or other. Or just to earn a nice few bob from the police funds. Those doing it for revenge, stitching up a rival they hadn't got the bottle to do themselves, would come running to Old Bill and prop up the target. I personally find that abhorrent. But, professionally, I had to set that aside, smile politely and get on with the job. I had to associate with these people, go out drinking with them even, spend a lot of time with them, get to know them, their motives, build a relationship. You had to do it by the book for the powers that be because their registration documents as informants have to be noted accordingly as to what their motivations are. My personal opinion is that they are shitbags of the highest order because I just don't believe in their ethos. But needs must in a dirty world...

Norris, of course, was one of them. When I first met him he

had already begun his career as an informant giving information to the Regional Crime Squad about a variety of crooked enterprises. I met him when I was doing undercover operations for the Central Drugs Squad at Scotland Yard. He was a very well-connected villain. It naturally followed that he was able to give information of the highest quality involving other like-minded and well-connected criminals. But he was notoriously difficult to handle, in as much as people were never 100 per cent sure of which side of the fence he was on, if indeed he wasn't playing both sides from the middle, running with the fox while hunting with the hounds. He was likely to prop up a job he'd be earning out of, getting his rake-off, then in turn would be rewarded by the police for grassing up his cronies. He was definitely having an each-way bet on many occasions. Grassing is bad enough, but that sort of double-dealing is grassing at its worst. I've often said that if there is a heaven and a hell and these grasses find themselves in hell, I just hope the Devil's got a witness protection programme. Even he is going to have a number that he's going to have to re-house.

Despite the fact that Dave Norris would stitch up friends and enemies for cash rewards, he was, in fact, quite a likeable bloke if you were talking pub mates. He was sociable, jovial, he had diverse interests ranging from fishing to greyhound racing, and was keen on women even though he was married and not averse to an away game with a bit of crumpet as long as Debbie never knew – a few plus points over the average grass. You could go out on the piss with him and quite enjoy yourself. A lot of cops who mixed with him did genuinely like him. For a lot of them, of course, he was their first insight into dealing with someone from the underworld, a real villain.

SCUM OF THE EARTH

Cops, by and large, are precluded from associating with villains. They aren't allowed to associate with gangsters except, of course, registered informants. I've always found that a bit of a contradiction because surely informants reflect the very worst of criminality. These treacherous bastards live in a twilight world; they straddle the fence and hop from one side to another depending on whatever circumstances suit them. It's got to make them automatically the most dangerous of any type of villain. Yet they are the only ones the police will authorise you to mix with ... people with just about the most confused set of standards you can ever imagine. Many, many police careers have been ruined by the mishandling of informants. They either suffer from Stockholm syndrome, metaphorically getting into bed with them, or rubbing them up the wrong way to such a degree that they lose their trust and therefore the source of the information they're depending on. I've never been able to fathom it out. Surely a copper is better off having a pint with someone he knows is an out-and-out crook but would never for the life of him want to be a grass, allowing them to share a conversation about any number of other things and getting to know each other's attitudes without ever having to bring up the subject of criminality. You're a cop, I'm a villain, we know where we stand, let's talk about the football or the racing or any number of purely innocent subjects. It doesn't work that way. Informants have given the police as many problems as results over the years. By their very nature, you never know with certainty which side of the fence they are on. I think sometimes they don't know themselves. Always an eye on the main chance.

Norris was, by and large, in the informing business for money, coupled occasionally with a desire to take out the opposition on his patch. He was originally a coalman as a young man but he soon decided that lugging sacks of anthracite around was far too hard a way of earning a crust when there was villainy as an alternative. He was suspected of involvement in armed robberies, though not convicted. He would do anything, in the 'Arfur Daley' sense, that would be a 'nice little earner'. He knew the 'right' people. He'd handle counterfeit currency or stolen goods, and he would be involved in drug deals; there was nothing that was off limits to him. He was utterly ruthless in the way he eliminated other criminal gangs by informing on their crooked activities.

Towards the end, he was doing so much work with the police that it became an open secret in south-east London that Dave Norris was a grass. It was an odds-on certainty that someday one of those rivals would take revenge. His name had been on a bullet for a long time. He had grassed so many people up that the police ran out of ideas on how to protect him from being identified as the source. He got careless. He didn't give a toss. He didn't think it out. He was so desperately keen to grass more and more people up and make money out of it, which he did handsomely, that with every passing day he was putting himself in more and more danger. I've always been a gambling man and I wouldn't have given him better than even money of making his next birthday.

Just half an hour before he was shot, he was fixing the meet with me to grass up yet more villains, another drugs gang. The word had been out for him for a long, long time. He was so active the police had had to set aside two batches of officers to deal with him. A colleague and I were handling him more or less on a daily basis for his drugs work, and long-standing colleague Jim Clarkson, a DI on the Regional Crime Squad at East Dulwich, was handling his other crime stuff – counterfeit currency, stolen gear of every variety, art thefts, this, that and the other. That's how prolific Norris was.

He was discussing a future job with Jim Clarkson over a few pints in the Fox in Belvedere on the night he died. I rang him in the bar there to check that he was OK for the next day's breakfast meet on a new drugs job he was putting up. That's how he worked, moving from one cop to another with more underworld information.

The next morning I picked up my colleague, DS Bill Trimble, a pleasant, quiet, former long-serving uniformed officer, not the usual hard-nosed Yard DS you sometimes come across, and we were driving to meet Norris for breakfast to discuss the job. The radio was on and that's when I heard it. When they gave his name, they'd got it slightly wrong – Maurice or something like that, but I knew.

A couple of minutes later, my mobile rang. It was my boss DI Charlie Eubank and he said, 'Blex, have you heard?'

I said I'd just heard an item on the radio with the name slightly different but I was assuming it was our man.

He said, 'Yes, it's him.'

I said, 'Well, best I don't bother going to the cafe then. Norris won't turn up now.'

Bill, my colleague, was absolutely shell-shocked, aghast at the news. I literally saw the colour drain from his cheeks.

That was the morning I coined the phrase 'better dead

than nicked', because there had been a lot of suspicion about Norris's dealings with informant handlers over the years. At one point, one trusted colleague and I were the only officers allowed to deal with him. A lot of people had been struck off the list of handlers because of suspicions they had been got at, backhanders going to and fro, palms greased. I can say, hand on heart, that I was saying that for other people's benefit, because I'd heard the rumours and I was well aware of some of the shenanigans that were supposed to be going on. I said that if he'd been nicked with a huge great parcel of drugs, he would have sung like a canary taking everyone down with him, in the job or out of it, who had ever taken a drink off him. That's the sort of person he was. There would have been no loyalty to anyone. He was a grass and he was always looking to cover his backside. He'd have taken everyone down with him to save his skin.

Bill fell apart. I had to take him to my flat and give him a large brandy. He knew Norris well. In fact, he was due to collect some money off him over a betting coup that had come off over the weekend. Bill was a big greyhound man and he'd given Norris a tip, and Norris had lumped on it large and he was going to give Bill a drink out of his winnings. Not corrupt, but possibly unwise in the circumstances.

As Bill sat there ashen-faced, I said to him, 'Come on, pull yourself together; he's only a dirty stinking grass who's got wiped out. It's not anyone we're going to grieve for.'

But Bill was really, really upset. To me it was another reminder that you must never get to like these people, never get too close. Never kid yourself they are real friends. You can pretend to like them, but once you walk out that door you don't have to carry it on.

By the time Bill had regained his composure and we had arrived at the office, there was only one topic of conversation and a murder squad had already been set up. I expected the murder squad boys to be all over me like a nasty rash given the circumstances and my involvement with Norris over the years. After all, I'd spoken to him minutes before he'd been murdered, but to this very day nobody from that squad has ever asked me a single question, ever. Bill kept going to the murder squad almost on a daily basis like he'd lost a friend, giving them all sorts of theories. But I couldn't give a fuck. Norris was dead, and I'd got other things to be doing. He'd given us some good information over the years, he'd introduced me to loads of criminal gangs so that I could infiltrate them posing as another crook, but he knew the risks.

Rumours had been rife a long time before his death that there was a contract out on him, with a £15,000 price tag to do it quick and keep it neat.

Months of intensive inquiries by the Yard uncovered the fact that the hit was carried out by a professional two-man team from the terrorist heartland of Belfast – Terry McCrory and John Green. London drug barons, possibly the ones he was about to grass up to me, paid the pair to travel over and carry out the execution. Norris was an easy target. He took no special precautions and seemed to think he was untouchable. The hit happened as he pulled up outside his home in Regency Square, Belvedere, in his flash four-wheel-drive Jeep and stepped onto the pavement. The black-helmeted assassins zoomed up on their motorbike out of the dark. Norris started to run towards his front door. He knew the day had come. He was chased by one of the gunmen and was brought down with a single shot. His wife Debbie, who'd been inside with their three kids, ran out shouting, 'Stop, please stop.' The gunman took no heed and pumped several more shots into Norris. He died on a patch of grass beside the pavement, a huge pool of blood flooding out around him, with Debbie sobbing her heart out as he died. She was pregnant with twins at the time.

I don't know whether she knew about Dave's informing, his philandering, or where he'd got his money. She loved him anyway. But informing had become like a drug to him. He was absolutely hooked on it, a serial grass who couldn't stop. He got a real buzz out of it, always wanting to be around the police, and know the outcome of his tip-offs. His murder, I'm afraid, was as certain as night follows day.

The two motorbike assassins and two accomplices are all serving life for Norris's murder. Scotland Yard had at first denied that Norris was one of their paid informants, but several of the better-informed daily paper crime reporters knew it and used it in their headlines the day after the killing. The Yard was finally obliged to confirm it once the case came to trial.

Norris was the second informant of mine to be murdered. I'm surprised there haven't been more. They play a dangerous game. A grass called Peter McNeil put up a large cocaine importation job to us in which we nicked two guys with known and confirmed links with the Mafia. Any kind of grassing is perilous in the extreme, but double-crossing the Mafia is suicidal. We knew there would be a contract out on McNeil but it wasn't until years later that anyone finally got to him; whether it was the Mob or not, I don't know. McNeil was another who was almost blatant about his informing. He had this sort of *laissez-faire* attitude towards it all and was another for whom his past was always going to catch up with him one day. He was shot as well. I never got to know exactly who did it, but you could have lined up the usual suspects from London to Llandudno.

The fact that so few grasses end up dead is probably a tribute to the police witness protection schemes and the expertise they employ in putting would-be killers off the scent. A lot of time and thought is given to that. There was a time, while informants and supergrasses were big news in the national press, when people said that if the underworld crime bosses managed to bump off just one of them, it would be enough of a warning to stop any others turning informant. But in my experience the fear of assassination is considerably weaker than the lure of what they see as easy money from the police and a nice protection package for themselves. Far from diminishing, the number of informants, and above all, the quality of informants, has continued unabated over the years. They are crucial to keeping the lid on organised crime.

If you were a gangster thinking of killing an informant, you'd need to be very sure of covering your tracks because you can be absolutely certain that the police are going to leave no stone unturned to find out who's done it. The big boys probably think it's not worth the risk of a life sentence for wiping out a heap of shit and simply write it off to experience. They'll be more careful in future. I've never shed a tear for any misfortune that's happened to any grass I've known. They play at Judas, they take the consequences.

THE GANGBUSTER

I was severely warned off talking about David Norris by a senior Scotland Yard police officer. It was made clear to me in no uncertain terms that I shouldn't drag all this up again. It's always going to be a sensitive issue within the police force but I'm afraid the Norris incident is relevant and material to my life and I refuse to be gagged over it. Norris was a top-grade informant and his story is a first-class illustration of the level of informing the police now handle, as well as all its complexities, its dangers, and its consequences. Norris is dead, but there'll be someone to fill his shoes.

I have spent many hours with many informants of all colours and creeds, male and female. I treated every one of them with the utmost caution, fearful in the knowledge that there are a lot of Old Bill languishing in prison now because of inappropriate relationships with informers. You must never let the tail wag the dog, or be seduced into their clutches by the lure of easy money and a glamorous lifestyle. Discipline is the name of the game; discipline with yourself, an emotional detachment which allows you never to lose sight of the fact that you are doing a job on behalf of the British public who rely on you to sweep the sewers clean.

The style of hit which took out Dave Norris was a classic gangland assassination which originated in Colombia among the feuding drugs cartels. Two men on a powerful bike, the pillion rider to do the hit, the driver skilled enough to be able to make an escape through even the most congested streets.

I had many dealings with various factions of the Colombian drug trade as they targeted European markets in the eighties. They had emerged as the most powerful and ruthless drugs suppliers anywhere in the world. They protected their empires ruthlessly, killing judges, lawyers, police and rivals with impunity. The US markets were saturated.

The drug barons of Bogotá set their sights on other outlets worldwide. They sent various people to Britain looking for fresh buyers, fixers and would-be dealers, to prepare the ground work for the huge surge in cocaine and heroin which was to follow up to epidemic proportions. The advance guard had no real UK base and were probably a little less careful than they would have been if they were established career criminals from this country. They put themselves out on a limb a little bit too often trying to make new contacts in the drug world. So they frequently came to our attention through the informer network. We were able to scoop up several Colombian-linked gangs before they could get established. But we were only stemming the tide if you look at the fantastic amount of cocaine that's about in London and other parts of Britain today.

Informants came out of the woodwork all the time. It could be from a number of sources; local cops, for example, executing a search warrant at somebody's house, finding a load of gear, and that person then facing a hefty jail sentence and choosing to turn grass to bail themselves out of trouble. A confidential word would be passed on to the judge in court enabling him to know of how much assistance the suspect has been and hopefully get a lesser sentence. It could be an aggrieved fellow villain who wanted to level the score after he'd been had over by some other crook, so he came forward and volunteered information. It might be your established informants like Norris, motivated primarily by greed; it might be a local nick that've got someone a bit out of their league and want us to take over. Occasionally, you could have a cold caller come in off the street, walk in and say, 'I want to talk to someone about so and so,' and then you suddenly find you've a got a live runner out of nowhere. In every case, you get the necessary authorisation, submit the paperwork and go and check it out thoroughly.

What you have to be most careful of in dealing with every informant is that they aren't actually setting up a job just to get a police reward for informing. It's the bread and butter of the investigation to get the ground work right. You have to be mindful at all times that you are dealing with the most treacherous dregs of society, and be aware of any potential scams that could leave you with egg on your face or worse. And there were occasions in which informants would be putting up work to you where they were trying to entice you to bend the rules, like saying, 'I know that in Fred Bloggs's deep freeze he's got ten kilos of cocaine. Can we go in and find five?' They want five for themselves to make it a double-earner.

I've had a job put up to me where my informant said there was £70,000 cash in a suspect's home and he was inviting me to act as a legalised burglar to go in and nick the money. Part of it would go into the police report, the other into his back pocket. I told him to get lost. This was the tail wagging the dog and I didn't want any part of it.

* * *

Because of my reputation in the world of undercover operations, I would get called to all parts of the country to assist in different inquiries. I and my colleagues were effectively on hire to any force that needed our expertise. Sometimes you would even be requested by name if you'd met someone on another job or they had received a recommendation from somebody who knew you. We had regular national training seminars at which undercovers from all over the country would meet for updates on techniques, exchange experiences and so on, so a network was formed through which you became known throughout the country as an expert in your field.

Between regular covert assignments, I used to lecture to other forces both in Britain and abroad on training techniques for would-be undercover operatives. I was fortunate to be selected to go to the finest criminal investigation and intelligence unit in the world, at Quantico in Virginia, USA, where the FBI and American Drug Enforcement Agency share a joint headquarters, the very cutting edge in the worldwide fight against organised crime. I spent my time predominantly with the DEA and US Customs learning new aspects of detection and investigation. It was a rewarding and fascinating experience and a frightening insight into the sheer magnitude of the global drugs problem.

At Quantico, we saw the DEA Operation Snowcap guys in training – a military unit to all intents and purposes – who were going down to Colombia to bomb drugs factories in pre-emptive strikes against the drugs cartels. Hard bastards, every one of them. Tough, fit, totally committed to hitting back at the Colombian drug giants, and doing a great job.

I remember Colin Baker, the ITN reporter, telling me once over a drink just what a lawless and terrifying place Colombia was. He'd been there only a few weeks earlier after some bombing incident or other during the drugs wars and had witnessed a motorbike team assassination which was later copied in London for David Norris's killing and several others.

Apparently, one of the big gangs had targeted a rival dealer and had found someone who lived in a similar block and had a similar lifestyle. They'd watch for a while and if the similarities were close enough to the intended victim, they would hit the other poor bastard for practice. They'd take out a totally innocent bloke in a trial run. It never made me keen to visit Bogotá. I don't think the Yard would have allowed us to operate in Colombia anyway, for security reasons. They did have a certain regard for our safety. I limited my dealings with Colombians to Earl's Court. There were enough to practise on, trickling in every year looking at the market place.

The police play the financial dealings with informers very close to their chest; after all, it's public money they are paying out to criminals. But I have been involved in several cases where five-figure sums have been handed over – £10,000 is not unique or even overly unusual. I had one very good informant – I'll call him Sebastian to protect his real identity – who was so prolific he must have grassed up just about everyone he'd ever worked with over a ten-year period. Everything he was paid was salted away in a high-interest bank account and when he'd accumulated enough he set himself up in an antiques business, did very well at it and has never ever grassed up anyone since. He's the exception – most just blow it on drink or drugs or flash motors.

The money is always paid in cash by a senior officer. You're never going to get a grass to accept a cheque, are you? Sometimes, an undercover operative like myself might be there to see the grass collect, if he chooses, but I normally avoided it like the plague. By then my job had been done, you're out of it. Whatever amount of payment is due is normally set by a senior officer. You can nominate a figure if you think the information has been a bit special, but usually it's out of your hands, and a good thing too. A senior officer, like a Deputy Assistant Commissioner or a Chief Superintendent, would count the cash out, and then the informant would stuff it in his pocket and get a warning about not sharing it out with his police handler. They are the successful jobs. While the police actively encourage the recruitment of grasses they give you no back-up support or help if it all goes tits up. It is a sphere which is open to a lot of abuse, as there is a great deal of potential for having a swindle of one form or another with an informant. And much as the bosses love the good results, they are more than ready to jump on you like a ton of bricks if there is any suggestion of impropriety in relation to one.

All in all, it's a pretty thankless task being an informant handler. You only really get the personal satisfaction of locking the bad guys up. I remember my police colleague, who attained the rank of Superintendent despite a high-profile internal investigation into his links with a top North London supergrass, being asked at a CID drinks party what he thought about all the allegations that he might or might not be a rascal. He replied, 'Some call me corrupt and some promote me.' Amen.

Chapter Seven

KNIFE EDGE

Danny Smithers – not his real name – was not a man you could ever say was at ease with the world. Big, sinister, angry: the threat of violence never far away. He was suspected of running a vast drug empire with tentacles in London, Liverpool, Amsterdam and half a dozen other big cities. He was a busy 'networking' criminal with nationwide links in the underworld here and abroad, a serious pro. He had a well-documented history of violence, was thought to have regularly ripped off other drug-dealers in brutal attacks and his name had cropped up in relation to a number of savage murders. An altogether nasty bastard.

I knew from the start this was going to be one of those undercover jobs with more than the normal quota of risks, and I wasn't wrong. We'd got a lead in to Smithers' activities through informant Dave Norris and I went undercover, in my favoured jeans and pony tail role of cool drug-dealer, to meet various contacts on the fringes of drug crime in London to worm my way slowly into the Smithers inner circle of associates.

They weren't people we could instantly identify by name or criminal records, but were, and this was not unusual, people known only by their nicknames, or even just descriptions – Mick the Limp, Fat Alf, that sort of thing, people who were said to be selling a bit of gear or looking to find buyers for gear. We had vague leads like, 'He's a bald bloke who lives at so and so and drinks in such and such a pub,' you know the sort of thing, all part of the jigsaw. These guys don't make a habit of proffering their names, addresses and phone numbers. But you have to start somewhere. It's a matter of digging, piecing all the scraps together to make your way up the ladder to the big guys at the top. It all adds to the uncertainty of the job because you just don't know who you are going to meet on the next rung, or who might try to throw you off. But being a bit scared wasn't a bad thing. It kept you on your toes, kept you alive. It was the old swan syndrome – on the surface you're cool, calm and serene but underneath you're paddling like fuck to stay afloat. You had to retain your cover at all costs, keep your composure, set up your credibility, try and pull the job off successfully. Most of all, stay in one piece. The adrenaline that coursed through my veins with each new assignment was addictive. I was hooked on the danger. And it was no less so than when they sent me after Danny Smithers. The buzz was there.

Initially, your informant is your lifeline to get the operation up and running. He is the link with suspects and will initially give you your credibility as he introduces you into the criminal circles he's planning to blow apart.

'Yeah, I know this geezer, he's kosher,' or something like that. Nothing over the top. With Norris, we'd worked together so often, we had almost a set routine like Morecambe and Wise, gags and all, if I thought a laugh helped my credibility. We'd only have to polish up on it and change a few details with each new target. If I was meeting a new informant, and didn't know them from Adam, I would need to get their background and preferences together – things like tastes, beers, food, habits, hobbies – that would give us some common ground to work on. Conversation lines would always include the obvious, like 'Where were you born?' 'Where have you lived?' 'Where were you brought up?' 'How much bird have you done?' 'What well-known crooks do you know?' that we could have a mutual chat about. But you've got to be careful; if they check you out with some top villain you've mentioned and he says, 'Never heard of him,' you could be in deep shit. All the time, the villains might be wanting to keep the informant in on the action while you are desperate to get him off the plot so that he can't be sussed out.

Undercover work was play-acting in a real-life drama and it worked best if you'd got a bit of a script to stick to. I liked to keep a couple of funny stories up my sleeve to break up conversations, keep it light, get them to like you as a bit of a funny guy, a crook with a sense of humour. You can't have it all heavy nose to nose, eyeball to eyeball confrontation. You have to try to take out any tension between you and the villains. You're trying to set up a business arrangement that's hopefully going to make you both loads of money. You want them to be comfortable with you. You're one of them.

It's vital that your snout has briefed you as best he can so that the enemy doesn't get suspicious. The villains will always assume you are an undercover cop. You have to convince them otherwise. And they don't hold back in checking you out. I've been thrown against lavatory walls and searched for hidden wires a good few times before they'd accept I was kosher.

* * *

I eventually met Danny Smithers after Norris and I had done the ground work around various boozers in South London. He was not an easy man to deal with. He oozed suspicion, wary of everyone. He operated around seedy, run-down pubs, and there was an air of constant menace about his lifestyle that made people uncomfortable in his company. I wasn't any different. He was a difficult character to deal with, to say the least, and I had to dig deep in my undercover box of tricks to convince him that I was a genuine drug-trafficker of some considerable muscle. I could speak the language, I knew the scene. We agreed a trade involving a kilo of high-grade cocaine.

I was now breaking new ground in covert police work in establishing a 'freedom to roam' policy rather than a static operation controlled by senior officers. I needed to be able to move with the action without having to gain consent from my DI or other controlling officer. I had to be able to improvise, move the goalposts if necessary. I'd found that if you were too stuck in your ways, refusing to leave a particular premises, for instance, because that wasn't in the game plan, the villains were going to say, 'Hold on, there's something wrong here, why won't he leave?' Perhaps they wanted to pull out and go to the pub up the road. They might want to move to a pub five miles away to meet someone or have a drink. You could argue that your money was on the plot so you didn't want to take it on to some other manor you weren't sure about because of the threat of robbery. This was often true, because the prospect of being ripped off in the drug world was ever-present and the Commissioner of Scotland Yard would not take kindly to you going back and saying, 'Sorry, boss, I'm forty thousand pounds light on the drug-buy money.' So I needed this flexibility, a right to roam in pursuit of villainy.

When the evening of the cocaine trade arrived, Danny Smithers was his usual brooding self. You could tell he was a hard bastard. I had to be careful. Don't say the wrong thing. Should I raise my game and portray myself as hard as him? That could easily lead to a clash of styles – not a good move.

Should I pay a bit of due deference, the 'respect' the West Indians are so fond of? 'Don't diss me, man.' OK by me. This could help massage his ego perhaps and, if he was feeling great about himself, and you'd made him feel great that a trade was on and that he was going to make some nice money, then you had the ability to manoeuvre him a little bit in the way you wanted the job to proceed. You were aiming for all the key factors to be in place without arousing the suspicions of this very distrustful man: firstly, that he would be nicked, secondly, that the gear was on the plot and finally, that you could make good your escape. If you've got him feeling happy, it makes things that bit easier.

'Another drink, Danny?' I paid my due respects without

letting him take me for a mug. The deal was on. We were now on a 'roaming plot', moving with the action. It could sometimes be difficult for the supervising officers to keep tabs on. You work to a broad plan; you go here, you go there, wherever is necessary. You are basically working on the hoof and they must alter plans at a second's notice to make sure you are still in their sights. The surveillance teams and the attack teams backing you up, always invisible in the background, have to have the brains and the flexibility to change the game plan with all changing locations and environments, a very difficult job which I really appreciated on so many occasions. I knew it could be difficult for them, and dangerous for me, if contact was lost, so I always tried to make matters as easy as I could for them, never doing anything in too much of a hurry, if we were on the move. I'd get to my car door and stop for a chat, either with my driver or one of the bad guys, or light a fag, blow my nose, any sort of delaying tactic to allow the back-up teams to keep with me. But this was not always possible. There was always a margin for error and black holes to fall into.

The trade was scheduled to take place at a pub in East London, just off the Commercial Road, at Smithers' request. Smithers was orchestrating the situation throughout, nipping in to see me, nipping out to make a phone call and, of course, wanting to see the money. I'd drawn £35,000 of the Commissioner's money for the deal and had it all bundled up in £100 lots. Whenever I drew big sums, I insisted, much to the annoyance of everybody on the squad, that it was all rolled up in the drug-dealers' special way. If it was in twenties it would be four notes then one wrapped over so that everything was in hundred-pound rolls. It made it much easier to count out and it was what the dealers expected to see. If you were sitting in a car with a dealer, you didn't want to be counting out every bloody note. It would take forever, so it was a case of 'Here's some I prepared earlier.' When it came from the Yard cashiers, it was all in neat bundles of £5,000. I'd get some of the lads to fold it all down in £100 wads for Charlie Big Potatoes because that's how I wanted to take it out. I knew the style because I was spending more time being a drug-dealer than a cozzer and this was how it happened in the badlands. I was totally into the lifestyle of a top drugs baron. I acted like a drug-dealer, talked like a drug-dealer, thought like a drug-dealer, behaved like a drug-dealer. That's what made it work.

Danny Smithers was satisfied and had his lieutenants in place. He called the cocaine onto the plot ready for the handover. I was given my directions to go out of the pub and down an alleyway and wait underneath a lamp-post where I could be seen. Then I would be approached.

I was standing there looking the part, big-time drug-dealer, heart racing, and adrenaline pumping. It was dark and it was cold and nothing happened for several minutes. You start wondering about a rip-off, a couple of big blokes appearing out of the murk, kicking the shit out of you and legging it with the money. It happens a lot but you never hear about it unless some poor bastard gets shot. You just don't get drug-dealers pitching up at police stations saying that they've been robbed of a large sum of drugs money. I was very aware of the risks and getting a tad lonely out there.

Then one of Smithers' cronies came shuffling up the alley, a little white fella with a woolly hat pulled down over his head. He looked half-pregnant because he'd got the gear shoved down the front of his jacket. He came down the alleyway – he knew who he was looking for, he'd been given my name and description – and he suddenly presented me with the package from under his coat, as they always do. He wanted me to take it quick. It was often pass the parcel with Charlie or smack in case of a bust.

'The money, where's the money?' he asked.

I said, 'Hang on, all you've done is present me with a bag of powder here, I've got to test it.'

'You know it's quality gear, it's real quality gear, now where's the money?'

'Now, calm down,' I said, 'settle down, we're talking about a lot of money here. I'm going to test this before you get to see a penny.' I opened up the package in the middle of the alleyway because there was only one way I could test the cocaine; you can't take a line, so you have to dip into the powder with a wet finger and then rub it on your gums. Because cocaine has anaesthetic properties – just like novocaine which dentists use – you can tell pretty well instantaneously whether it's good gear or rubbish by how quickly your gums go numb. It's like the early stages of a dental injection, a tingling then an anaesthetic effect. It hit me very quickly. I thought I was in the dentist's chair. This was quality gear. Creamo.

We were all set for the bust and I gave my signal to the waiting back-up squad: off with my Kangol cap and hold it in my right hand. That's what they'd been told to watch for and I expected the heavy clump of police boots to be thundering up the alley, guns drawn for action. Nothing happened. I waited. And I waited. Nothing. Houston, we have a problem. At this point, I have a couple of options. I can break cover and nick him. But that jeopardises the informant, risks losing the arrest of Smithers, could blow the whole operation. Alternatively, I can stall for time. So I told the geezer, 'No, I'm not sure, I haven't got a feeling yet. I'm gonna have to have another dab, mate.'

So I do it again, playing for time. The quality of the cocaine was never in doubt but I had to buy a bit more time. I was thinking that I'd had a bloody great surveillance team on me all day but they sure don't seem to be with me now. In fact, they'd lost me when I went down the alley and they didn't have the nous to send somebody down to see what was happening. So I had another dab. And by now, my mouth is so anaesthetised I thought I'd copped a right-hander from Lennox Lewis. You could have ripped my teeth out one by one and I wouldn't have known. I wouldn't have felt a thing. I thought, if I have to take another dab I'll seize up. It was like my top lip was stuck to my gums. Then they finally sent someone down the alley to see what was happening. The bad guy and I got into a sort of huddle and lit up a fag as if nothing was going on, like we were just having a chat. But chatting had become near impossible. My mouth was like after you've had a tooth out. I could hardly speak a word it was so numb. I managed to mumble that I wasn't happy and I was going to have to give the gear back to him. He knew it was good gear, he'd probably had a toot himself before the trade – so what sort of twat he thought I was I don't know. I had no choice but to pull out. If back-up couldn't be there on time to nick him, it would have to be the one that got away. I started to move off muttering, 'Fuck, fuck, fuck,' under my breath. I was fuming. I'd set the job up, I'd got the gear on the plot, where were those tossers?

I was disappearing into the night and the dealer was walking out of the alley when all hell broke loose. The heavy mob arrived. Someone was shouting, 'ATTACK, ATTACK, ATTACK.' They chased and caught him nearby. Then he nearly died from an asthma attack in the street. They ended up calling an ambulance for him and it was touch and go for a couple of days. He subsequently sued the police for damages but lost his claim. Talk about chancing it – he'd been caught red-handed with half a kilo of coke!

Smithers ran a spurious defence after his case went to a retrial and was eventually acquitted of conspiracy to supply drugs and possession of drugs. There is a Scotland Yard report in existence which called it an 'outrageous defence which totally confused or at least misled the jury'. Smithers is now in prison for other offences. If he wants to sue me for mentioning his involvement in the East London case I'll see him in court.

* * *

Like many of the cases I was involved in, I was not asked to give evidence because my guv'nors wanted to retain my anonymity for future operations. If they had a strong enough case without me, they'd keep me out of it altogether. That way, the villains would never know I was an undercover cop. If it was necessary, I'd do it from behind a screen if the trial judge was amenable.

On another job involving a big cannabis ring, I found myself negotiating with a small army of villains. I've never known any job in which so many people were involved.

I was again posing as a buyer and the gang reckoned they could supply me up to forty kilos of good-grade hash. As it happened, they didn't have the ability to get the full quota and they only brought ten kilos onto the plot.

We were again on a fluid, roving brief and went to North London for the trade. Suddenly there were six, seven, eight people involved, a bloody battalion of fingers in the pie. I wasn't negotiating with one of them; I was negotiating with the whole fucking lot of them. I couldn't hear myself think.

I'd spent days working around the Holloway Road, getting dragged round pubs here, there and everywhere, meeting other people, trying to penetrate the gang. I finally ended up in a shop somewhere. Again, it's late at night and it's dark and I'm involved in a lot of heated negotiations over the cannabis with the bloke who's running the place. The whole place is adorned with knives, machetes, swords, every sort of weapon.

Anyway, it was gone 9.00pm, the place was closed to the public and I was locked inside with this mad bastard and his fearsome choppers. Tempers were getting frayed; it was boiling up into a nasty situation. They were insisting that I brought the money into the building. I argued that I wasn't bringing in the cash in case it got nicked and I was thinking, fuck me, I'm in a knife shop, I've got to be careful here. The bloke I was talking to was a daunting fucker; a shaven-headed, big, tall fucking lump. He ran the place and was basically putting the deal together. I wasn't budging from my standpoint until I'd seen the hash. They were getting shirtier and shirtier.

Then, suddenly a car screeched up outside the shop and I was bundled out and slung into the back seat. As we were driving round the block, they produced the cannabis and said, 'Right, there's the fucking gear, where's the cash?'

THE GANGBUSTER

They'd expected me to do it all nicely nicely on trust and weren't happy that I'd insisted on seeing the stuff. But I had to satisfy the police criteria for making an arrest. I had to risk needling them. I looked at the hash and it seemed fine. And just as quickly as I'd been bundled out of the place I was shoved back in it, and the car drove off with the gear inside. I thought the Old Bill shadowing me would have missed all that and wouldn't know where the cannabis was being kept. I thought they would have considered that too risky. So now I was totally incommunicado. The bloke turned round to me, bolted the place back and front and said, 'Right, if you don't bring the money in here there's only one way you're going to leave this shop.' 'Oh yeah?' I said. 'With six of them in your back,' he continued. He was looking at the knives on the wall, and proper fuck-off knives they were. So I thought, it's only a poxy job and not worth dying for, and told him I'd call up the money from my mate who was round the corner with it in his motor. I rang my pal – another undercover officer, of course – on my mobile and started talking utter fucking gobbledegook. He was asking me questions and I was giving him stupid answers hoping he'd twig that I was in bother.

We had agreed one pre-arranged danger word at the start of the operation. If I mentioned it, he would know it had all gone horrendously wrong and he would need to alert the cavalry. I gave the password – in fact it was two, 'poxy BMW', which you could slip easily into a conversation – and told the knife loony the money was on its way. I said my mate was a little way away and would be there in a few minutes. That was a bluff upon which my life could depend. I knew the money wasn't going to come round. The tension in the shop became absolutely unbearable.

Everyone was hyper, him and three or four other guys, they were all on edge, jittery. I made another call on the mobile. 'Are you on your way, get a move on?' I knew he wasn't in a BMW but I said again, 'Are you in that poxy BMW?'

That left him in no doubt we had a crisis. I managed to get myself slightly away from the front door because I knew what was going to happen next. And it did.

BANG!

It was like a fucking bomb going off as the Old Bill launched into the front of the shop, taking out doors and windows with sledgehammers. One of the biggest blokes you've ever seen took out the reinforced front door with a couple of mighty swipes. The drug gang thought they were about to be ripped off.

'Are these yours? Are these yours?' they asked.

'They're fuck all to do with me,' I lied. With that, they all started legging it to the back of the shop which was great because it was bolted and barred like Fort Knox and they were all desperately trying to get the door open. The attack team ploughed through the front door and captured them all at the back of the shop, trapped like rats. With that, I was out through the hole and scarpered off the plot.

Unfortunately, there wasn't a big stash of drugs in the shop, just a couple of little bits which were samples and that was all they got charged with possessing. The bloke round the comer with the main drugs was arrested and identified and stood trial separately. The bad bastard who had threatened my life never stood trial because no drugs were found on him, but he was the real orchestrator of the deal.

We wanted to protect the undercover operation and our

source. My giving evidence in court would have given it away. I must say I was a little bit aggrieved because he'd held me captive and had threatened to stick fucking great knives in my back. I'd been kidnapped, in essence. I did make my feelings known to the management and said I was willing to give evidence, but they said 'No'. I just had to bite my tongue, walk away and hope to God I never met him on another job.

That is always one of your greatest fears. You walk into a drugs operation and there in front of you is someone you've met before on a previous job who's either served their bird or hasn't been arrested. They don't necessarily know or suspect you are Old Bill, but when it all went wrong last time you were there, and you're tainted. You keep a register of everyone you come across and try to cross-reference them with every new job that comes along, but it always remained a risk. In the drugs world, there are thousands and thousands of people at it out there. That's the depressing side of things. You would have thought that in the ten years I was doing undercover drugs work, one of those compromising situations would have cropped up. But it never did, partly through luck and partly through the care we put into researching each operation. Drugs involve people right across the social strata, from toerags in the gutter to members of high society. I've even been in the homes of TV personalities, famous and notorious personalities, orchestrating drugs deals, not necessarily with their knowledge but in their houses with people close to them. I've crossed every stratum and met people from virtually every walk of life, educated, gentrified even, during my drugs investigations.

It's quite phenomenal how many people are at it. A ton of

cannabis is smoked in London every night. Kilos of cocaine are snorted up people's noses every week or smoked as crack. Millions of ecstasy tablets are taken every weekend across the country. And people do it because it's fun. That's how it all starts – for fun. Then comes dependency and addiction and suddenly it's not fun anymore. But that old dope dealer is still out there and willing to sell you the gear you've got hooked on, and then you've got to find the cash to pay him. That's the start of the rot. You're on the slippery slope to ruin.

Personally, I'd like to see the decriminalisation of certain drug offences. If you are nicked with an eighth of cannabis, a gram of cocaine or one ecstasy tablet, I cannot see the point of the police hauling you off to a police station, taking about four hours to process you, costing plenty of money and reducing police resources. I would like to see that level of drug-taking reduced down to the level of a parking offence. If a policeman stops you on the street and finds you in possession of a drug for personal use, he should be able to issue you with a parking-type ticket with a £40 or £50 fine which you must pay within a month or something similar. That would free up the cop to go about his business again after fifteen minutes as opposed to four hours spent in the police station plus any subsequent court hearing. The more people a copper is able to deal with in the course of a day, the more chance he has of pulling someone with drugs who will say, 'Actually, I'm willing to tell you where I got it from,' and then you could be into the dealer, then possibly onto the importer and the international gangs.

These were the big fish I was after now and every lead into the gangs could be vital. I did a lot of work in South London and met a lot of black guys involved in, or on the margins of, the drugs business. A person's colour or race had by now become unimportant to me. There are good guys and bad guys, end of story. But it had been difficult to erase the memories of my early days pounding the beat on those South London streets – I'm talking late seventies, early eighties – when racism was not only institutionalised, it was bloody compulsory.

The first day I ever went out on the streets I was exposed to impropriety of the highest order. I was totally naïve and inexperienced in the ways of policing that existed among some officers at that time. I went out with my 'parent PC' and other officers to raid a blues party at a disused premises in Peckham. It was the big thing among the West Indian community at the time. Find the premises, get in stacks of booze, a DJ and some really loud reggae music, plenty of ganja, charge a tenner a head on the door and dance the night away. It was OK if you were part of the scene, but a real bummer if you lived nearby and got Bob Marley thumping through your walls for eight hours.

I knew Peckham was a lively nick when I was posted there after Hendon and was chomping at the bit to get some action. I had testosterone coursing through my veins and I wanted to get out there and make my difference. Because I badgered and pestered so much, I was eventually allowed to go out on this raid. And what an eye-opener it proved to be.

I was solemnly told to stick to my parent PC – my puppy walker, in effect – and not let him out of my sight. 'Don't get involved in nicking people because it's your first day out. Do what he does and, if he needs help, give him help.'

So we went crashing in through the doors of this blues party, pandemonium all round, drugs hitting the deck so people don't get nicked in possession. I stuck tight to my parent PC and he went straight up to the fucking great sound system and pulled what looked like a long hat pin out of his kit. Then he systematically pierced the speakers with it, wrecking the system with barely a mark showing. Better than belting the fuck out of it with a truncheon, he reckoned. Then he went to the record collection and started smashing that up, too. What do I do? This is my baptism of fire on my very first operation. Do I say it's wrong, do I partake in it? The pressure was such that I went along. Then I quickly learned about 'flying ganja': drugs which had been dumped on the floor mysteriously found their way back into the pockets of the suspects, most of them black, and they were charged with possession. It was unbelievable, but it was common practice in those days. They might have got lucky and put the drugs back in the right pockets sometimes, but you can bet your life they didn't always and they certainly didn't care.

Derogatory words like 'coon' and 'sooty' were bandied about all the time. If you didn't join in the banter, which I now have to admit to, to my great shame, then you were looked on as an outsider, you'd be ostracised and distrusted, your career would go nowhere. Then, years later, some of those people who'd been with you doing those things would go on to have glittering careers and end up being holier than thou and telling people how they should or shouldn't behave towards the ethnic minorities. Some of us have very long memories.

Chapter Eight

STAGE FRIGHT

We were parked up right near the Royal Court Theatre just after Christmas and I was giving a performance to be envied. A deal was about to go down for a £14,000 package of cocaine. Then the dealer started hinting that I might be a copper trying to set him up. On the basis that attack is the best form of defence, I rounded on him angrily.

'If you're insulting me by saying I could be Old Bill then you can just fuck off out of this car now. Go on, fuck off.'

I was hurling it at him from the top of my voice. Desmond looked startled. In his rich West Indian patois he tried to calm the situation.

'No, no, no, man, I'm not insulting you, but you know we have to be careful.'

I retorted, 'Yeah, yeah I know but just grow up and let's get on with the trade.'

It was a risk I had to take. He might have pulled out and

cleared off. But he didn't. The lure of £14,000 persuaded him to put the thought of underhand dealings to the back of his mind. He looked greedily at the wedge of cash we produced from the boot of our maroon 5 Series BMW, one of SO10's pool of luxury motors we used on undercover operations.

'OK, let's do it,' he said and sprinted off to collect the package of cocaine that was up for offer.

Desmond should have gone with his hunch. Minutes later he was flat on his face on the deck in Sloane Square with Customs Officers and police on top of him. It was another nicking which emanated from my favourite location for sting operations, the Royal Court Tavern, opposite the Royal Court Theatre. There always seemed a nice irony about staging our operations among London's theatrical clientele, blissfully unaware of the real life dramas going on under their noses as they sipped their G and Ts before curtain up.

The Christmas decorations were still inviting goodwill to all when I was first introduced to Desmond the dealer, and leg man for a far bigger cocaine racket spread throughout London. I'd gone in through the side door in Sedding Street and walked up to the bar where my colleague Richard was waiting. We had just ordered a couple of pints when a tall, slim black man in his mid-thirties came in. He was wearing a black cardigan, grey patterned trousers and black Kangol flat hat. Cool dude. He walked over and Richard introduced us.

'Desmond, this is Peter who I told you about.'

We shook hands. Desmond said, 'Hello, Peter, it was you I was expecting to meet. Sorry about the time. I couldn't find this place.' His voice was rich and deep.

'Well, at least we've met now,' I replied with a touch of nonchalance that I hoped would put him at ease.

'So, you want business?' he said.

'Yeah, if it suits me,' I told him. He was keen.

'Me tell you, man, this is the best coke you'll find. Come, let's talk.'

We walked outside.

'Look, you can have sixteen ounces today and then two kilos at the weekend. Is that OK?'

I told him, 'Look, I'm on wages you know. It's not all my money, so I'll have to speak to my people. We can handle sixteen ounces, no problem. How much do you want for it?'

He wanted £16,000.

'Too much,' I said. 'We'll only pay fifteen maximum.'

Desmond went into sales mode. 'Try some,' he said. 'Take this sample and see what you think.'

He reached down and pulled a small plastic bag of powder out of his right sock and handed it to me. I slipped it in my coat pocket.

'You check it out and if you like it and want to do business, I'll call you later.'

I said, 'All right, call about six o'clock.'

Too late, said Desmond, could we make it about 4.00pm and do the trade that night? I agreed. 'Sweet,' he said as we parted company, and I set off for Scotland Yard to get the cocaine tested.

Desmond rang at 4.30pm. I was with another undercover officer who was pretending to be part of my cocaine network. My colleague, Graham, said the gear was not of the quality we normally dealt with. Because it was poorer strength, we'd need more of it, and the top price we'd pay was £12,000. After a bit of haggling, it was agreed we'd stump up £14,000 cash. We agreed another meet at the Royal Court Tavern for the trade.

'You will have the money?' asked Desmond.

'Definitely, no problem,' I said.

'Good, so it will be quick?'

'Yeah, nice and quick and no fuck-ups.'

'Cool, no fuck-ups.'

I arrived with Richard just before 8.00pm and we parked in Sedding Street. In the boot was a Christmassy silver carrier bag with £13,500 stuffed into it in used notes from Scotland Yard's undercover fund. I went into the pub and bought a drink. Soon Desmond came in and beckoned me with a nod of the head. I followed him to the rear door of the pub.

'So you got the money?'

'Yeah, it's here. You got the coke?'

Desmond said it was close by. So was our money.

'Do you want to see it?' I asked.

'Yeah.'

I told him that once he'd seen the cash he'd got two minutes to bring me the cocaine or I'd fuck off.

'I'm not going to sit about when you know where my money is,' I said.

We walked towards the BMW.

'When you've seen the money, I ain't going to sit around like a plum so you can blag me,' I insisted.

'No, man,' he said.

We got into the back seat behind Richard.

'I thought you were on your own.'

'Don't be fucking stupid; Richard has an interest in this as well.'

I told him again that once he'd counted the cash he'd only got minutes to produce the coke before we cleared off.

'It's very close by,' he said.

I said I'd go with him. He looked shocked. 'My other people will see you,' he said, getting agitated. 'I'll go an' get it.'

I said I'd wait in the pub. 'You bring it to me there and we'll do a quick exchange there and then at the car.'

Desmond agreed. 'We must be careful,' he said. 'I don't know you, and we have to be careful of the police, you know.'

He was looking round for imagined danger.

'Once I've got the parcel the risks are all mine, so don't start that bollocks,' I said testily.

'I've been speaking on the phone and the police could have intercepted and put you in, see what I'm saying?' he added nervously. How close you were, Desmond. My angry response to his suspicions seemed to placate him and the deal was back on course. Richard produced the goody bag with the cash in.

'There's thirteen and a half thousand in there,' he said.

Desmond raised his eyebrows. 'But I agreed fourteen thousand.'

I said, 'Yeah, but I've taken £500 out for me to have a drink out of this and that's that.'

Desmond grinned. 'OK,' he said, flicking through the wads of notes and seeming happy.

'Off you go and get the coke ... I'll be in the pub,' I said.

He was gone no more than two minutes. He came in and said, 'Come, let's go.' He looked around the bar again, failing to pick up on any of the surveillance team dotted around with their beers and crisps. We went out of the side door into Sedding Street.

'Let me see it then,' I demanded. From inside a long coat he was wearing against the cold December night he produced a black and brown ladies' handbag with a long strap. I took it into a stairwell adjacent to the pub, pulled out a sock and a rag and saw the coke in its plastic wrapping.

'Yeah, seems all right,' I nodded. 'You walk up to the car and throw it in and Richard will give you the cash.'

Desmond said, 'Yeah.'

'If this gear is light or shit,' I warned him, 'you'll be hearing from us one way or another, you understand.' I was in drug-dealer mode and this is what he would expect to hear.

'Yeah, there's no problem with this,' he said.

At this I heard the heavy clump of Customs Officers' boots and saw them right behind Desmond with back-up cops not far away. I legged it. And the curtain came down on Desmond's big deal. He was later jailed for cocaine trafficking.

* * *

For success in the complex arena of undercover policing, it was necessary to move in with streetwise conviction, to hone your cover story to perfection, to make the opposition believe in you as a real person. I had to be more than just a bloke buying some gear. I needed flesh on the bones of my character.

To that end, I built up a series of background stories that would stand up against the most intense scrutiny. I love a pint. So whenever I was in a pub, I endeavoured to learn as much about the licensing trade as I could. Peter the ex-publican was always a good cover. I learned how to change a barrel, how much a barrel of ale cost, what your profit margins are, how to feed spirits from the off licence through the optics without the brewery and VAT man knowing. Or sometimes I'd pretend to be a former free-house owner and I'd talk about the scams I'd worked, like 'skimming' off the top or buying dodgy bootleg gear and selling it. I could say, 'Yeah, I was in the pub trade for years,' if villains were asking, and know that I could keep up that front.

I also used the cover story of being a former pop group manager. I had a friend who had a relative involved in the management of various groups and had recently taken over rock legends Status Quo, one of Britain's most durable groups. He felt there were some serious financial irregularities in the accounts and came to me as a friend for advice. I was never a fraud investigator and never could be. But I knew a man who was, a good pal called Bob Webb stationed at the Yard's fraud squad in Holborn at the time. He was a financial expert, and knew his subject inside and out.

We went in our own time to meet the Status Quo management team and Bob went through the books. He advised them where there might be a bit of a black hole and what action they should take.

I was amazed at how comparatively little they were worth after all their years in the pop business. I think they pursued civil action to recover some of the missing money. This was wonderful material for me. It gave me a great insight into the workings and pitfalls of pop management. I was firing questions all the time, learning about royalties, percentages, live shows and so on, building up yet another cover story in my repertoire of authentic-sounding characters for my underworld forages against crime.

I was never one for mixing with other Old Bill all the time and I kept a wide circle of friends outside the police force – car dealers, publicans, builders. And all the time I listened and learned as they talked about their work, paid a lot of attention to what they said and, unbeknown to them, would go out the next day on an undercover job and purport to be a builder, or whatever. I'd know about costs, what a day's wages for a plumber was, a chippie, a sparks or a labourer. Terrific cover. You'd make sure, of course, that the villain you were looking at wasn't a master builder himself. That could have got tricky. But it was horses for courses. You chose your cover story to suit the villains you were dealing with.

The SO10 undercover unit was setting up businesses itself at the time. There were second-hand shops staffed by undercover officers to nick villains and fences selling stolen gear. They nicked hundreds of people selling bent goods. They set up a mobile phone shop on one occasion. Cloning phones had become such a major industry they wanted to get at the guys behind it. I spent a good deal of time with the lads running the shop so that I could learn the machinations of the mobile phone industry and its various scams. 'Yes, I've got a mobile phone shop.' Another great cover. And the bonus was that if the villains then wanted a phone cloned or new chips fitted, I could go back to the shop and get it done. That would put me in well with the villains and set me up nicely for bigger deals in drugs or whatever.

I'd try to get hold of snide gear – fake designer wear that

is, confiscated in police raids – and take that along to meets with crooks.

'Here you are, mate, a couple of nice Tommy Hilfiger T-shirts for you. They're snide but who cares?'

They end up thinking, not only is this geezer a drug-dealer but he can fix your mobiles and get moody T-shirts. Ace bloke.

I gave some T-shirts to a couple of blokes trying to sell me counterfeit currency. They loved it. They were selling me counterfeit notes. I was giving them counterfeit clothes.

Another favourite cover was ex-football pro. I said I'd fallen on hard times after a bad injury and was now carving my way through life doing a bit of drugs, this, that and the other. I've always been bonkers about football and I could rattle off footballers' names, matches and times and places. I'd never claim to have been a QPR player because they were my team. I'd always profess to be a former player with a club I didn't like and I'd slag them off something rotten all the way through the conversation – what a bunch of arseholes they were, the chairman was a slag, the board were shit-arses who'd let me down and fucked up my insurance pay-out. My career was ruined, they just left me on the scrap heap and now here I was a drug-dealer. It all made the wheels of deception grind that little bit easier.

Chapter Nine

TOP DOLLAR

I didn't know whether to laugh or cry. I'd put my neck on the line to intercept a gang planning to flood $1 million in fake notes onto the money markets and I had landed up in court facing a spell in nick myself. To be honest, it was the end of a job that had been doomed from the start, so perhaps I shouldn't have been too surprised at standing in the witness box and seeing the three men arrested in the operation laughing like drains as they walked free and me facing the wrath of one very irate judge threatening me with porridge for my troubles. And all because I was honouring the most sacrosanct of our obligations – to protect the informant.

You'll have gathered by now I don't have a lot of time for grasses on a personal level, and you won't find any on my Christmas list, but it was vital that we sustained the integrity of the job by never, ever, jeopardising the identity of our informants if it was humanly possible.

THE GANGBUSTER

A grass had come forward on this job and said he could introduce me to a bloke who could supply me with $1 million in high-quality forged notes. To me, this would be an archetypal undercover operation where I would pretend to be a top London gangster with the knowledge and contacts to be able to shift such a huge quantity of counterfeit notes, and enough financial clout to put the cash up front to buy the consignment. We were talking big, big money here – around £100,000 – to get the deal up and running. I'd dealt with counterfeiters before and found them to be, in general terms, a better class of criminal: more cerebral, less paranoid than, say, drug-dealers, but criminals none the less. I was more than happy to do the job, variety is the spice and all that sort of thing, little knowing that it was destined to be an abysmal fuck-up from beginning to end.

I was introduced to a guy, stockily built, a likeable enough London rogue, and negotiations started well over a few drinks. I impressed him with my imaginary portfolio of dodgy international dealers who would launder the dollars for me and secure a decent rake-off on the investment. After several weeks of protracted negotiations, we drew up plans for the hand-over.

These jobs can be slow starters quite often because the villains always start off the way they want to do it; you say the way you want to do it and you have to negotiate, cajole and gradually create a situation which suits both parties. I must say, though, I wouldn't personally have chosen the location for the exchange of dollars for cash – Tesco's car park, Sidcup. Not exactly the million-dollar touch. But the counterfeiters reckoned it was a satisfactory location for all concerned because it gave good access to the M25 and being a busy suburban supermarket afforded ample cover for our transaction to take place without attracting undue attention among the baked beans and two-for-the-price-of-one washing powder offers.

The quality of the notes was pretty good, the paper was right and the serial numbers had been varied to avoid immediate suspicion. I was posing as an international money launderer who could shift the $1 million by shipping it initially out to Africa, using it on various moody deals, then pulling out with a profit before the shit hit the fan. I said that other batches of the fake notes would go to other countries where the dollar was king, make a nice few bob for us and we could get out again before anyone rumbled the fact they'd got a fistful of dodgy dollars.

The senior officer who would normally be in charge of the arrest operation was tied up on another job so a pal of mine was standing in for him and was the operational commander on the ground. His team would be strategically placed all around the car park, disguised as cleaners, trolley collectors, anything that was in keeping with the location, ready to make arrests when I gave the signal. But what you do need in any undercover operation, whether you are the undercover operative or you are the operational commander, is trust in one another, an unquestioning belief in the abilities of your team-mates. If you don't have that, you can't have a successful working relationship. It's absolutely vital. The officer in charge and I got on well enough and, even though he had not been the operational commander on a big job before, I felt happy that he would be competent enough to do his side of the job.

I drove into the car park in my Renault, parked up and awaited the arrival of the guy who was going to supply me with the $1 million. Very cleverly, the gang brought only $100,000 in forged notes, and not the full million, onto the plot. It was a tester – if he takes the $100,000 and nothing goes wrong, we'll bring the remaining $900,000. This hadn't been catered for in our pre-operational briefing, and the villains, like so many times before, hadn't read the script. Bastards. This was where your instincts kicked in, the need to have flexibility, initiative, and the ability to think on your feet.

I was re-evaluating the situation in my head. It was still not going too badly and I'd taken possession of the first $100,000 and put it in the boot of my car. I'd just got to keep my cool, and my credibility, and I was sure the rest of the cash would come rolling in. There was no way I was going to back it to them. I told my contact I'd sit and wait for the rest. No problem. We chatted about not very much. He assured me the fake notes would be on the plot pretty soon. I'd hang on in there.

The surveillance teams waiting to move in to make arrests at the conclusion of an undercover operation should only ever do so at a pre-determined signal from the man under cover, whether that is a physical or transmitted signal. This depends on the trust factor.

My contact and I continued negotiations over the remaining $900,000. I didn't see a problem with me sitting in Tesco's car park with $100,000 of bent money in the boot of my car. I assumed the rest of the team were cool about the situation as well. It stood to reason in my mind that once the final hurdle was overcome, and the rest of the money was produced, we would have evidence as to the true severity of the crime, which was what the whole undercover operation was about. We needed it to prove that this was a major-league deal, not Mickey Mouse funny money.

I was just sitting there calmly awaiting the arrival of the dosh, when the next thing I knew all fucking hell had broken loose. Now, I hadn't given my agreed signal, or any signal at all. But we now had police coming from everywhere, leaping over walls, climbing over fences, charging through people and I thought, shit, this has gone pear-shaped. I had it on my dancers as fast as I could to get away from the scene. I legged it over the front wall of the car park, down to the A20 where I knew there was a factory where I could go and hide. I was fuming. Why had they called in the cavalry when the job was only half done?

What I subsequently found out was that they saw me taking possession of the parcel. In the heat of the moment, the mist came down and the 'Go, go, go,' signal to attack was given.

The net result was that three minor players, acting as fixers and go-betweens, were arrested nearby while the starring players, sitting in a car unseen and unidentified by the surveillance teams, realised what had happened and discreetly vanished from the scene with the $900,000 in duds, wiping their brows in relief and saying, 'Haven't we just had a stroke of luck.' So, when the dust settled and we all went back for our debriefing, the only question I wanted answers to was what the fuck had happened.

So, instead of a million-dollar bust backed up with top-grade evidence of international fraud, we ended up with a half-baked case involving just $100,000 in fake notes. Not best case evidence to back up a prosecution and it was with no great surprise that the case was eventually thrown out at Croydon Crown Court and the three defendants walked out scot-free.

But what I hadn't banked on was the judge threatening to send me off to jail for contempt of court because I refused to name the informant who had put up the job. I'd been reliably forewarned by some of my fellow officers that Judge McHale wasn't the most pro-police judge who'd ever sat. I knew it might be a rough ride.

When you are undercover, you tend to lurk in the shadows much of the time. A court appearance is no different. You still don't need your face to be on show. You are taken in through secret entrances, you are kept hanging around in bare offices, not able to have a bite to eat or cup of tea in canteens, you are only brought on when it's your turn to give evidence. You feel like a pariah.

Before I was called, the prosecution made an application to the judge in closed court that I should be allowed to give my evidence under a pseudonym so my real identity would not be made known to the defendants in the dock. Judge McHale ruled in his wisdom that if I was going to give evidence in his court, I was going to give it under my real name. Thank you very much, Judge McHale. The senior police officer in the case, who was trying to sew this dog's dinner together as best he could, came to me and said that the judge had ruled I must give evidence under my real name. He said, 'I'm giving you the opportunity now to choose whether you do or you don't.'

'Well,' I said, 'if I don't, what happens?'

'Well, the case will be slung out and that will be that.'

I could tell by the way he was looking at me that he wanted me to do it. He was asking me pleasantly but I knew they would be very disappointed if I refused to go in the box. And, on top of that, I might have got the reputation of a prima donna hanging over me for the rest of my career and I wouldn't have wanted that. So I said, 'No, I'll go and give my evidence,' which I duly did. And a rough ride it certainly turned out to be.

A Mr Francis Sheridan was appearing on behalf of the defendant. He was an advocate with whom I had crossed swords many times in the past, invariably when I was in an undercover role, so much so that it became common for Mr Sheridan to receive my statement of evidence under some completely moody name, then turn round to the officer in the case and say, 'Oh, will Mr Bleksley be appearing?' He knew my style and I knew his. He was a mighty, formidable adversary in court, sharp as a razor, and had a fantastic knack of lulling you into a false sense of security then hitting you with an absolute crippler which could make you wobble in the witness box. He proved to be no less skilful on this occasion.

He fought hammer and tongs for crucial disclosures relating to the first meeting with the defendant, such as: was the informant who had set up the job, and who had been there to introduce us, one and the same person? I steadfastly refused to identify who that person was.

What Mr Sheridan was doing was going on a fishing exercise in the hope that I would have to admit that the person was my informant, so it would indicate to the blokes in the dock who it was who'd grassed them up. On this occasion, we had agreed as a trial tactic that I would only disclose the Christian name of the person who'd effected the introduction with the gang – a man given the code-name Richard – but to give nothing more about him, whether he was an informant, another undercover police officer, or anyone else. Mr Sheridan knew this was the weak link and he would have to attack it. And attack it he did, ferociously. I've kept the court transcripts, which read like this:

> Sheridan: 'Do you agree that it would be wholly wrong for you to withhold any information that may mislead the court in order to protect anyone?'
>
> Me: 'I am not here to mislead the court in any way, shape or form.'
>
> Sheridan: 'Do you agree that it would be wholly wrong for you to do so, bearing in mind your oath to tell the truth, the whole truth and nothing but the truth?'
>
> Me (feeling slightly vulnerable in pony tail and casual gear as opposed to the more conventional clothes a police witness would normally wear): 'I am not here to mislead the court and have no intention of doing so.'
>
> Sheridan: 'Do you also agree that it would be wholly wrong of you, as a police officer, to counsel, procure, or incite the commission of a crime?'
>
> Me: 'Absolutely.'
>
> Sheridan: 'Can you help us? When did you first meet Richard?'
>
> Me: 'I cannot answer that question.'
>
> Sheridan: 'Who introduced you?'
>
> Me: 'Again, I do not wish to answer that question.'
>
> Sheridan: 'Do you know Richard's full name?'
>
> Me: 'I do not wish to answer that question.'

I could see exactly where Mr Sheridan was coming from. He was getting nowhere in this game of verbal ping-pong. So he asked the judge for a ruling, a matter which had to be dealt with in the absence of the jury, at which Mr Sheridan presented his argument for the judge ordering me to answer the key questions – who Richard really was and whether he was the informant.

After what seemed an eternity of legal wrangling, at which I was not present, the judge decided that he would direct me to answer those compromising questions that could so easily place my informant in danger.

With the court reassembled and the jury back in their seats, Mr Sheridan was back on the attack like a dog with a bone.

> Sheridan: *'Mr Bleksley, when did you first meet Richard?'*

Here we go again, I thought.

> Me: *'I do not wish to answer that question.'*
> Judge: *'Was that the question you last asked?'*
> Sheridan: *'The three questions I asked yesterday were: When did you first meet? Who introduced you? And what was his name?'*
> Judge: *'Yes, well, would you care to have a go at them in reverse order?'*
> Sheridan: *'Certainly. What is Richard's full name?'*
> Me: *'I do not wish to answer that question.'*
> Judge: *'I direct you to answer.'*

I knew now I was in troubled waters as Mr Sheridan sensed a victory in this battle, with the judge now firmly behind him.

> *Me: 'In view of your direction, Your Honour, I would respectfully ask for an adjournment in order that I can speak to senior officers.'*
>
> *Judge: 'No, I direct you to answer.'*
>
> *Me: 'I decline to answer, Your Honour.'*
>
> *Judge: 'You understand the consequences or possible consequences?'*
>
> *Me (knowing we are now talking contempt of court and a possible stay in HM Prison Brixton): 'Your Honour, yes I do.'*

Frankly, I didn't give a shit about being banged up. What I did care about was my professional integrity being compromised. So I stuck to my guns.

Mr Sheridan persisted with his fishing trip, no doubt hoping to hook a killer whale.

> *Sheridan: 'Who introduced you to Richard?'*
>
> *Me: 'I do not wish to answer that question, Your Honour.'*
>
> *Judge: 'Why?'*
>
> *Me: 'Because I do not wish to answer any question in relation to the man Richard, as I fear that should I do so any possible source of information may be revealed.'*

Would I continue to stay silent over Richard's identity even if the judge ordered me to reveal all, asked Sheridan. Yes, I said, I certainly would.

A bid by prosecution barrister Mr Pitt to have yet another

legal argument on the subject without the jury was quickly dismissed by Judge McHale. Mr Sheridan resumed the attack with the key question we all knew he wanted to ask. Was Richard an informer?

I, yet again, repeated parrot-fashion in a crazy cross-examination that was going nowhere fast, 'I do not wish to answer that question, Your Honour.'

'Well, are you going to answer any of my questions?' Mr Sheridan enquired.

He should have known the answer by now! I replied cagily, 'I don't know what questions you are going to ask.'

Sheridan: 'Is he a villain?'

Me: 'I do not wish to answer that question, Sir.'

Sheridan: 'Has he been granted immunity from prosecution?'

Me: 'I do not wish to answer that question, Sir.'

Sheridan: 'Has he been paid by the police?'

Me: 'I don't wish to answer that question.'

Sheridan: 'Is he a regular, so far as you know, in his dealings with the police?'

Me: 'I do not wish to answer that question.'

Right, that was it for the exasperated Mr Sheridan. He turned to the judge for help to try to resolve this impasse. And he got it.

Judge: 'I direct you to answer counsel's question – Richard's name.'

Me: 'Your Honour, being fully aware of all the possible

consequences involved, I do not wish to answer that
question and I would seek leave to consult with a senior
police officer.'

In other words, I'm not going to stick up my informant's
name for some sort of retaliation in the future.

Judge: 'Do you say Richard is an informer?'
Me: 'I do not wish to answer that question.'
Judge: 'I direct you to answer it.'

His Lordship was seemingly running out of patience and
clearly not happy at my lack of deference to his authority over
the court and all those in it, including humble witnesses like me.

I wasn't going to bottle out now, that was for sure. 'With
respect, Your Honour,' I repeated for the umpteenth time, 'being
aware of all the circumstances, I decline.'

That was it, interrogation over, reputation intact, consequences
to follow.

'You may withdraw,' said Judge McHale and added, slightly
ominously, 'Do not leave the precincts of the court.'

According to the transcript which I read later, Mr Sheridan
went for the jugular once I had retired from the battlefield. It
was, he argued, unfair on his client that I was blanking all the
questions about Richard.

Sheridan: 'I invite Your Honour to take steps to see
that assistance is forthcoming, however draconian that
action may be, to require the truth to come out.'

Judge: 'I think, Mr Sheridan, one has to acknowledge the fact that, since the abolition of thumb screws, no judge has the power to take steps to elicit the answer. All I have the power to do is to punish a witness who is in contempt of court.'

Sheridan: 'Then I ask you to exercise that power because I am being denied any co-operation to establish the truth. The prosecution remain silent and the officer completely refuses to co-operate with this court. It is wrong, it is unfair and should be stopped.'

This was a first for our prosecution counsel as well. 'I have never been in a situation where a prosecution witness, a police officer, no doubt for perfectly good reasons, has refused to answer the questions posed,' he told the judge.

So what to do with me? Nothing too hasty, he told the assembled lawyers. Any contempt of court proceedings against me should best be dealt with by another judge in another court with me represented by another lawyer. But what he didn't want was another fiasco with me in the witness box stone-walling everything that was thrown at me.

'I think there is something inherently obnoxious about that,' he said. 'It is not a state of affairs which I think should be allowed to continue.'

The case was adjourned overnight with me off to seek advice from senior officers and police lawyers and hoping to God they'd be backing me in the morning. God certainly wasn't backing Mr Sheridan on his journey to court; he was four hours late having been trapped in a monster traffic jam on the M25 within a hundred yards of his exit but unable to reach it. Shame, I thought, but this was the geezer trying to get me banged up, so I wasn't too upset at the stay of execution.

Next move was from our barrister, Mr Pitt. It came as no surprise considering the court room stalemate between myself and Mr Sheridan.

'We have considered the position overnight and the Crown propose to offer no further evidence against the accused and ask that he is discharged.'

That was it – he was off the hook, acquitted on the direction of Judge McHale. Inevitably, the lawyers for the other two accused men rapidly followed suit and successfully applied for their clients to be discharged as well. They argued that it was apparent that I, as the chief police witness, would continue to refuse to answer any questions about Richard's identity and background put to me on behalf of the other defendants. And they were right, of course.

The judge ruled that I had declined to answer questions about Richard 'with courtesy and without any arrogance or anything of that kind', which was something of a relief. But there I was – no toothbrush, no change of underpants, I'd worked undercover in a potentially dangerous situation, knocked my bollocks out and all the defendants had walked and I was the only one left. I'd tried to play the white man, tried to protect my source and I was likely to get a spell inside. To my relief, however, the judge decided not to hand out any punishment there and then.

He told me, 'It seems quite inappropriate that I should deal with this matter in a summary way and I shall direct that proceedings for contempt of court be brought and be brought before another judge. The court has said on more than one occasion that these things should not be dealt with in haste and I take the view they are better dealt with by another judge.'

My counsel, Mr Pitt, asked if that meant I was bailed to appear at another court at another time.

'No, he is not bailed,' said Judge McHale.

I stood there and thought, oh fuck, I'm going to get banged up as well now, but he quickly clarified the position by adding, 'As I understand it, he's finished his evidence and is released in the normal way.' That, I thought, was a bit of a result. At least it won't be B and B in Brixton tonight.

The accused lads all seemed to have a bit of a chuckle over the whole fiasco, especially over my particular predicament. There were only a couple of minutes between them coming out and me joining them outside, and I could see they were having a bit of handshaking and back-slapping and all that sort of thing, and one of them called across the concourse as I was with a fellow officer.

'Oy, you.'

He looked across and said, 'Yes?'

He said, 'That Peter Bleksley ... he's a lot better than any of your grasses.'

My colleague said, 'Oh yes? Why's that?'

'He keeps his fucking mouth shut.'

Everyone smiled and gradually they all dispersed, and I was left standing with the threat of legal proceedings and a potential prison sentence still hanging over my head.

I subsequently received a letter from the Attorney General's office saying I was going to be charged with contempt of court.

I thought, sod it, let them get on with it. But that was followed a couple of months later by another letter saying the matter was being dropped because it wasn't in the public interest and I never heard another thing about it. I like to think that whoever reviewed the case came to the very sensible conclusion that putting a copper in the dock for protecting his informant would achieve absolutely nothing at all.

At the end of the day, no real harm had been done. It just stood to reinforce the many and varied problems that beset the job of being an undercover officer.

* * *

The trendy pony tail look I favoured at that time had become one of my favourite disguises. It was acceptable for all sorts of different jobs in the shadowy world of villainy, but in the bewigged and begowned portals of our courts of law you could feel seriously unloved and out of place. But that's the way it had to be. My pony tail, my designer jeans and my leather jacket were as important to my role as the legal manuals were to the lawyers. I could be scruffy with a pony tail if, for instance, I was involved with a low-life drugs gang. If I was in the Windows on the World restaurant on the twenty-eighth floor of the Hilton entertaining over lunch or an evening meal I would have the hair slicked, be suited and booted and look the part of a high-roller. If I needed to look like an oik buying twenty grand's worth of cocaine, I could have the arse hanging out of my trousers but the pony tail would still look OK. It wouldn't matter. I could take the pony tail out if I wanted to and I had the biggest fucking mass of curly hair you've ever seen. I could look like Marc Bolan at the drop of a hat. I could be as smart as I wanted to be or as scruffy as I wanted to be. It was all about dressing up, dressing down, playing a role. Beards and moustaches came and went. The nagging concern that is always in the back of your mind is that you might be recognised at the wrong place and wrong time, and I always tried to keep one jump ahead of that possibility.

Chapter Ten

THE GREAT PROVIDER

Yes, I have to put my hands up to nicking drugs from Scotland Yard. Regularly and systematically. Heroin, cocaine, cannabis, ecstasy, speed – you name it, I had it away. I did it because I had to. If that sounds cock-eyed I must explain that, as one of the leading undercover drugs investigators in Britain, I was frequently asked to lecture at training courses attended by trainee officers from forces throughout the UK. The Government, police authorities, Customs and society in general were reeling from a massive upsurge in drug-taking and drug-trafficking in the eighties and suddenly everyone was taking the subject very seriously. The problem was way past a few rock stars getting smashed and a bit of puff being smoked socially. It was boom time for businesses with no hint of the great crash to come, money was plentiful and heroin, cocaine and cannabis were being smuggled into the country at unprecedented levels. Consignments of smack were even arriving in London courtesy of the Russian Mafia who saw rich rewards for their filthy trade in all the big European capitals. Cosmopolitan London was top of their list. It was nothing short of a drug explosion.

Police forces across Britain came under mounting pressure to increase the strength, sophistication and effectiveness of their drug investigation teams. At Scotland Yard's Central Drugs Squad – unquestionably in the forefront of the battle against the big-time crime barons – manpower was increased dramatically in a very short space of time from a squad of twenty-four officers with three detective inspectors to a team of sixty officers with six DIs and continued to grow year after year to become the massive part of the National Crime Squad it is today.

The war on drugs became as big a topic in the UK as it had been for years in the USA. They say we are usually ten years behind America with every social phenomenon. They were right about drugs. Crack cocaine was already a major problem in dozens of American cities and was wiping out hundreds of young lives needlessly week after week. Cannabis dealers were floating up the English Channel almost daily with tons of the stuff, then sneaking off back to their Costa del Sol bolt-holes to enjoy their ill-gotten gains. Heroin and cocaine traffickers were devising ever more cunning ways to get their contraband past Customs. It became vitally important that, if the British authorities were to combat this menace in any sort of effective way, they must upgrade manpower and training right across the board. That is where I came in.

As an undercover officer, I was dealing with drugs cases on a permanent basis and my expertise was drawn on to help train other officers in the tricky task of drug-related operations – a real minefield in police terms unless you knew exactly what you were doing. Cases across Britain were being dealt with on an ad hoc basis by individual squads with no formulated policy or pattern, no logging of the operations or the operatives; they were still doing it willy-nilly. There was a pressing need to centralise the entire crime-fighting network and do it fast.

So the undercover unit at Scotland Yard, the Crime Operations Group – or COG as we called it – was set up to head the battle in 1986. Because of the increasing success we'd had against the drug barons and against big-time crime in general, COG became the pivotal unit in amalgamating all aspects of training and operations. It also took on board the witness protection programme to look after informants who might be in danger after grassing up fellow villains. They instituted the register of informants, and really became the heart and soul of undercover operations in the UK.

The first training course specifically for undercover officers was established in 1987. Twelve of the most experienced undercover operatives in the force were to be guinea pigs as part of a plan to devise a national structure for the increasingly important area of covert policing. I was one of the dirty dozen. It was more of a melting pot than an instructional course because they were teaching us a lot we already knew, but at the same time they were countenancing our views as to how it could be shaped, altered, adjusted or developed for various grades of undercover officers and would-be undercover officers, ranging from very experienced and partly experienced to totally inexperienced. They were looking for a format which would benefit all those who would be following on into this dangerous field of operations. They wanted to train people specifically for drug-related operations where extra manpower was so crucially needed, to teach the identifying of drugs, how to detect them by smell or touch, how to test them to ensure it was genuine gear, and so on. I was the officer with the most experience in this field, a wide knowledge of most drugs and a string of good undercover 'kills' under my belt. It fell to me to explain the various techniques of drug testing to my fellow officers on the undercover courses.

The most basic thing for them to know was the street testing of all kinds of drugs. How to know what gear you were dealing with, and how to keep your credibility as a dealer, pusher or whatever you were posing as, intact, and not make the bad guys suspicious. You had to go out there and be a drug-dealer, not some witless prick playing at it. You had to know the gear and know the lingo.

It was here we hit the first major snag. It was pretty pointless lecturing people about illegal drugs when you hadn't got any drugs in front of you to show them, to let them handle, to smell, to know what it was likely to do when someone shoves it up their nose or into their veins. When you're undercover, it's not just identifying what the drug is, you've got to be able to know precisely what its effects are, what its possible side-effects are, what is good gear and what is shit gear.

Cannabis, for example, comes in a Heinz 57 of varieties – in slabs, in oils, in bars, soaps or slate, or rocky or ricky – there are dozens of names for it, and you've got to know them all if you're not going to get caught out. If you're with people who have been drug-dealing all their lives and you don't know what you are talking about, you will very quickly be sussed out.

THE GREAT PROVIDER

I used to impress on the students all the time how important it was to know what you were doing: be familiar with the drugs, how to handle them, know the language of the drug world. When a gram of cocaine is presented to you in a wrap and you've got to open it out and look at it, it would be a dead giveaway if you did it all wrong and tipped the bloody lot all over the floor. A lot of the young officers on the courses had never even seen a wrap of coke, let alone opened one. A wrap is put together in a special way that users and dealers know, and so must you.

While I was doing the training courses, it was fair to say that I had a somewhat testy relationship with the Metropolitan Police Laboratory in Lambeth, South London. I would regularly go on an undercover job, and pick up a sample of heroin, cocaine or other drugs. I'd have a wallet full of cash to buy a sample on the spot and a whole lot more of the stuff later if it was OK gear. What I then needed to know by the time I had my next meeting, sometimes only a couple of hours later, was the quality of the drugs, so I could let the dealer know whether I was interested in continuing with the deal or not. It was often not possible to test the drugs in front of them. You couldn't if you were in a hotel, a bar, a club, or some sort of public arena. You couldn't start running up a bit of heroin or washing up cocaine to get the purity level. You had to say, 'Right, I'll take the gear, thanks very much, I'll test it when I get home and I'll come back to you when I know whether it's any good.' Never would I seem to be too keen to want to do the business. I mean, if it was shit gear it would only be the police who would want to buy it to get a nicking. You had to have quality gear if you were playing drug-dealer.

I'd take the samples to the Metropolitan Police lab for testing.

That was the official procedure. It was a time-consuming rigmarole of making out paperwork, sealing the drugs in a special bag, entering it into the register, filling in the details, and constantly looking at your watch all the time in case you're not going to get back for your meet. You really didn't want to be doing this. You are doing a covert operation; you don't necessarily want anybody at the lab to know who you are and you don't want the time-wasting.

The problem was, they were scientists through and through. And, of course, they adopted a very scientific standpoint to everything. That was all very well and good and I appreciate that was the way they had to do things, but for the practicalities of an undercover drugs operation it could be a nightmare. And sometimes it was necessary to side-step the rigid formalities of the world of science and do a bit of DIY drug research which would tell me exactly what I needed to know. If I had a gram of cocaine, I could walk into my own kitchen with a bit of bicarb and a drop of water, wash it up and bring it down to base cocaine to tell me what purity I was dealing with. I could do that in one minute. If I went to the laboratory, they'd say, 'Oh well, it takes several hours for us to do our standard procedures for drug testing,' and they only get you a purity banding – between 30 and 50 per cent or 40 and 60 per cent, which was far from precise. That was useless to me. I'd got the bad guy sitting waiting somewhere, thinking I'll be back in two hours to tell him how I rated the gear. I couldn't have risked blowing job after job through delays, so I managed to get the lab boys to give me a quick banding test instead of the precise analysis which would have given me down to 97.3 per cent purity, for example, which was about as good as it gets. Even that took a lot of persuading. They didn't understand the urgency of it, though there was one scientist there called Jim Cowie, a lovely fella who was on our side and who sympathised with the predicaments we found ourselves in from a practical point of view and tried to help. But, of course, he had the hierarchy above him who were still very constraining and there were endless arguments with some of the scientists. I would say, 'Look, I need this done urgently,' and they would say, 'It's going to take hours and hours,' and I'd say, 'Why don't you let me do it here? I'll show you a test that will tell me what I want to know in a matter of minutes.' They'd say, 'How can you do that?' I'd say, 'Easy – I'll mix three parts coke to one part bicarb, mix it up, moisten it, microwave it for thirty seconds and wallop ... that's how it is.' 'Oh yes,' they'd say, 'all right, we can see how that would work, but if there are artificial caines in there – lignocaine, procaine, this, that and the other as opposed to cocaine – your test would not be so precise, would it?'

Well, I had to accept that, but if I was a fucking *bona fide* drug-dealer my test wouldn't need to be that fucking scientific.

This was the mentality I had to fight against all the time. It wasn't helpful to anyone out there trying to catch drug-dealers, which was our sole priority. It was so bloody frustrating. At times, I used to feel I was banging my head against a brick wall. We did our best but sometimes we just had to bypass the system. The bureaucracy and the dogmatic scientific standpoint, which they frequently could not be shifted from, put up too many difficulties and too many barriers. So we frequently had to resort to doing it ourselves.

Then we'd get problems like testing a sample of cannabis

we'd picked up. You can tell it's cannabis OK by warming it up a bit, have a sniff, have a crumble, but how do you know if it's any good? Cannabis is one of the drugs where the proof of the pudding is in the eating, or in the puffing as the case may be. Books have been written on the cannabis varieties; there's dozens of different resins – slates, soaps, Afghan, Thai, Moroccan black, herbal (any number of different types of herbal) – I mean, you had to know them all. And to know it, you had to try it.

Because the lab was then confronted with a new set of circumstances, a new type of copper doing a new type of operation, they could make life difficult. They always seemed to look at you as though you were doing something utterly and totally wrong: these long-haired, hippy-looking undercover chappies are not what policemen used to be. We were supposed to be on the same side but we were often worlds apart. Their attitude was, 'My God, you're going out buying drugs. You're in the police; you're supposed to be going out and arresting people for having drugs.' That's the attitude that existed.

So we had no choice if we were going to get results. We'd utilise the scientific facilities if it was convenient, otherwise we'd go off and do what we had to do with our own inventiveness. If that meant putting together a joint and smoking it, that's what we did. Hands-on work. Practical puffing. We weren't doing it at the Yard, of course, not all nipping into the gents for a joint. You can imagine them seeing some spaced-out cop and saying, 'We know what squad he's in.' We were more discreet, but I remember going into the Yard canteen after one testing session and having a fit of the uncontrollable giggles as we demolished the dish of the day.

THE GREAT PROVIDER

It's fair to say at that stage I was probably the most knowledgeable drugs officer in Britain. I became an expert in all types of illegal drugs, from smack to magic mushrooms. I'd had some drugs grounding in America, sampled coke in California. I'd spent my adolescence in South London where drugs were freely available, affording me real-life experience of the burgeoning drug culture which helped equip me better to hit back at the drug barons invading Britain with ruthless determination. I made it my business to know drugs because it was my business to know drugs. I had to know what I was doing at all times. People would ring me up from within the police and say something like, 'We've had a strange parcel down here we've not seen before. Can you get over and have a look? It might be of some use to you.' If I thought it might help with my drugs education or broaden my knowledge in some way, then I would.

I remember when Thai sticks were first found in this country, I had a call from a pal asking me if I wanted to have a look. I'd go over and sneak in through the back way at the nick where the stuff was all bagged up. My pals would say, 'Have a look at this.' I'd say, 'Terrific, we've not seen that before,' or maybe we hadn't seen it for some time and it was useful to know it was back on the streets. I'd ask the officers to ask the bloke they'd found it on where he'd got it, where it came from, anything that would serve to increase my knowledge of the drugs scene worldwide.

Drugs are such a trend-orientated thing; today's hot drug will be passé tomorrow so you needed to keep on the ball as to what was new, what was in and what was out. I used to read publications worldwide relating to drugs, everything I could lay my hands on. You can never know enough on the subject.

Although my relationship with the laboratory wasn't exactly brilliant, I used to go to their library where they had various books which had been seized in raids giving details of drug production, drug cultivation, drug usage. These had been confiscated by police in various operations and eventually found their way through the system into the laboratory library, and I used to avail myself of that as often as possible to help me stay at the cutting edge.

One of the books that became the 'bible' of drugs officers was called *The Cocaine Tester's Handbook*, by the American High Priest of drug culture Adam Gottlieb, who also wrote *The Pleasures of Cocaine* and works about cannabis. I've still got copies of these books and I find them as illuminating, and in some respects as frightening, as on the day I first leafed through them in the eighties. They treat cocaine and hash almost with reverence. Though, to be fair, Gottlieb does state that the objective of his works was to 'convey the impartial facts of the uses and abuses' of cocaine and not simply to promote its use by all and sundry. Make what you like of the following extract, written in the mid-seventies on the West Coast of America:

We are living in an age of decadence. It cannot be avoided. It is an inevitable part of history and progress. The everyday demands of survival have slackened. Illusory moral values are in a state of rapid collapse. Leisure and luxury are becoming more and more abundant, and this abundance no longer permeates only the upper crust, where it usually resides, but is seeping downwards through the middle and lower classes.

THE GREAT PROVIDER

For many who nurture hopes for the future of our world, decadence is a frightening word. It conjures visions of the final days of civilisation blackened by distorted orgies and a sick disregard for life ending in the deglorification of Greece, the collapse of Rome and the angelic or extra-terrestrial destruction of Sodom and Gomorrah. Decadence seems always to be the prelude to a fall. But then isn't the fall harder the higher we climb? It may be that decadence is merely one of the highest states of civilisation and that its dangers lie only in its vertiginous altitudes.

It is the author's personal philosophy that if there be any teleological purpose (evidence of design or purpose in nature) to man's existence on earth and in his power to progress, it is that he should achieve a successful form of decadence and learn to live in harmony with it. The life-game then would be, at least in part, to sustain a decadent situation for as long as one might expect any civilisation to last, and perhaps longer. Such an accomplishment requires a great amount of self-knowledge and the ability to keep positive and negative forces in balance. It is not the author's intent to probe in depth the philosophy of decadence at this time, even though he has many profound notions on the subject. The thought is suggested here because cocaine is so much a part of the New Decadence and, like decadence itself, can either elevate or destroy us, depending entirely upon which we permit it to do ... The path of cocaine as it stands in the streets of today offers dangers not only inherent in the pharmacology itself, but in the bizarre assortment of adulterants which are added to it by black-market middlemen. This is what happens when a popular substance is made illegal. We have lived this nightmare before and we still have not learned.

This book contains information on the nature of cocaine, how to use it, not abuse it, what substances are used to cut it, what the dangers and drawbacks of the various cuts are and, in some cases, how to remove the cuts and purify the cocaine by a relatively simple kitchen procedure. At some date in the near future, it is hoped these chapters on cuts will become obsolete or merely of historical interest. This could only happen if cocaine is legalised and its purity controlled as is that of other foods, beverages and drugs that are commercially available. The sooner this happens, the better, because the Golden Age of Decadence towards which we are inevitably moving can succeed without disaster only in an atmosphere of freedom, knowledge, and respect for the lifestyles of others.

From my many years' involvement in drug investigation, I suppose Mr Gottlieb might have a point. But I guess he's never had to deal with the greedy scum who trade in coke and other drugs and play Russian roulette with people's lives in the process. Or perhaps he's never seen some broken and paranoid coke user who has lost everything through addiction. I have, and all I wanted to do was bust the bastards who made it possible.

To that end, I became the main lecturer in drug detection

and usage in the eighties and nineties as well as going out on hundreds of undercover busts myself. But what I realised very quickly at the drug seminars was that it was a virtually pointless exercise because I wasn't allowed any real drugs in my tuition programme. I needed the drugs to be able to educate the police students fully, to show them exactly what to do. So I went to the police laboratory and asked them kindly to supply me with a quantity of the various drugs I needed on the training courses – for example, two grams of cocaine, a gram of heroin, five gram of cannabis (resin, herbal or both), an ecstasy tablet, an LSD tab, and so on and so forth. But such was the bureaucracy of the laboratory and their failure to grasp the fact that they weren't going to get it all back neatly packaged, led them to pull the shutters down and say they wouldn't supply me. They still had this air of suspicion about covert operations. 'Oh, those two bags of cocaine will be £120 in their pockets or they'll be out of their brains by Tuesday.' That's what they seemed to be implying.

Where did that leave me? I had my own credibility to think of. I couldn't stand up in front of a class of trainee drugs investigators and give what was basically a fucking useless lecture with no practicalities – that was pointless. So what did I do? I 'acquired' my drugs – nicked, borrowed, whatever was necessary. I didn't give a shit. If some of my mates had pulled off a job involving cannabis and there was an eighth or a sixteenth of a gram of puff lying about, or a bit of coke that could be unaccounted for and would be invaluable for my training purposes, then it would mysteriously disappear. No paperwork, no hassle, just a nod and a wink and I had the material I needed for the lecture room.

I often wondered what would have happened if I'd been searched walking out of the nick with a pocketful of stolen drugs. 'Training purposes? Tell that to the beak.'

I had to get the drugs through my own resourcefulness because the system forced me to. We weren't about to go partying on it. It was all for legitimate purposes. But I had a wry smile when I drove through the gates of Hendon to lecture undercovers about illegal drugs when I had a pocketful of drugs myself, obtained illegally. Thankfully, the management on the course took a more enlightened view. They knew, or at least suspected, what I was doing, but turned a blind eye because they knew their students were benefiting from it. There are still a lot of good undercover cops out there today using the benefits gleaned from my nicked gear. But Christ knows what might have happened if I'd had an accident on the way to Hendon and been rendered unconscious. They'd have carted me off to casualty and cut my trousers off to find a stash of dope and they'd say, 'No wonder he's had an accident.'

* * *

My training reputation had spread far and wide and I like to think I was playing a significant part in hammering the drugs gangs. For instance, I had a call from the Belgian police asking me to lecture their undercover operatives on the latest techniques.

They couldn't have organised it better: I had my requisition translated and when I walked into the lecture room there it was, all the drugs and paraphernalia I required neatly laid out for me. The Belgian students had the best possible assistance to make the lecture a success. It was entirely different from having to beg, borrow and steal it on my home ground. I was treated like a lord, listened to with great respect and, when the lecture was over, all the remnants were scooped up and any losses caused by demonstrating drug uses and so forth were written off by the senior officer in charge. No fuss, no problems.

Our courses in London became almost legendary – once I'd sorted out my lack of drug samples – and forces throughout Britain sent trainees to us to gain undercover expertise, from county drugs squads, from Regional Crime Squads, inner cities, wherever there was a need to equip officers for covert work. A lot of forces, though, fell into the trap of selecting the wrong sort of people for the job: 'Oh, he looks the sort who'd be a drug dealer ... eyes too close together.' They were selecting people merely on the cosmetics of the job. But at the end of the day, what someone looked like was irrelevant. Some of the best undercover officers I've known look the straightest guys in the world, but once they were in role they were brilliant. It's what comes out of your mouth, how you act, what you know, at the end of the day that is the crux of whether or not you are a good undercover cop. They recruited a number of black guys to start with in the belief that they would suit the job, but a lot of them just weren't up to it. They were a danger to themselves, let alone anyone else working with them.

One training course I went on ended up with me being nicknamed 'The Great Provider'. I was chosen for a place on an undercover training course organised by Greater Manchester Police, a force with a good reputation for being at the cutting edge of training techniques. I travelled up to Manchester in

1993 to take part in the course, partly as an observer, partly as a participant, with the aim of taking back anything we could utilise in the Met or giving my expertise as and when required to other students. Manchester's VO2 Covert Operations Unit had built up a good reputation. Where they were doing things which would be of use to me, I'd take it back to London.

One night they took us out on the piss, then out for a curry and it was getting towards two in the morning. Something made me start to smell a rat, just by looking at the other instructors. I thought they had definitely got something up their sleeve. We got back to the training centre at about half-past two in the morning and I was ready for kip. I hadn't been in bed very long when bang, bang, bang, the door was nearly knocked off its hinges.

'GET UP, GET UP, GET DRESSED,' someone yelled.

'You've got twenty minutes to make it to the lecture room.'

We'd only had a couple of hours' sleep; some were really hungover, and some of us had paced ourselves a bit. We were all frog-marched into the lecture room, strip-searched and relieved of everything except the clothes we stood up in – cash, credit cards, keys, mobile phones, pens, watches, everything was taken. We were all frog-marched out again and stuck in the back of a blacked-out Ford Transit van. We had no idea where we were going. We were driven off not knowing what direction we were travelling in and, after about an hour and a half, they started dropping us off one by one. At one point, I knew we were at Leeds Bradford Airport because I could hear the noise of aircraft. I was crossing my fingers I'd get tossed out there; what a terrific place to get turned out. Every facility there.

THE GREAT PROVIDER

I wasn't that lucky. In the end, I was the last to get dropped off, down a dirt track in the middle of nowhere. As I was hauled out of the back of the van, I was given typed instructions saying, 'You must not break the law apart from begging,' with 20p taped to it. That was your survival kit for the day – 20p. I had to get ten business cards from the village where they had dropped me – Burley-in-Wharfedale in Yorkshire – some hypodermic needles from a needle exchange at a Manchester hospital and make a phone call to base at a specific time for further instructions from our taskmasters.

I thought, what a load of bollocks. If they were looking for a bit of initiative to help me through, then I'd oblige them. There I was, an out-and-out townie, looking like a sore thumb at 6.30am with poxy instructions in my hand saying not to break the law. Sod that. I had a quick look up and down the village street, and saw my breakfast in the shape of a nice pint of milk standing on the doorstep of the local solicitor's office. Wallop, it went down a treat. I didn't take their only pint of milk – they had two – so no one had to miss their morning cuppa. Then I found myself a nice bench in the local churchyard and had a snooze for an hour. What else was I going to do in the back of beyond?

I woke up and there was a geezer walking through the churchyard smoking a fag.

'Excuse me, mate, I couldn't ponce a fag off you, could I?'

He looked half scared to death. I think he thought he was about to be mugged.

'Yeah, yeah,' he said, very nervously, 'have a couple, have three or four.' Then he toddled off looking mightily relieved he hadn't been hit over the head and robbed of his wallet.

Getting the ten business cards from the village businesses wasn't a problem. I said my parents were moving there and I was getting information about local shops and services. Getting to Manchester, which was fucking miles away, might be more of a challenge. What should I do? I'd got a bit of a reputation for thinking on my feet, so now was the time to prove it. I had a mate who'd met a girl on holiday a couple of years earlier and had a passionate fling with her. I knew she lived not far from Manchester. So as the church clock was striking eight, I found a phone box and called my mate, reversing the charges. I told him where I was.

'That girl, Linda, you met on holiday … she lives round here somewhere doesn't she?'

'Yes, she does.'

'Have you got a number for her?'

'Yes, yes, but what the fuck are you doing? You're supposed to be away on a course. What's going on, Blex?'

'Never mind,' I said. 'I'll tell you about it when I get back to London.'

He flicked through his personal phone numbers and read out Linda's. I scrawled it down on a piece of paper with a pen I borrowed off a woman walking past. Contact with anyone you knew was supposed to be strictly forbidden. That was made clear from the start. But I thought; fuck this for a game of soldiers.

I dialled the operator and asked for a transfer charge call to Linda's number. I kept my fingers crossed as it rang. No one answered. I gave it another thirty seconds, then a sleepy voice said, 'Hello?' She recognised me from our couple of brief meetings and accepted the call. I'd phoned at what I thought was a reasonable hour.

'Hello, Blex. What on earth are you calling for at this time of day?' she said.

I didn't know, of course, but she'd been out clubbing until 6.00am and had had only a couple of hours in bed. I said, 'Lin, if ever I needed a friend, now is the time.'

She lived in the posh part of Cheshire, in Wilmslow, where all the footballers have their mansions. Her parents were pretty well heeled and I knew she had a car of her own. With all the powers of persuasion I could muster, I managed to talk her into getting out of her comfortable warm bed and driving the forty miles to where I was. She arrived at about 11.30am and picked me up from a pub car park on the main road which I knew she couldn't miss. I'd spent the time waiting for her dossing in the beer garden in the sun. I don't think it was quite what the instructors envisaged any of us to be doing. They thought we'd be slogging it on foot or bumming lifts on lorries.

Anyway, Linda's little Fiat Panda swung into the car park like a vision. I gave her a little welcome hug and explained what was going on. She thought it was hysterical. She thought it was great that I'd stuck two fingers up at their Boy Scout course and said, 'Great, I'm game for the rest of the day.'

We headed off for Manchester and she got petrol for the car and bought me a welcome egg and tomato sandwich. Then she cashed a cheque and gave me £15. Joy of joys, I was solvent again. Then it was back to her parents' home where she cooked a nice spaghetti lunch which I washed down with some cool beers from the fridge. I was made up. I didn't want to be smug but I couldn't help thinking about those other poor sods out there with their 20ps all trying to get back home from some remote location, all playing the white man in their blistered feet. Lin drove me into the centre of Manchester to fulfil the task of acquiring some needles. I said, 'Don't take me right up to the hospital; drop me half a mile away. They are bound to be watching to see if anyone's cheating.'

Any breach of regulations, even with this fiasco, would have led to instant dismissal from the course. I'd probably never work undercover again, and I'd be blacklisted because I'd let the side down. My guv'nors at SO10 would not have been amused. It was a risk I was prepared to take. I crept into the hospital through a side entrance and got the hypodermics by saying that I'd just moved to Manchester from London with my girlfriend and was trying to wean her off heroin but she'd gone back on it.

Mission accomplished, I said goodbye to the lovely Lin. Then I had a couple of hours to kill. I was way ahead of schedule and didn't have to ring in for further instructions until 7.00pm. It started to rain, as it tends to in Manchester, so I retired to the shelter of a Coral betting shop. I thought I'd look at the greyhound meetings from Catford and Walthamstow showing on the SIS screens. There was a beast I liked the sound of in the 3.17. I put a cautious £1 on to win. I knew I couldn't afford to lose too much of what cash I'd got. It romped in at 4-1. I picked another dog a couple of races later, got all brave and stuck £2 on to win. Another £7 in winnings. My modest kitty had now swollen to £25. Another £2 bet and I'd picked a loser. One more try and I'm back on target with £2 on a 3-1 shot which won in a photo-finish. That's it, £30 up and I was away to meet my other valiant soldiers.

I found the phone box from which I had to ring in for my

next set of instructions. The instructors no doubt expected to see me exhausted, bedraggled, broke and starving. Well, I'm not, guys. I've had a lovely day, got a decent lunch in my stomach and £30 in my pocket. My orders now were to go to a rendezvous point where I would meet up with the others.

Well, I've never seen such a sorry sight in all my life. They all looked tired, drained and knackered, one had blisters on his feet where he'd walked about thirty-five miles, others had bleeding feet, and they looked totally pissed off. One guy told me about the joy he had felt when he'd found half a Big Mac in a bin and had scavenged it for his lunch. I stood there thinking, poor sods. What has it all been about? We were all training to be undercover operators, not win a Duke of Edinburgh gold award. Its relevance at that point in time seemed nil. But they hadn't finished yet. They gave us instructions to conduct a surveillance operation on some 'suspects' in a nearby pub and report back on our findings. That could have shafted everyone. How would they carry out surveillance inside a boozer when they hadn't got tuppence between them for a pint? Some had managed to beg a couple of quid for food during the day but only had pennies left. Undaunted, we set off for the pub. As we neared it, I turned to them one by one, handed them a couple of quid so they could order up a pint and some peanuts and carry out the surveillance exercise to the satisfaction of the instructors, and without some stroppy barman saying, 'You can't sit in here if you're not buying a drink.'

The final stunt of that bizarre day was to make all ten of us, mainly police but with a couple of Customs guys, walk back on foot to the training centre through the gloom and the rain.

It was about two miles; we'd been up since the crack of dawn and they were taking great delight in driving past in their police cars giving us a load of stick out of the windows. It was a pretty dismal band of adventurers – dismal bar one. I was still as fresh as a daisy at the end of the day's exertions. I was able to keep morale up with a bit of Cockney banter as we trudged back to base. As we neared the training centre, where I knew everyone would be waiting, I said, 'Right, we are all going to present a united front and fuck 'em.' They had tried to break our spirits and I wasn't having any of that, even though my own spirits weren't even cracked let alone broken. In we went, heads held high, as though we did this every week without batting an eyelid.

The Customs blokes were extremely pissed off with the whole thing. They could see no point in it at all. Most of the cops were equally baffled by the merits of what seemed to most a complete waste of time and effort.

'Stay cool,' I urged, 'don't let them think Big Brother has won the day.'

We agreed to put it down to experience, and perhaps not be available when the next course came up.

Finally, I had to explain to the instructors how I was able to provide everyone with a couple of quid for the pub drinks and where I had got it from when I started the day with a mere 20p piece. I couldn't tell them the truth. So I contrived this elaborate story about a person I had confronted and had asked to borrow money from. I said I'd given him moody details, claimed I'd been on the piss all night and lost my wallet and that I'd promise to send back every penny when I got home. He'd taken a shine to me and handed over a tenner. With that, I said, I'd had a flutter and got the rest of the cash in winnings. Pure initiative. I didn't dare tell anyone about Linda, of course, because I didn't know any of them that well and there was a danger of getting grassed up and dispatched back to Scotland Yard in shame.

The guy who ran the course, Harry Mercer, laid on a bit of a party after the final debriefing. He listened politely to individual stories of survival, how people had begged and borrowed to get back to base. Then he said to the assembled group, 'Of course, when you got back to Manchester you met with The Great Provider, didn't you?' I knew he was suspicious. But he also knew he was dealing with a professional liar and I wasn't about to cough the truth.

As soon as I got back to London, I sent a cheque and a big thank you card to Lin in Wilmslow. She was my cracker when I needed her.

Chapter Eleven

STEAM CLEANED

'You want how much?' The guv'nor was aghast. 'At least three hundred and fifty thousand,' I said. 'You know, just over a third of a million.'

We were dealing with the *crème de la crème* of international criminals and only big bucks would snare the big players. I needed the cash to tee up a potential cocaine deal worth millions. This was a high-flying international organisation that brokered every type of valuable commodity in any part of the world. Valuable stolen art works and multi-national counterfeit currency already featured in their portfolio of crime. Now they were in the blue-chip drugs business. Wall-to-wall cocaine, up to thirty kilos a time in regular consignments. And they had an Amsterdam-based banker to launder their proceeds through undetectable channels designed to baffle even the most astute of investigators.

THE GANGBUSTER

The gang had already been under scrutiny by another undercover team who were interested in their activities on the art world black market. Paintings had been stolen to order and were being offered to unscrupulous collectors all over the world. They had been busy, too, printing and circulating fake notes in half a dozen currencies. Once drugs entered the equation, a separate covert inquiry was decided upon. That's when I met The Dutchman – smooth, cultured, knowledgeable, a true cosmopolitan crook.

The undercovers who had already infiltrated certain areas of the gang's activities knew who was likely to be drafted into the operation to move the drugs investigation forward. They had painted a colourful but not unflattering picture of the London dealer who would be interested in buying big parcels of coke.

'He's a bit lairy, but he knows what he's doing. And he's very security conscious.'

They'd more or less taken it for granted that I'd be the drugs expert nominated for the job and they were right.

The Dutchman – urbane, educated and fluent in English and three other languages – originated from Amsterdam but had lived in London for several years. We were introduced in a bar in north-west London. He sipped cognac, I downed a pint. He was easy to deal with. A refreshing change from the inner-city scumbags I rubbed shoulders with so much of the time. We were soon talking cocaine deals as casually as if we were discussing a shipment of tinned tomatoes as we strolled across Hampstead Heath keeping clear of prying eyes or over-attentive ears. His people, he said, would be in a position to supply me with enough cocaine to keep London's snorters happy for years.

'How much do you want? I can get twenty or thirty kilos at a time,' he said.

'Sounds good to me.'

We got down to the fine print of where and when.

'You must first meet my business partner,' he said. 'I think you will like him. Then you can show us that you have the money ready.'

The scene was set. The Dutchman was happily anticipating a brand-new venture. I reported back to base that we were now in a go situation and I would need to draw at least £350,000 cash from the Commissioner's vaults. The raised eyebrows soon lowered as I explained what a major league operation we had latched on to.

'OK, Blex, let's go for it.'

First, I needed to rent a decent flat where I could set up a meet with the crooks to show them the money. I needed it to look like my everyday home. I carted over boxes of my own possessions, photos and knick-knacks to place around the rooms to give it that lived-in look. And the technical boys were briefed to get in there and wire it up before the start of business.

The Dutchman's business partner, a well-dressed type who could have arrived from a City of London stockbrokers but had flown in from Amsterdam especially for the meeting, was courteous and business-like.

'Hello, Peter, it's nice to do business with you. I understand you can handle large quantities of the merchandise.'

'Yes,' I said, 'if it is of the right quality I can take as much as you can get.'

'Good, we can get plenty. Have you got the money ready?'

We drove to my rented flat in a West London block by a circuitous route that would have left them mystified about its exact location. I back-tracked, I ducked down side-roads. I stopped, reversed and turned around, all anti-surveillance tactics I'd learned at SO10. They'd been told I was security conscious, and I was proving the point.

'I need to be sure there is no one on your tail,' I told them, 'cops or otherwise.'

They looked suitably impressed. I'd taken the BMW twice round the plot when I suddenly pulled up and said, 'We're here,' and ushered them towards the door. I let myself in, nodding to a neighbour on the way as if I'd been living there for years. I undid the double security locks and we went inside. I pretended to carry out an electronic scan to check whether the place could have been bugged. Joke, really, I knew it had. I made a phone call on my mobile to summon a couple of undercover guys who were acting as my minders – really hard-looking, fucking great giants of men. These were part of my team, I told the Dutchmen. They were certainly the sort of tasty blokes you wouldn't mind having around if there was a problem.

'You can't be too sure these days,' I said. 'A lot of people are getting robbed.'

The Dutchmen were suitably impressed. I saw them look at each other and nod as if to say, 'This guy knows what he's doing.'

I pulled a black travelling holdall from a cupboard in the bedroom and unzipped it in front of my Dutch visitors. The guy who'd just flown in fingered through the notes, testing them like he might know a thing or two about counterfeit currency.

'Yes, these are good, Peter. How much have you got?'

'There is three hundred and fifty thousand there and more where that came from.'

There were more nods of approval and handshakes before we parted. 'It is good, Peter. We will see you tomorrow for some business. In Amsterdam.'

This was all happening in the middle of the afternoon in West London and they were making plans to meet me at the Hilton Hotel at Schiphol Airport at 9.00am the next day. You can't say, 'Sorry, but I can't make it.' And you certainly can't say, 'Er, sorry, I'm on surveillance duty in Woking tomorrow …' You've just got to go with the flow. It was back to the Yard as quickly as possible to seek authorisation for the trip from a senior officer. I needed to liaise with our Dutch counterparts, to tell them I'd be working on their patch in the morning, and put all the logistics of the operation into motion. I'd already got a false passport and documentation in the bogus name I was using, Peter Mitchell, company director. It was part of the standard SO10 undercover kit.

I spent the rest of the day, until after 11.00pm that night, sorting out plane tickets and putting the final details together for the venture into enemy territory.

I was at the City of London Airport at the crack of dawn, buzzing. I strode through the terminal, *Financial Times* under my arm, looking every inch the British businessman off to Holland on a routine business trip. Inside my briefcase I had headed notepaper, letters, invoices, all the paraphernalia I needed to back up my cover. Nothing was left to chance in these hazardous exploits.

I didn't catch the flight the Dutchmen would have expected

me to. I needed to be there earlier. There was work to be done. I caught the earliest plane I could. I needed first to contact the Dutch police. They were required to give me their official list of rules and regulations that would govern my investigative activities on Dutch soil. It was all laid down by magistrates and had to be adhered to or consent would be withdrawn. I went early because I thought the bad guys might have spotters out looking for me on the planned 8.55am arrival. I needed to slip through earlier unnoticed, liaise with the Dutch police then meet up with the Dutch gangsters in the bar of the Hilton. It was a race against time.

It went well. I strolled into the Hilton only a couple of minutes late and met my Dutch contacts.

'Good flight?'

'Yes, fine.'

'OK, we'll take you to meet some of our people.'

I suppose I asked for it in a way, but the bastards did to me exactly what I had done to them in London – only ten times worse. It was, in short, fucking terrifying. They put me in a top-of-the-range Volvo, screeched off and took me on a merry-go-round of a journey at high speed, ducking, diving, and trying to disorientate me like I'd done to them.

Well, I tried to look cool, like I did this all the time. In London, I never had a problem jumping in a car with someone I didn't know because I was born and bred there. I'd always know roughly where I was going. You could drop me anywhere and within a couple of minutes I could go to the end of the road and know where I was. This was a whole lot different. It was what we called a dry-cleaning run, an anti-surveillance technique to make sure no one is sticking with you. I was totally thrown. I hadn't got a fucking clue where we were going. I was trying to look calm, as though 80kph in a built-up area didn't faze me, as though I didn't mind running the odd light on red. It was like the Dutch fucking Grand Prix. All the time I was trying to clock buildings, rivers, tower blocks, any landmark that might tell me where I'd been. Except that the same landmarks kept cropping up time after time.

I now knew I was dealing with premier division criminals; no more Mr Nice Guys. All the time I was thinking perhaps this was all a scam to keep me hostage until the £350,000 had been paid. It had happened several times among the Dutch drug gangs.

The gang suddenly drove into a car park and stopped. This was the meeting place, they said. My heart jumped. No one was there. Then suddenly, wallop! They shoved me into another car and off we roared again. If it was a kidnap, I thought, I'd need to know where I'd been taken. I was busy looking everywhere but trying at the same time to hold a normal conversation.

'Have you been to our red-light district?' one of them asked.

'Yeah,' I said, 'I have, but I don't like paying for it.' I thought I'd best compliment them on their anti-surveillance techniques rather than let them think I was worried.

'I do like working with professionals', I said after another particularly devious manoeuvre. 'I've been having a look myself and I don't think anyone is onto us.'

We were now in a commercial district. I was trying to catch the street name. Then we stopped outside a bank. We went quickly inside and I was introduced briefly to a man who was every inch the bank manager. Grey-haired, smartly-dressed, a little aloof. The conversation was brief, almost non-existent. It was, 'Right, you know him, he knows you,' and we were on the move again. As we headed back to Schiphol by another roundabout route, it was explained that he was the banker who would launder the drugs cash, convert my £350,000, when I brought it over, into guilders or invest it in the gang's phoney businesses. These really were proper crooks. And I knew I had to be doubly careful being on foreign soil. I was on their territory with no back-up. I was in company but, by fuck, I didn't half feel lonely.

I was mightily relieved to be able to settle back into my seat for the flight to London knowing I had infiltrated a gang operating at the very highest level of international crime. I gave the Dutch police a full briefing. I gave my own bosses a detailed run-down. We sat and we waited for the bomb to drop. Nothing. I waited for a call from the London-based Dutchman. Nothing. I waited for word from across the North Sea. Nothing. The job just disappeared into a black hole.

I was never given a proper explanation but the clear implication had to be that corruption had thwarted our investigation. I'd given the Dutch police a leading drugs gang and a bent bank manager on a plate. But, as far as I could establish, he'd never been arrested, never even been questioned. It left a very nasty taste in the mouth. Was this the Amsterdam establishment closing ranks?

The Dutchman in London made contact after several weeks – we'd let him run so we could keep an eye on him – and he seemed fine so I was happy I'd not done anything wrong in the inquiry. He seemed as puzzled as me that the cocaine trade had been shelved. The whole business remains as much a mystery to me today as it did then.

* * *

STEAM CLEANED

Corruption has been and, I fear, always will be, a sad fact of life in the police force. I've turned down offers that could have made me millions. Informants have suggested that, when we raided the home of one coke dealer known to keep a stash of £100,000 in his deep freeze, we hand in only £40,000 and split the rest. Informants have put up propositions that when I went into a drugs job in which six kilos of heroin would be found, I could say it was four and we'd share the other two between us and make a nice few quid. Invariably, each time I'd turn round and say, 'I didn't hear that,' or 'Look, mate, we haven't had this conversation, get my drift?' You could see the looks on their faces, the palpable disappointment, when they realised I wasn't up for a fiddle. They thought we were going out there to earn a bit, and why not? We go out there and infiltrate these people, we're all in it together, we've put ourselves on the line here, now come on, let's just have a little weed out of the gear. They have no scruples about it at all.

I've turned down every proposition ever put to me, but I've had to be very, very careful. If you upset the informant, if you don't go along with the scam, he might not want to work with you and the whole operation could fall flat on its face. They always make it sound so easy, so fool proof. Be it money or drugs that mysteriously go missing, there aren't many villains likely to say, 'I've been robbed – I had six kilos on me, not four,' or 'I had a hundred grand in there, not forty,' because the more they had, the more it would implicate them in the crime. So they keep quiet. And who would believe them anyway, when two or three fine, upstanding members of Her Majesty's police force stand up in the witness box and give their version under oath? Of course we didn't nick the stuff, Your Honour. Perish the thought! It's the oldest defence in the world to say the cops are bent. Not hearing any slippery propositions in the first place was always the best way of dealing with it. An informant can't then go back to his handler, who would be in on the scam, and say, 'You've got to sack this bloke 'cos he's not playing ball.' It stopped things in their tracks before it got out of hand. I just wanted to get on with the job of nicking villains, not robbing off them.

I think a lot of informants assume that because you are playing the part of a villain, you must be a bit of a villain. The better the undercover guy is, the more likely he is to find himself being offered dodgy dealings. They think you really are one of them, not just Plod playing the bad guy.

I must admit, I've seen systematic corruption and suspected even more. But what do the public perceive as bent? What do they regard as a bent copper? There are many different levels as to what people will accept. They will tolerate having a box of paper clips and a packet of A4 out of the office. Every level of society has a tolerance level regarding corruption in whatever walk of life.

But bent cops are always a no-no. The police are expected to be paragons of virtue in everything they do. But what people often fail to remember is that the police are plucked from society. They are not a separate society; they are a reflection of society. So to expect that there won't be any misdemeanours taking place, and expecting some sort of idealistic, whiter-than-white police service, is pure naïveté on the part of the public and foolhardiness on behalf of the police authorities.

My area of expertise, the deep undercover mission, was more

prone than most police departments to the spectre of corruption and it sometimes took great strength of mind to turn down the offer of easy money or the temptation to 'go native' and join the villains in money-making enterprises. On the face of it, they always seemed to be having a much better time than anyone else – better homes, better cars, better holidays, and didn't even have to get up in the morning to clock on for work. But underneath you always had a sort of satisfaction that it wasn't going to be Easy Street for them much longer because you were there to see to it. I was there to take them out. That's the way I liked it.

But what can happen, even when you resist all temptation, is that you can still get tainted because some other bastard on your team is doing a double-reverse ferret.

A pal of mine on the undercover squad did a job on a dealer in possession of 30,000 tabs of LSD. He went back to the nick and wrote up his evidence immediately after the event in accordance with police procedure.

His statement said, 'I saw and counted thirty thousand doses of LSD, thirty sheets each containing a thousand doses,' it was all done and dusted and he submitted it to his supervising officer for his signature. When the arresting officers came up from the charge room a couple of hours later, they said, 'Right, we've charged him, twenty thousand tabs of LSD, all done.'

What could he do, what could he say? His evidence had been totally compromised, and he could see what was likely to happen. Six months up the line, he would be standing in the witness box at the Old Bailey telling how he saw 30,000 tabs when the accused is charged with possessing only 20,000. 'How can this officer's evidence possibly be believed, members of the jury?' Acquittal, internal investigation and his name tarnished throughout the job. We were, effectively, the cops' own crooks in our game, playing the part of villains to catch real villains. We knew the risks. We knew the temptations. I was always gutted if I knew blokes were going over to the other side and letting us down.

I often found myself the 'tail-end Charlie' on operations when my knowledge of the drug involved required special expertise. Another undercover officer might have already infiltrated a drugs gang but wanted me pulled in at the last minute to be the tester. Everybody knew that I was experienced in handling all types of gear. Some undercovers were equipped to go in and infiltrate but when the parcel arrived on the plot they didn't have the confidence in their own abilities, or sufficient knowledge of the drug involved, to test it themselves to see if it was the real stuff. I would arrive as the trusted 'mate' who knew about these things and would sample the drugs and give an honest opinion. I'd pop along with my holdall containing my scales, all the drug paraphernalia, the weights and what have you, and do what I had to do in the way they wanted to see it done, by an expert. I was the professional at this. My bag and I got called all over the show. With us travelled the spectre of temptation. You might meet an undercover cop who was already inside the gang and he'd say, 'It's going to be eight kilos of heroin they're bringing you this afternoon, but, er, between you, me and the gatepost, we'll say five, eh? Don't worry about it, we'll call you in a week's time and we'll meet up and all have a nice drink.'

His proposition got short shrift from me. 'We haven't had this conversation,' I replied in time-honoured fashion. And the deal, I'm glad to say, usually went through straight without any gear going AWOL and with the villains all getting banged up without the knowledge of being stitched up by bent Old Bill. I couldn't help thinking over the years there should have been one or two police officers doing bird with them.

Whatever my knowledge or suspicions I never grassed any of my fellow officers up. That's the way I was. I didn't mind what names people called me as long as one of them wasn't grass. I knew the temptations out there. How easy it would have been just to say OK and make more money in an afternoon than I was likely to earn in a year as a straight copper.

Huge sums of money were part and parcel of my everyday life and the opportunities were there, the enticement factor immense. They had a cash room at Scotland Yard where you'd go to pick up the dosh and I was a regular customer. I was always drawing big sums, £50,000 and up as regular as clockwork. And the distrust within the police always used to entertain me. The money had to be signed for, counted, and signed for again by the commanding officer. It was then counted again to make sure that what you'd been given by the cash room staff was all there, then you'd go out and use it on the plot and it's all got to be accounted for and signed for again at the end of the day when they want to put it back. You had to be so careful to prove the continuity of who you gave it to because, on more than one occasion, it would get back to the cash room and they'd say, 'No, we haven't got fifty thousand pounds here, we've only got forty-seven thousand five hundred.' Then the shit would hit the fan and everybody would come to you straight away as the officer dealing and have a little look. Fortunately, because of my reputation I never used to get seriously grilled over it and I'd say, 'Well, you'll just have to work backwards and find whose hands it's passed through. But don't look at me.'

I don't think they ever managed to nick anyone for thieving the Commissioner's cash. The perpetrators would have been too careful.

If you were handling these huge sums of money almost every day, and you'd got bills or a mortgage to pay or needed a holiday or whatever, you had to be straight, and strong. You could find yourself spending months and months targeting someone suspected of running a major scam, who lived in a fucking great house, drove a top-of-the-range Merc, ran what appeared on the surface to be a successful business, and lived the life of Reilly. After months of tedium, and sometimes danger, it all ended in a huge search of the place and there was a fucking great Joey full of scratch. The Old Bill were resentful of the fucker anyway; he'd got all these ill-gotten gains, so was it to be on-the-spot fining? Into the cash stash and away with a nice wedge of spending money. It was hardly surprising that a bit of dough went walkies now and again. I knew it happened, but it wasn't my scene. Where's my big Jag and mansion?

Although the job was great if you judged it on the mind-blowing adrenaline rushes which were part of the territory, there was certainly no cash incentive to stay on the straight and narrow. My basic rate of pay as a detective constable was peanuts compared to many of the geezers I was put in to investigate. There was no extra five or ten grand a year for going undercover. Fuck all. No danger money, nothing for putting your head on the block day after day, nothing for being the leading specialist in my field. You took home the same as any other similarly ranked officer who walked out of the nick in the morning and spent eight hours plodding the streets looking at his toecaps. Same with the desk wallahs who sat doing fuck-all all day while I'd be out there getting shot and stabbed and infiltrating the bad guys.

There were expenses but, as often as not, you'd be out of pocket on a job and have to do a bit of creative accounting on your expenses to balance the books. They always wanted provable expenses but you can't do that when you are cruising round with villains; you can't ask barmen for receipts or suddenly demand that the taxi driver gives you a signed tab. The villains are going to suss you out double quick. There was a bit of overtime once, but that got whittled away eventually in financial cutbacks. The penny-pinching became unbelievable in the end. I told them, 'Excuse me, I'm out there pretending to be a fucking high-flying, hard-case gangster ... I can't do it on a tenner a day.'

Several members of the squad made approaches to the powers that be for more money – at least a clothing allowance to help us do the job in as professional a manner as possible. If you were in a position where you were frequenting high-class hotels and eating expensive meals as part of an undercover job you had to look the part. If you pitched up in a Marks & Spencer suit you'd look suspicious right away. Dressing up or dressing down was important; people judge you on first impressions. And you never get a second chance to make a first impression, do you? You always had to be very aware of that, and dress according to the people you were mixing with. Be one of them.

There was always some bitching and whingeing about some sort of allowance and eventually the police very graciously let us go up to the prisoners' property store in Cricklewood in north–west London and have a root through to see if there was anything there which might be useful. It was stuff that had been confiscated, marked 'not claimed'; a lot of it was a load of old tat, a right load of old garbage. It was laughable, some of the most skilled detectives at Scotland Yard rummaging through old bin bags for something to wear.

I was described in several of the Yard's annual appraisals as 'an imaginative dresser' which was sort of true anyway. I always liked to dress stylishly – some might say a bit garishly – so the clothing problem didn't affect me so much. If I looked the part on an undercover job, it was out of my own pocket and not through the largesse of Scotland Yard. My old grandad always used to say you judged a man by his shoes. I don't know how relevant that is today, but when I went out on a mission I was very conscious of everything I was wearing, from my Gucci watch to my favourite make of Dolce and Gabbana designer-label jeans. They had to be right if you were going to convince the bad guys.

Several blokes on the squad had relationships with friendly jewellers where they could go to borrow some decent kit. If you went to a meet wearing ten or fifteen grand's worth of jewellery it was good for your kudos. I was never a great one for jewellery so I never bothered with it myself, but it certainly helped a few of the others establish their credentials.

I heard various rumours about corruption at high levels at Scotland Yard but nothing I could ever prove, not that I'd go running to the CIB boys anyway. One incident I am sure is true involves a colleague who went undercover to infiltrate a notorious North London criminal gang suspected of being involved in all sorts of villainy from murder to robbery to drugs. The twist was that he'd managed to convince the gang bosses that he was a bent cop prepared to help them out when in fact he was as straight as a die with every intention of getting evidence that would put them behind bars for twenty years minimum. He spent a lot of time drinking with them, getting close, and convincing them he was bent and up for any sorts of deals. He came back into the office four weeks later shaking and told me, 'I walked into the pub today, Blex, and they said, "We know you're not a bent copper and we know you're working undercover. Now consider yourself lucky, get out of here, fuck off and be grateful we haven't put our hands on you."'

He was shell-shocked, absolutely fucking gobsmacked; he knew how close he'd been to taking a dip with a concrete overcoat or propping up a motorway bridge. What he did tell me sickened me to my boots – the gang had been tipped off about his undercover role by a senior officer at Scotland Yard who'd been paid a £50,000 bung in cash. It blew the whole fucking job right out of the water and put an officer in grave danger. That senior officer was never questioned, never arrested, never charged and has now left the force. He's no doubt got a nice retirement home on the Costa with a fair bit of added bunce in his retirement kitty. But I wonder how his conscience is.

Chapter Twelve

ROBBING HOODS

I've got a scar on my face that serves as a permanent reminder always to expect the unexpected. The knife that sliced me just under my chin came within an inch of severing my windpipe or puncturing my jugular. It all happened in a split second as we raided the headquarters of a drugs gang in Tooting, South London, when indecision almost proved fatal.

I had been drafted into the job, not as the undercover man this time, but as back-up to a West Midlands undercover cop investigating a team of Indians suspected of dealing in heroin. I knew the squad was short of troops and volunteered my assistance. The uniformed senior officer running the job hadn't had a lot of experience in covert work so I was there to offer him any expertise I could.

The operation went like clockwork to start with; a police hit team moved in and scooped up two of the gang in the street as cash and drugs were exchanged. The heroin package was safely retrieved. So far so good. Premises had been identified during surveillance from where the dealers had been seen toing and froing. It needed checking, and quick.

I suggested to the operational head, a lovely fella but new to this kind of job, that this was a place which had to be searched as a matter of some considerable urgency. In fact, I was pleading with him to get the placed turned over right away. 'Let's attack now,' I said. 'We know the villains have been in there, we mustn't wait another minute. Let's go now. Right now.'

But he was still reluctant to launch a full-scale attack. 'Let's wait and see, let's hold on a bit longer,' he said.

I knew what might have been going on in those premises. If somebody had been left in there, another member of the gang, he would be expecting his colleagues back by now with all the money. They'd gone off and done the deal as far as he was concerned, and should be coming back with the cash pretty soon to divvy it up. The longer we left the attack, I argued, the more likely anyone in there would start to get jittery. These were premises we should attack without a minute's further delay.

Under considerable pressure, I finally persuaded the operational head to allow us to move in. It was now a full half-hour since the bust had taken place. The dealers should have been back within ten minutes with the money. Anyone left in the flat could be getting severely twitchy.

Without further delay, I led the assault up to the fortified front door. It was a flat over a shop and access was via a metal staircase to the rear. I went clunk, clunk up the dimly-lit stairway trying to make as little noise as possible. It was difficult on the metal stairs. I wanted to check out access, and decide what the best method of attack would be – kicking the door in, or if we'd got another Fort Knox on our hands then we'd have to withdraw to get battering equipment to storm in. I felt I could do it OK myself.

Suddenly, the door flew open and ... wallop! The fucker came at me with a knife and stabbed me in the neck just under my chin. It happened in a flash.

I acted instinctively and reached out and grabbed him, dragged him out of the house and wrapped him over some metal railings on the walkway. I got hold of his hand and he was still clutching the knife, all covered in blood – my fucking blood. I was thinking, oh shit I wonder how bad it is, and kept him pinned down until there were enough troops behind me to hold him and stop him doing any more damage with the knife. I'd exercised proper caution, but the bastard had still caught me unawares.

I put my hand to my neck and it was pouring blood. I didn't know whether this was it, the end of the line for P. Bleksley, detective constable. I didn't know whether the knife had cut the jugular or what untold damage he had done. He had really lunged at me, really hit me one. I reckon he had thought we were robbers on the stairs after the heroin money, shat himself and panicked.

The wound was throbbing and the pain was getting worse. I was a bit in shock. I needed medical attention and I needed it quickly. Unfortunately, I didn't manage to get in a retaliatory blow on my attacker but, as I sat down waiting for the ambulance to arrive, I could hear all these screams and wails coming from round the corner as they carted him off to the nick. If he got a pasting, I didn't waste any sympathy on him.

Because I didn't know how bad the injury was, I didn't want to breathe in and inhale any blood. Somebody had grabbed a scarf and wrapped it round the wound, and I kept it pressed tight 'til the ambulance came and I went off to St George's Hospital. They were on emergency standby at the A and E department because the message they'd got was that a policeman was coming in with a knife in his neck.

The duty doctor, a somewhat hard-faced lady, took a look and said, 'Oh, you'll live, don't panic. Just a few stitches.' I was mightily relieved to hear that. The knife, which had a 6in double-edged blade, had fortunately hit me a glancing blow under my chin, ripping open a 2in gash. It could so easily have been another story. It gave me a severe bit of grief for several weeks; my face came up black and blue, and the scar, on the underside of my left jaw, will be with me for life, a salutary reminder that you never know what's round the next comer or behind the next door.

The knifeman was charged with causing me grievous bodily harm with intent and sentenced to five years in jail. Ironically, the two other members of the heroin gang were acquitted at their trial of conspiracy to supply drugs. If my bloke had kept his cool and not gone for me like a madman, he'd probably have got off the drug-dealing as well. Tough, ain't it?

* * *

I got my first taste of learning to expect the unexpected on my very first job with the Central Drugs Squad undercover division. And what a baptism of fire it turned out to be.

ROBBING HOODS

It was 1985 and I had arrived at Scotland Yard bright-eyed and bushy-tailed, the new kid on the block anxious to do well. I knew I had a vast amount to learn about the workings of Scotland Yard. It was all very well being a detective at a local police station, but now this was premier league. I was confronted by things I never even imagined the police did, let alone knew how they did them. It was a vast new arena to enter.

The job carried a lot of kudos; I was a young man who had made it to a Scotland Yard squad at a relatively early age, twenty-four, and I couldn't wait for the action. It came after just three days.

'Right,' said the DI, 'there's an undercover job going down in Regent's Park this afternoon and you are on it.'

I sure was. I was briefed as to what the job was all about – so and so from the unit had infiltrated this massive drug network operating in central London; the gangsters were going to supply the officers with three or four kilos of heroin in the car park of Regent's Park zoo, and when the gear arrived we would all leap out and arrest the villains. I thought, fuck me, this is real cops and robbers. There was a suspicion, said the boss, that some or all of the gang might have firearms, so caution at all times. There were going to be armed officers dotted about in various disguises, from road sweepers to porters, and although I was firearms trained, I wouldn't be carrying a weapon myself. It was the policy for an officer to go out unarmed on his first ever job for the squad.

It was a biggish team going out on the operation and the plan was for most of them to be hidden away in a big bus, ostensibly an executive-style tourist coach visiting the zoo with a party of day-trippers. It had smoked glass windows for extra cover. We would all be lying hidden on the floor or upstairs out of sight of the gangsters or anybody else curious about our activities.

Fuck me, I thought as we waited expectantly for the action to start, this is a rush. This was my initiation into the world of undercover operations. Pure excitement.

I was crouching in the bus with the other officers, and I'd got my radio tuned into the events, listening to the commentary second by second, minute by minute, to what the baddies were doing, what the police were doing. We seemed to have the situation buttoned up tight. Then, all of a sudden, the shit hit the fucking fan.

'ATTACK ... ATTACK ... ATTACK.'

Events had suddenly gone haywire. The bad guys had decided that they were going to rob the undercover police, thinking they were a team of second division crooks, and blag the £70,000 that was supposed to be used to buy the drugs. What had prompted them to change tactics I don't know, but I did discover that suspicions had crept in during a previous meeting between the two sides when the villains had asked an undercover woman detective to take her bra off as they checked her out for hidden devices like a mini tape recorder or transmitter, and she had refused. Her modesty had decreed that she stayed fully clothed. I think the gang probably went away from that meeting thinking, well, she won't get her tits out, that's a bit iffy, a bit prudish for a drug-dealer looking at a £70,000 trade. They probably thought they'd be an easy touch and decided to roll them instead.

The gang approached the undercover police team, two men and the woman, sitting in their car at the appointed meeting place in Regent's Park. Suddenly one of them produced a plastic squeezy bottle and sprayed ammonia directly in the face of the driver through the window. They opened the boot, grabbed the £70,000 and legged it. This hadn't been anticipated at all, a huge chunk of the Commissioner's cash being robbed from his own police officers.

We all poured out of the bus and various other strategic hiding places and stormed into action. There was absolute fucking bedlam. The injured driver was lying on the ground clutching his face and screaming in agony thinking he'd been blinded; the four villains had all scarpered in different directions; the police were panicking because the bag with £70,000 in it had vanished; and people were legging it all over the show in complete chaos. I was in the thick of it, just loving it. This was what I'd joined the cops for. I was young, fit and mega keen and I soon caught up with one of the villains bolting away from the car park, past the zoo visitors, mums, dads, kids and tourists. I got to within a few feet of him as he headed for some trees and bushes, low-level cover for him, where he probably hoped to hide. I was gaining on him stride by stride. Then he turned and levelled a gun at me. He hissed, 'Fuck off, you bastard,' and I thought, shit, he's going to shoot me. But I'd got up such a head of steam and was travelling like an Olympic fucking sprinter so there was no way I could stop. I ducked to one side and just carried right on straight at him. He could see I wasn't going to stop and started running again, and then – crunch – I hit him with an almighty fucking bang and sent him crashing to the deck. He slammed down like a sack of King Edwards. That was it, he was nicked.

Firearms officers examined the gun and it turned out to be a loaded .22 pistol, a lower-calibre gun but quite deadly enough to have killed me from that range. That was my first day in action with the undercover unit.

I learned a lot in a very short space of time. It was a wonderful education for me in my chosen career, but sadly it involved another officer receiving serious injuries to his eyes. It was painful but there was no lasting damage done. He received treatment at Moorfields Eye Hospital but was later able to resume his police duties after a period of sick leave.

The police squad were also fortuitous in not having to suffer the massive embarrassment of having to admit to losing the £70,000. The tabloids would have loved that. The cash was recovered from under a tarpaulin inside the zoo where one of the villains had slung the bag as he legged it. He'd seen the opportunity to dump it as he fled and obviously hoped to return later in the dead of night to retrieve it. But there was bedlam for a while. Once the crooks had been handcuffed and bundled off to be charged, there was a colossal fucking panic to find the missing seventy grand. People were looking everywhere. Blokes were running round for about twenty minutes shouting, 'Find the money, find that fucking money.' After it had been found and some sort of normality had returned, I remember the DI who ran the job, Mark Leyton, saying at the debriefing, 'Gentlemen, today is the day that I discovered adrenaline runs down your leg.' That did sum it up for all of us. And Mark Leyton, of course, had been looking at the prospect of his entire career ending in humiliation if the £70,000 had not been recovered.

The whole incident taught me that things are never black and white, and if Sod's Law can strike when you least expect it, then it will.

I sat drinking a few pints with a pal later that night and I said, 'I can do this undercover stuff, and no fucker is ever going to rob me.' I just couldn't wait to go undercover myself. It wasn't very long coming, just a matter of days. They wanted someone to volunteer for a drug infiltration and my hand shot up like an Exocet missile.

In the years that followed, I worked all over the UK and abroad, often with female police officers in undercover roles, and I can't praise them enough for their skill and courage. It could be an arduous enough job for experienced male officers; for some of the female officers, it could sometimes be nightmarish. I wasn't surprised, for instance, to hear that the girl who went undercover in the Rachel Nickell murder investigation in Wimbledon was forced to retire because of stress. I knew Lizzie James, although that wasn't her real name, and had every admiration for her abilities. To ask her to go undercover and befriend the man suspected of the murder, Colin Stagg, must have tested her emotional capabilities to the limit. I know she was deeply upset when the case was thrown out at the Old Bailey and the undercover 'honey trap' was branded reprehensible by the judge. I'm glad she's now got a decent damages pay-off from Scotland Yard.

Another female detective I worked with – we'll call her Diane because that was the undercover name she normally used – travelled with me to Darlington in Durham on a drugs job, pretending to be my courier, taking the money up north and bringing the heroin back down south to London. It was a job we'd been asked to do by the local police who'd been tipped off about an Asian gang dealing smack in a big way – or big, at least, by their standards – and wanted an experienced undercover unit to go in and do a buy of half a kilo of heroin. In London, we probably wouldn't have rated half a kilo a major job. To a provincial force it was a serious and worrying element in an upsurge of drug-related crime. So it was 'Call in the Yard,' and Diane and I headed north by train.

The trade had been arranged to take place at Darlington railway station. Normally, stations were a good place to meet and conduct drug deals because of the volume of people who would be about and you could mingle with the crowd. They also had left-luggage lockers for stashing drugs or money. That was, of course, until the advent of wall-to-wall CCTV cameras, so prevalent in all public places now. I believe the statistics suggest that an individual can be picked up on a CCTV camera over 200 times in a normal working day. But that's now. In the eighties, there weren't nearly so many, and a station was still a good, sensible place for doing criminal business.

We settled into our seats for the Darlington trip, coffee and sandwiches to hand and Diane keeping a wary eye on £16,000 in a case. I was met at the other end by one of the heroin dealers by the name of Mushi – or 'Mushy Peas' as we called him – and we started the transaction with me acting the big-shot dealer from up the Smoke and Diane as my gangster's moll. Then there was the usual hiccup – the drug parcel was not there yet, we'd have to sit and wait blah blah. The times I'd heard that.

Almost at once, Mushi was alerted by a bloke standing on the opposite platform. He took a second look then ducked out of sight and asked me, 'Do you know that geezer over there?' He pointed out a guy in jeans and a casual jacket standing there apparently just minding his own business and waiting for a train.

'No, don't know him from Adam,' I said.

'Well, I fucking do,' he replied, 'he's Old Bill. I know that for sure because he trains in a gym in Middlesbrough where I train.'

I could see the alarm bells ringing in his head. He insisted we left the station and I had to tell Diane to stay put in the buffet with the money. I wasn't too happy about it but she was cool with the situation. We went out of the station and walked about a bit doing a lot of anti-surveillance around the neighbouring streets ensuring that neither of us was being followed. Mushi seemed satisfied everything was OK and the gear finally arrived on the plot. By that time, thankfully, the bloke on the opposite platform had disappeared and Mushi assumed he'd just been waiting for a train. But he was, in fact, one of the surveillance team put in by the local police to back Diane and me up. It was either a stroke of luck, or a canny move on his part, that he'd disappeared off the plot when the time came to do the deal or it wouldn't have gone down and everyone's time would have been wasted. He must have realised that if he just stood there and trains came and went, he was going to stick out like a sore thumb, so he'd backed off.

He wasn't the only back-up cop there. There were undercover officers in British Rail clothes with the fluorescent vests tinkering about at the end of the platform; we had a bloke dressed up in the full BR porter's uniform complete with peaked hat. There was plenty of support still safely in place. We finally went back to the station, looked for a toilet where we could do the business and checked that Diane was still OK with the cash.

It was a typical run down neglected station; only half the bogs had a lock on them and we had to test each of them 'til we found a cubicle with a secure lock where I opened up the parcel. It was wrapped in the standard drug-dealer's way, a bag within a bag within a bag and so on. I pulled down the toilet seat, put the package on it and carried out my tests to see if it was OK gear. I sampled a little bit by burning it on the silver foil I always carried with me on these jaunts. I nodded and told him I was happy with it and pulled out some masking tape to make the package secure again for transportation to London. Then, much to his delight – and with his help because I wanted to get his fingerprints all over it – I started to shape the parcel into something which could be concealed on the female body, i.e. a fucking great cock, a dildo. We were in this tatty bog together and I couldn't stop him laughing.

'My girl's got to courier it for me so I've got to make it into a shape so that she can stuff it,' I told him, very much tongue in cheek but he didn't know that. We were wrapping more tape round this huge dick-like object and he was in fits. He said, 'It's impossible, she'll never get that up there.'

'Don't you worry,' I said, 'she's on the game and she's had bigger than that up there.'

By now we were both pissing ourselves with laughter.

'It'll make her eyes water,' he said and fell about again.

'And she'll have a smile on her face all the way to London,' I said.

We finally got this huge dildo-shaped parcel neatly taped up and I asked him to hold it until we got back to the buffet to get the money from Diane for the swap. Of course, we never made it back to the buffet. As we strolled along the platform, I gave the signal, and Mr Station Master and half a dozen hairy-arsed Old

Bill jumped him and carted him off to Darlington nick. I made my escape in customary fashion by diving into nearby backstreets then linked up with Diane later.

I must say, she wasn't overly impressed with the scenario I'd put forward to Mushi. What if, she said, it had all gone wrong and she had ended up with the elongated parcel and had an excited Mushi waiting to know if she'd managed the concealment?

'Well,' I said, 'when duty calls …'

If I remember correctly, the gist of her reply was along the lines of 'You must be joking, Blex,' but a tad more colourful. Good girl was Diane.

Mushi, whose real name I never knew because my role was to go in undercover then vanish and not to concern myself with the prosecution side and the paperwork, was charged with drug trafficking and jailed for a substantial period. We had a laugh but, at the end of the day, it was another bit of scum off the streets.

On another job, I was sent on a 'romantic weekend' in Bruges in Belgium as part of an undercover infiltration of a drug gang run by some German and Belgian crooks. A female member of the team and I had to carry out a recce of the city so that I could be seen to be familiar with it when we met the gang there for negotiations. I'd told them I knew Bruges, but in fact had never been there in my life, so it was important to buff up quickly, get to know some bars, a hotel, some clubs. It was the kind of detail that made SO10 such a potent crime-fighting force. We needed to get our faces known a bit and get the lie of the land so we knew what we were talking about. So a good recce was essential before meeting the bad guys to talk drug-dealing.

We went in our undercover roles as a trendy young couple,

a bit flash, money to spend, on a weekend trip to a very lovely city, much like thousands of others who go to Bruges every year. We hoped we'd be noticed. It would be convincing cover if we returned and a barman said, 'Hi, Peter, hi, Sue, nice to see you again.' Because it was just a recce, we took our official police ID as well, which we kept carefully concealed in our car but which we could produce if we hit a snag. We needed to have an each-way bet on this one.

We drove out there on the ferry from Dover in a lovely Jag from the Yard's pool of undercover motors, enjoyed a really pleasant weekend and achieved our goal, ready to move the drugs operation on a further step. I think we must have done the job too well because on the way back we got a pull at the Customs at Dover. They obviously thought we were at it in some way or other. I don't know whether they'd been tipped off by the police in Belgium or something of that sort, but they were determined to give us a tough time by searching the Jag inch by fucking inch. Fucking marvellous, I thought. I could just have produced our police ID and sorted it out in minutes. But I thought, fuck 'em. They were being really stroppy, tearing all my bags apart, really giving us the third degree. They'd seen our fake IDs we used for the Bruges trip so I started spinning them a token yarn about where we'd been and why. I knew it was only a matter of time before they would eventually find our police ID. My female colleague Sue started off looking a bit apprehensive about why I hadn't just shown out to the Customs boys. Then she started getting a bit panicky.

'What are you doing?' she said. She had been expecting me to take the lead and produce the ID cards and tell the Customs who we were, save everybody's time and get on with it. But because I hated the Customs so much I just sat there and let them get on with it. I thought, bollocks, I'd got nothing better to do on a Sunday afternoon and I was beginning to enjoy sitting there and watching the Customs blokes waste their time. They demolished our fucking car and, of course, after about an hour, found our warrant cards securely hidden under the spare wheel in the boot. This Customs geezer looked at me and you could see he really wanted to rip my fucking head off.

'Why didn't you tell us from the start who you were instead of wasting our time?' he demanded.

'I like watching people work, actually,' I told him.

They were really, really pissed off. OK, it was a bit of a laugh at the expense of Customs, and you will have gathered there was no love lost between them and us, but the downside was that the Jaguar had to be abandoned as an undercover vehicle and taken out of the Scotland Yard pool, and our false identities used in Bruges had to be scrapped because everything was now on the Customs computers. If they had seen us going out again they would probably have stopped us again wondering what we were up to. We had to kill every scrap of identity involving that trip. But it would have happened anyway, even if I had declared our true status from the off. They'd still have had everything on computer and there was always the danger that we might be compromised sometime in the future. You don't want any false identities on record anywhere. Or genuine ones, come to that. In my line of business, you could never be too sure.

* * *

THE GANGBUSTER

I've got tremendous respect for the women in the undercover unit, as you will have gathered. They do a fantastic job. It's about a 70:30 ratio of male to female but they are equal in ability every time. Apart from classic cases like Lizzie James in the Wimbledon Common murder inquiry, undercover women officers are brilliant against fraudsters and white-collar crime. If you are doing a job in a plush hotel, an attractive woman on your arm can often allay suspicions. If you are there smartly dressed with a fashionably dressed woman, people aren't going to give you much of a second glance.

When we were on the trail of The Dutchman, for instance, we knew he was a bachelor living alone in London and I asked him if he fancied a night out on the town. I said my girlfriend had got a mate and we could make up a foursome if he fancied it. He was pretty keen on the idea. I got it OK'd by the bosses, then picked the two best-looking girls on the undercover section to come along. I told them the score, that The Dutchman was involved in a big-time drug gang and I was purporting to be a top banana drug boss here with hundreds of thousands of illicit pounds to spend, and they were happy with that. It was all part of adding to the credibility of the role I was playing, to get The Dutchman convinced he was onto someone with big bucks.

I told the girls we were going to a top-notch venue for the night and when they turned up at the Yard ready for the off, they looked absolutely fucking magnificent. They had really put themselves out.

I'd picked the Windows on the World restaurant on the twenty eighth floor of the Hilton Hotel for our night out. I loved the place anyway – I'd been a few times before – and I'd booked a nice window table with fantastic views right across the capital at night. Basically, if I was ever going to impress a top drug-dealer, this was the place and the girls were the business. The Dutchman was hopping. We had a fantastic meal with loads of champagne. Top stuff. The girls looked such crackers that, as soon as they went to the loo, he said to me, 'Her mate, is she a working girl?' and was sex with her going to be nailed on?

That posed a bit of a dilemma for me.

'Oh, no, no,' I said. 'She's not a hooker, but you know, play your cards right and you never know your luck!'

I knew she wasn't going to shag him, that *is* beyond the call of duty. But I was hoping she would be able to flirt with him, give him an enjoyable evening, give him a promise for the future which would never happen because I was expecting to have him nicked by then.

We had a fantastic night; The Dutchman was putty in our hands, but the boss running the job nearly choked when I showed him the bill – nearly £550 for the four of us. We'd had bubbly and the works, I'd successfully convinced The Dutchman I was a major-league drug-dealer and it was money well spent in my opinion. You certainly couldn't have taken a crook of that stature into a McDonald's and had a Happy Meal for four. All in all, it was one of the more pleasurable evenings' work in the often sordid world of drug-dealing. One theory, when the investigation fell flat over in Amsterdam and The Dutchman was left free in London, was that he'd fallen head over heels in love with our undercover girl and became more interested in getting into her knickers than dealing in drugs. It's ironic, I suppose, after all that expense, that neither the job nor the police girl's knickers came off.

Chapter Thirteen

ROZZERS' RAMPAGE

Posing as an IRA henchman brought me solemn respect in my underworld dealings. But it didn't stop me getting poleaxed by one of my own mates in the middle of a huge drugs bust. It was probably stupid, on reflection, to infiltrate a heavyweight drugs mob by saying I was buying the stuff on behalf of the Provos but it made sure nobody ever asked too many awkward questions. Even my Cockney accent didn't seem to ring any alarm bells.

It was well known that the IRA was into drugdealing on a massive scale to launder cash to buy guns, so it was an acceptable ploy. The North London firm I was into were selling consignments of speed – 'whizz' or 'Billy Whizz' as it was known – like it was a supermarket special offer.

I moved in undercover after a tip-off that they were 'at it' on such a scale they were producing literally millions of amphetamine-based tablets every week. They were hitting the London nightclub scene or wherever else there was a ready market for pep pills. The mob was fronted up by a bloke who was being referred to on the underworld grapevine as Mr Speed. It was known from intelligence reports and tip-offs that they were supplying big, wholesale batches of the tablets, thousands at a time, to middle-men dealers. The supply was so consistent they were either making the stuff themselves or were very close to the machinery and chemicals that were being used in some secret drugs factory.

Finding a pill machine and putting it out of action was regarded as a premier prize. It was with this object in mind that I got myself involved with the firm. It was, like most undercover ops, a 'gently, gently' job, getting yourself accepted by the villains, establishing your credibility, building up the character you were supposed to be, acting the role of bad guy. It sometimes got so effortless it was worrying. Getting 'in character' had become so second nature to me I sometimes reckoned I was more convincing as a villain than Frankie Fraser. But that had to be good, not bad. That's what I was paid to do.

I didn't say in as many words that I was working for the IRA. A few casual mentions of 'the boys over the water' and people drew their own conclusions. I met members of the gang at various North London pubs and slowly got bits of intelligence and information out of them over a few beers and a bit of calculated chat but there was no hint as to where the pill machine was hidden. As word leaked out that I was supposedly a dealer acting on behalf of the Provisionals, I earned enough respect to stop them getting too nosey about my background, though Christ knows what the IRA would have done if they had known I was using their name in vain. A bullet in the back of the head or a shot through the kneecaps would probably have sorted it for them. The villains in my sights were a bit older than me and believed I was a young, up-and-coming criminal star who was up to laundering considerable sums of money for the terrorists through drugs. The sort of bloke you wanted to keep in with for the future. Obviously going places in gangland.

Mr Speed and his cronies agreed to supply me with 16,000 speed tablets as a start to our 'business' arrangements. When a deal like this was arranged, it took a team conference to set up the details, such as back-up, armed or otherwise, arresting officers, drivers and so on, to make sure it all went smoothly. We were dealing with top crooks and we'd got to be on top of the situation.

When the day of the trade came down, I required a driver who would pose as one of my IRA associates on the deal. Out of the blue, I was asked by the undercover unit if I would be prepared to take out an inexperienced but highly-rated cop who they reckoned might have a big future in the squad. No problem. So I met the guy, got to know him in what short time we had available and, yes, I felt he was up to the job. He looked like a hoodlum, spoke like a hoodlum, and conducted himself like a hoodlum, all bonus points in our line of work. I felt I would be able to take him on this job with little risk of disaster, briefed him up a bit, and gave him a spot of quick-fire training –a few handy tips on keeping a step ahead of the villains, that sort of thing. It was agreed that we'd do the trade in a pub car park in Holloway, North London. We all turned up at the agreed time. The villains were shown the money we had brought along to buy the drugs, supplied by Scotland Yard, of course, and they brought the parcel of drugs on to the plot. We had agreed a pre-arranged signal with the back-up team for them to steam in and make the arrests. In this case, it was me scratching my right ear, something that could easily be seen by any watching cops – or so I thought. My new driver, my minder as the villains thought, was sitting in the car while I was doing the business. I got into the back seat with one of the bad guys and examined the parcel. I obviously couldn't count out 16,000 whizz tablets one by one; it would take all fucking day. I took a sample count of what a hundred looked like and compared it to the rest of the bags, gauging it by eye and by weight. You weigh a hundred and then weigh one of the big bags and calculate it accordingly. It all looked genuine stuff and the bust was set to go. I gave the signal expecting the troops to come storming in and nick the whole team red-handed. But nothing happened. There had been some sort of problem getting their act together. A familiar story, unfortunately, which had dropped me in the shit before.

So now I had to play for time, drag the scenario out. I had to take the geezer to the boot of the car and show him the £15,000 in used notes, with a view to actually giving it to him if necessary, but it was merely tactical time-delaying. The object was not to go out actually buying drugs but purporting to buy them, don't let go of the dosh until the cavalry have charged in.

So I was standing at the boot of the car, things were getting a bit tense, and I'd gone into deliberate slow motion as we wondered where the hell the sodding back-up had got to and calculated how much longer we could string it out before it became a monster cock-up.

I was at the back of the car with the boot open when it suddenly happened, late but welcome. The back-up swarmed in. But my new trainee's judgement went right at that very moment. All he had to do was sit tight, wait for the arrests to take place, and then get us out. Merry hell broke loose with people arriving from all directions, running everywhere, shouting orders, waving guns. The villain obviously thought it was a rip-off or a robbery.

I was leaning in the boot trying to delay showing him the cash in case he made a grab for it. Mayhem broke out on all sides with people shouting and running. With that, the villain made a grab at the money and tried to make off with it. So I grabbed him and we got embroiled in a ferocious tug of war over this bag of money. I managed to wrestle the bag off him and sling it back into the boot.

With that, my trainee partner hit the accelerator and the boot lid came smashing down, straight on to my head. The boot corner hit me right over my temple and my head just pinged open. I was seeing stars and there was blood spurting everywhere. My driver braked again almost immediately so I was able, even in my concussed state, to get the money back in the car and shut the boot. Part of the agreed scenario was for me to leg it and now I had a chance to escape, which I did before anything else went amiss. I was still under surveillance by the back-ups and they saw me running up the road with blood pissing out of a gaping hole in my head. They thought I'd been shot or stabbed or hit with a cosh. Messages were flashed back to the Yard saying I'd been badly hurt and ambulances were dispatched to find me. But I found my own way to the Middlesex Hospital in central London, had six stitches put in the wound and was left with a headache for a week. And, strangely enough, never worked with my inexperienced driver again. His glittering career in the undercover squad ended before he'd cleared the bottom rung.

The incident proved once again the importance of trust on undercover missions. You get to know the guys you'd trust with your life and those you wouldn't trust to carry your shopping from Safeway. Trust and comradeship play a massive role in the police force, particularly in small, specialist units like COG. And they can come into play when you least expect it.

When I was at one nick, I worked with a mate who had a reputation as big as a bus in the Old Bill. We got on like a house on fire. We were great friends, on or off duty.

Much to everybody's surprise, the nick where we worked had a little gym down in the basement and after work we used to go down there and beat the fuck out of each other in the boxing ring, have a shower then go out on the piss together. People could never suss it out. We were real buddies. His great boast, repeated to me not long ago, was that there wasn't a policeman on earth who'd spent more on prostitutes than him. I mean, he was notorious. And this was while he was a serving police officer. We used to do everything together – work together, drink together, fight together, fuck women together.

One night, we were at a leaving function together – they were always coming up as people were posted about in the job or retired – and my mate said to me, 'You'll never guess what happened to me last night.' Now, with this guy, you don't even start to guess because it could have been anything. All I knew was I'd seen him for a drink the previous night and he'd said,

'I've got the raging horn, Blex. I've got to go down Earl's Court and find a bird.' Not unusual. So he told me what happened.

He'd gone down to Earl's Court, picked up one of the local brasses and gone back to a hotel room. But because he'd taken a load of booze on board, he wasn't able to get it up. As far as he was concerned, 'If I can't perform, I don't have to pay.' That was his thinking and he wanted to keep his £50. She had different ideas and started screaming at him to hand over the money. A big row broke out and suddenly he was surrounded by her pimps, three big geezers, Maltese or Cypriots. He managed to bluff his way down onto the street, where he felt safer, and continued arguing the toss. One of the pimps pulled a knife and held it to his throat and told him he'd got to pay whether he'd had a shag or not. At this point, he pulled out his warrant card and said, 'Do you know who you are doing this to?'

They didn't give a toss and demanded that he paid up. So he got the money out of his pocket and pretended to drop it on the floor accidentally. One of the pimps bent down to pick it up and my mate hit him with a belting right cross. He was a good boxer, and the blow knocked the geezer spark out. Then he had it on his toes, leaving the £50 behind.

The pimps chased him all round the back streets of Earl's Court, still keen for some aggro, but he managed to give them the slip.

But, all in all, he was not best pleased and he now wanted to go back down there and exact some retribution. And, of course, who did he want to go along with him, but yours truly.

We hadn't really got a plan and I didn't know what we were going to do, but I thought I'd better trundle off with him.

When we'd worked together once, a defence barrister had asked my mate in the witness box, 'Is it right to say you are the brawn of this partnership, and DC Bleksley is the brains?'

He replied, 'Oh, no, no, no ... Blex can smack 'em as hard as I can.'

He always was a fearsome handful, and one of the older and wiser detective sergeants who had seen us having this agitated scrum down at the leaving do had immediately suspected that something dodgy was afoot. He came over to us and demanded to know what was going on. So we told him the brief story of what had happened to my mate and he said, 'Well, all right, just leave it, don't do anything rash, don't do anything quickly and we'll hatch a plan to sort things out in a sensible and proper way.'

He wanted to set up a proper observation and nick the girls for soliciting for prostitution and the pimps for living off immoral earnings. That's what the wise old sage decided and we nodded our agreement. But once we were outside my mate said, 'Bollocks to that, let's go and sort them out.'

We were trundling down the Earl's Court Road a bit later when he nudged me and said, 'That's her.' The tom was hanging about at the entrance to Earl's Court tube station, where a lot of them touted for punters, and my mate was on his way over to her before I could stop him. I thought he was just going to go over to her, remonstrate and get his money back. But he walked straight up to her and with no further ado went BANG and slapped her straight in the mouth. I thought, oh, fucking hell, this is not in the plan.

The pimps appeared from everywhere – doorways, the drains, whatever – and we were surrounded by the vice bosses of Earl's

Court all steaming angry. My mate was fuelled up and I'd got a drink on board and so we were suddenly going at it like maniacs trading punches with the pimps, putting the boot in. A couple of them then ran off into a newsagent-cum-convenience store with a fired-up copper in hot pursuit. Well, he was my mate, I was in it to the hilt now so I had to leg it behind him. We steamed into the shop and it was literally like a scene from a movie. There were punches being thrown, shelves of goods being sent flying across the floor and we were giving them a right pasting, I mean we were both good boxers and they got our best shots. I dug one and he went straight back into a shelf sending cans of beans, tins of tomatoes and whatever all over the place. My mate got hold of another one and was banging his head into the fucking frozen food cabinet. The geezer running the shop was screaming and playing merry hell. It was absolute carnage, total chaos.

After a couple of minutes, my mate obviously felt we had exacted suitable revenge and we'd better get out. The shop owner was still kicking off and a crowd was beginning to gather. We came out into Earl's Court Road where the traffic was jammed solid in the one-way system. The tart was running up ahead of us and there was a police car stuck in the jam. I grabbed hold of my mate, trying to be sensible, trying to be the brains of the team again, and said, 'Come here, let's just see what happens before we do anything.' With that, we could see her bending into the police car obviously telling them she'd been duffed up by some lunatic. She was followed by the pimps, holding heads, limping, giving it all that, showing them what happened. She was pointing up at us and nodding and saying, 'That's them.'

At this point I said, 'Right, let's get out of here.'

We skidaddled off down the tube, split up, jumped trains and went our own separate ways.

It turned out that the police car was from a neighbouring police station and not our nick where everybody knew us. Just our luck, because they would have had to deal with it impartially as was their duty. Allegations of assault and battery involved pulling in about eight or nine witnesses, as well as the victims, to give statements in evidence. The brass and her pimps spent all night making these fucking great statements of complaint. She put it all in there, that he was a copper who had tried to shag her the previous night but couldn't get it up.

The next day, my mate was off but I went in on normal duty and the place was a hot-bed of rumour. As soon as people heard, they were saying, 'If there are two bastards who would go and get involved in something like that, it's those two.' So I hung around keeping my head down and my ear close to the ground. I was expecting the shit to hit the fan at any moment.

When there was a spot of internal bother, you could have the complaint investigated locally or by the specialist Complaints Investigation Bureau at the Yard, and that could be really nasty. Dear old Basil Hadrell, the Chief Super who had been landed with the papers in the case and was overseeing the investigation, had, through a trusted colleague, put the word out that if whoever is responsible comes forward, it could remain an investigation at local level and it wouldn't have to go up to the Yard. The go-between took me aside and said, 'Look, was this you two at this shindig? From the descriptions and the *modus operandi* it could only be you two.'

I said, 'Yeah, it was.'

He said, 'Right, if you are prepared to admit it, everything will be kept local and you won't have to face all the flak you'll get at the Yard.'

I managed to get hold of my mate on the phone and said, 'Come on, you've got to come in. We'll put our hands up and go for as much damage limitation as possible.'

We were up before the uniformed Chief Inspector who'd been designated by Mr Hadrell to investigate the case at about 6.00pm that night. He just asked us, 'Were you involved in an incident at the Earl's Court Road at approximately midnight last night?'

'Yes.'

'Right, I've no further questions to ask at this time.'

He said he would conduct his inquiries and we would be dealt with later.

Curiously, we never heard another word. The matter was completely dropped much to our relief. There was no official explanation but we were given to believe that one of our colleagues had gone down there and sorted things out with the tart in a more amicable way than me and my mate. I can imagine them saying, 'Well, look, after all, at the end of the day, you are a prostitute and these other people are living off your immoral earnings ... do you think it wise to proceed with these charges?' They all disappeared soon afterwards and haven't been traced since which was a result as far as my mate and I were concerned. The officers on the case tried to find them a few months later to re-interview them, but they still refused to come forward. No action was taken, but an internal report did suggest that 'the greatest care' should be taken that the two of us never worked together again because in the two and a half years we had operated as a team, we had each accumulated a total of thirteen complaints – twelve while we were working together.

My mate disappeared off to the Flying Squad and I went to the Central Drugs Squad. That was our somewhat spurious reward, a couple of premier squad postings. We counted ourselves very lucky. The only time we ever saw each other after that was over the occasional pint.

* * *

Another fiasco I was involved in came when I was on a major undercover operation in South London and had ended up at Sutton Police Station as my temporary base. When you work undercover you are itinerant and you can end up in any nick for briefings, evidence collecting, interviewing, and your face is not generally known. But when a Yard squad descends, word usually gets about that something is on the go. You get used to the itinerant life, moving about all the time, working at different stations and hopefully you have the communication skills to get along with people you don't normally work with on a daily basis.

One day, we'd just conducted a search as a part of a big robbery inquiry and had gone into Sutton nick – not exactly one of the biggest in London – and while my colleagues were dealing with a prisoner we'd arrested I ventured out to the front counter to which members of the public have access. I was looking for some forms and they were usually kept handy in the front office.

I heard a commotion and a woman burst into the front office heavily out of breath saying, 'Help me, you've got to help me.' It's not my job to deal with it. I'm a Scotland Yard detective and I'm dealing with something else. I look round and see two bone-idle, fat old fuckers sitting there doing nothing, just getting on with their business, ignoring this bird. I turned round.

'Somebody going to deal with her?'

'Well, all right, yeah, in a minute.'

I thought, you ignorant fucking toss pots. All the time, the woman was pleading for some assistance.

'Help me, please, help me.'

Nobody else was doing anything. I approached her out of a sense of duty, although it wasn't my place, and said, 'What's up?'

'I'm a store detective, come with me, come with me.'

I could see she was getting more distressed by the second, so I leapt over the counter and went into the street with her.

'I'm a store detective,' she repeated breathlessly. 'Little fella, beige bag, he's nicked a portable TV.'

She pointed down the street and way, way in the distance I could see this little fella disappearing round the corner with a fucking great beige holdall.

'OK. Leave it to me,' I said and I was off down the high street like shit off a shovel. There I was, supposedly the elite of Scotland Yard's undercover drugs detectives, scooting after a shoplifter.

Pretty soon, I'd caught up with the geezer, about 5ft 6in, covered in tattoos – up his arms, round his neck, across his forehead. I ran up to him and said, 'OK, mate, I'm Old Bill, I know you've just nicked this telly.'

He said, 'Yes, right, OK, mate. No problem, I'll come with you.' I took the beige holdall off him with the TV in it, in case he did a runner, and grabbed him by the arm. I thought, I'm really going to get the piss taken out of me when I get back to the Yard.

We were walking back towards Sutton nick when, like a

shining beacon, along came local plod. He was about nineteen, brand new out of training school, and up he came to do his duty. But I had made a fatal mistake. I'd got the beige holdall.

The baby bobby ran up to me and said, 'I've reason to believe you've been shoplifting and there's a stolen television in that bag. I'm arresting you for theft. You do not have to say anything, blah, blah, blah.'

I was standing there, holding on to this shoplifter half my size, and I was totally gobsmacked. I said, 'You're having a laugh here, aren't you? You've got the wrong bloke. I'm actually from Scotland Yard and I've arrested *him* for shoplifting.'

He looked totally baffled. 'Have you got a warrant card on you?' he said.

'Yes, I have.'

'Will you show it to me?'

I looked him straight in the eye. 'So you are proposing that I put the bag down, let go of him, get my warrant card out to show you ... by which time he will have legged it again. Then you'll believe I'm a copper and we can all go running off after him again.'

He wasn't budging. 'If you refuse to show me your warrant card, I can only assume you are lying. I've got to arrest you.'

So he took the beige holdall from me, doing exactly what I'd done a few minutes earlier. I still had a hold of the little fella, the young bobby got hold of me and there were three of us walking abreast up Sutton High Street. Just then, along came what I thought would be my saving grace – the store detective. She went straight up to the baby bobby and said, 'What are you doing, you stupid boy?'

He nodded at me and said, 'I've arrested this man on suspicion of shoplifting.'

'He's a policeman,' she said. 'He came to my help when I was in your police station.'

To my amazement, he said, 'Well, it's too late now, I've arrested him and he'll have to stay under arrest.'

She said, '*He's* the shoplifter ... the little fella.'

So the bobby said, 'You take hold of his other arm then.'

Now there were four of us abreast going up the street, him holding me holding him holding her, forcing members of the public out of the way, almost obstructing the highway. Even when we got to the front door of the police station, he wouldn't let go. Because we couldn't go in four abreast we had to go in sideways. It was one of the most ridiculous scenarios I've ever seen.

When we finally got through to the charge room, the duty sergeant, who knew I was from the Yard, took one look at us all holding on to each other, grinned, and said, 'I'm really looking forward to hearing this.' The baby bobby gave a detailed account of how he had made the arrests and everyone just fell about in hysterics and took the piss out of him something rotten. I think he's probably a chief superintendent by now!

I wasn't sorry to get back to our base at the Yard after that fiasco, and it gave my mates in SO10 a good laugh. If you're in the Met, then the Yard's where you want to be if you've got an ounce of ambition. I loved it. And as a relatively young detective attached to one of the glamour squads, I can only say that Scotland Yard is shaggers' heaven. I suppose it's a little bit like war-time – you're doing a job that has more danger than most and when you're off duty you're looking for relaxation in the shape of a pretty girl and a nice few pints.

There was a workforce of 3,000 employed at the Yard with many attractive, unattached females among the civilian ranks. Work hard, play hard, that's what a lot of coppers do.

Inevitably, our squad had quite a lot of dealings with the Yard's Press Bureau, the section which deals with the media, papers, TV, radio, whatever, on a day-to-day basis, fielding questions and issuing information. There was a certain amount of scepticism towards one another, because we sometimes felt they were useless and didn't give our squad the publicity it deserved, didn't argue our cause well enough, and the Press Bureau in turn would think we were bone-headed paranoids or publicity-seeking prima donnas. I think, by and large, both standpoints had a degree of truth to them.

I had quite a lot of dealings with one of the girls who was quite high up in the bureau and we used to go out for drinks and meals and argue the toss about the virtues of us and them. We'd have a good old argument then wind our way back to the Yard and try to find an empty office to have a shag in. A lot of people were at it. The crumpet there was a joy to behold. Married men were all shagging; the single blokes were all shagging their brains out. It was great fun. But some nights you just couldn't find a sodding office to do it in. You'd go round rattling all the doors but they'd be locked. I don't know whether it was others at it or just security but on one such occasion we were forced to resort to the basement where all the cars were kept. All sorts of motors were there, facilities for changing number plates for covert operations, all sorts, so we decided to do it in the back seat of my vehicle. Not ideal and not as good as one of the guv'nor's offices with a nice big desk to shag over, but better than nothing.

So we thrashed about in my car for half an hour and had a decent sort of shag, her arms and legs hanging out of my motor amid the passion. Although we got on well, she was awfully full of herself and really did look down her nose at most of the lower rank Old Bill. She earned bundles of money and took a delight in pointing that out to us.

A couple of days after our basement shag, I had a mate's leaving do coming up. I thought, right, I can have a bit of a wheeze here. The basement garage didn't have a CCTV camera installed – though I think it might have one now – but the Press Bureau bird didn't know this. So I rang her up and said, 'Look, we've got a spot of bother here. You and I were caught shagging on the CCTV cameras.'

Well, she sounded shattered, petrified. So I said, 'The inspector from the information room is a friend of mine and he's managed to swag the tape for me. But he needs to be rewarded for his efforts.'

By now, she was absolutely stricken with panic.

'What does he want, what have we got to do?'

I said he loves scotch and he loves vodka, which were coincidentally the two drinks we were short of for the upcoming party.

She said, 'Leave it to me, leave it to me.'

I said, 'Well, I'm willing to get one.'

'No, no, I'll get them, leave it to me. You make sure you get the tape and then we can destroy it.' She could see her lucrative career going right out of the window in a seedy scandal. 'All right, all right, I'll make an excuse and get out of the office.'

She came back a couple of hours later with a lovely 40oz bottle of scotch and a lovely 40oz bottle of vodka. I said, 'Right, I'll go up and see my mate, get the tape and destroy it.'

Of course, I went straight upstairs to the squad office and said, 'Right, lads, we're OK for the booze. Let's go and have a party.'

I don't think she ever twigged that she really wasn't the star of her own porn movie on CCTV. But it was a risk she couldn't take.

Chapter Fourteen

YARDIES INCH IN

I was eyeball to eyeball with the Yardie gangs very early on in my undercover career. And I soon realised that this was a new dimension in organised crime. Young, black and angry, these second-generation West Indians had a ruthlessness that could see them wipe out a rival just because he didn't show enough respect, a world where street cred was a currency higher than cash.

Yardies originated from the back yards – or crime territories – of Jamaica, where localised gangs had dealt drugs and enforced 'protection' for generations. In Britain in the eighties, they had grown into a feared underworld organisation, breaking into the crime scene with vicious enthusiasm and a penchant for violence that was truly terrifying. But unlike the sprawling power of the Mafia or the Chinese Triads, they tended to operate in tight-knit gangs with more emphasis on street cred and community respect than establishing money-making power bases. Factional wars were not uncommon. Rivals were wiped out with almost casual savagery, by gun and by knife, the root cause often so obscure as to be incomprehensible.

So it was with special interest that we listened to an informant who came to us with inside information on a Yardie gang moving seriously into organised drug-dealing with the accent on supplying big heroin consignments. The team, based in South London, were putting out feelers for buyers of big amounts, raising fears among Scotland Yard's drug experts of an explosion of smack-dealing and its inevitable consequences.

With the West Indians, we had normally found that because the West Indies are a source nation for cannabis, that was their main commodity. They sought out their own transport, distribution and sales. And as cocaine markets expanded, Yardies wanted a piece of that action, too. With the geographical proximity to the South American cocaine suppliers and the United States, where demand for coke was incessant, a lot came through the Caribbean islands. They had lucrative cannabis and cocaine routes up and running. What they didn't have as a source drug, or potential route drug, was heroin. But that's what the Yardies were planning to break into, according to our informant, with supply links set up to the Golden Triangle poppy fields and other heroin-producing Asian countries. We were intrigued because it was widely known that there was no love lost between the West Indian and Asian communities. They were notoriously loath to get involved in any sort of business deals together, let alone drugs. So we reckoned something big was on the cards. Our intelligence reports at that stage suggested the Yardies were leaning towards helping out some Nigerian heroin suppliers who had been going into a lot of drug deals and getting ripped off, getting robbed by *bona fide* gangsters, over here. They'd been dealing with London gangs to sell smack then finding themselves getting rolled over at the last minute and taken for every penny. Of course it broke our hearts to hear about it! So the Nigerians were actively recruiting some hard-case West Indians in London to look after their interests. This was the three-sided situation I was confronted with: London-based Yardies, Asians and Nigerians all involved in a trade offensive to distribute the world's deadliest drug. Then I met the ferocious Levi, the 'main man' in the enterprise and just about as hard as they come. I could see why the Nigerians rated him the kind of muscle they needed to protect their deals.

Levi was the name by which I knew Keith Valentine Graham, aged about thirty, with a form sheet showing previous convictions for offences of violence and for drug-dealing. I was introduced to him by an informant, using my normal M.O. of top drug-dealer able to handle substantial quantities of just about any gear, particularly smack. The fact that Levi was black and I was white made things a little uncomfortable for a while, but greed got the upper hand and the prospect of some lucrative deals ahead persuaded him I was trustworthy. But right from the off he made it clear that he was calling the shots. No white honky was running this show. I met him first time at the informant's premises and right away he made it clear these were the only places we ever used. It wasn't up for debate. 'You understand?' he scowled.

'If you say so,' I shrugged. That, of course, immediately threw up operational difficulties which called for serious discussion at our pre-operation briefings. Do we take out this dangerous drug-dealer or do we let it run because of the dangers inherent in using the informant's premises?

We weighed up the pros and cons, consulted with the informant, the man most at risk, and I was told, 'Do what you've got to do. We must take Levi out.'

After several weeks of dealings with him in the summer of 1985, it became obvious to me that Levi and his mob represented a classic case of disorganised crime.

For example, on the first occasion that we had the heroin trade fixed, I had everything in place – I had my money on the plot, I had the attack team in place, everybody sorted and dotted around the location, hidden away where they couldn't be seen. They turned up, and obviously they'd gone with the Nigerian suppliers this time because Levi had a Nigerian with him. We were all set to go, then they told me they hadn't got the gear. They were due to supply half a kilo of pure-grade heroin. We'd fixed prices and all that and then they arrived empty-handed. For a moment, I was thrown. Was it on or was it off? Or was it some sort of scam with me in the middle?

It seemed to me that they were simply having difficulty with their suppliers, a problem of actually laying their hands on the gear and getting it to me. A 'distribution problem' they'd probably have told me about if they had bothered to say anything at all. Communication skills were zero. I had to try to work things out for myself. They wouldn't tell me anything.

'What's going down, man?' I asked.

Nothing.

I had to try and figure it out myself. They were nipping

out to make phone calls, coming back, and nipping out again somewhere for half an hour. I couldn't catch much from the heavy dialogue. There was a lot going on and time was getting scarce. It seemed to me that if they were having some practical difficulties with their side of things, and the gear would be produced eventually, I just had to sit tight and wait, hoping the troops outside wouldn't get restless. This lasted for hours and hours. The tension was getting unbearable but I was sitting there doing my best to look Mr Cool.

Normally in a situation like that, I would have got up and walked away. But I had this gut feeling that it was still going to happen. Despite all the hold-ups, the toing and froing, all the phone calls, all the farting about, I was still sure it was on. Now, that was all well and good for me; I was sitting there sipping a few beers waiting for things to finally happen, but ever mindful that outside we had a large number of highly-trained police officers waiting unseen, ready to storm in for the arrests. By now, they might just have started to become a bit edgy, a bit restless with all the unexplained delays. I was painfully aware that I was the linchpin in the operation and everything depended on me. It was a heavy responsibility to bear, as well as having to deal with the low-life drug-dealers. I had to retain my cover. Don't let them know you're worried.

All the time, a voice in the back of my head was saying, 'Hold on, Blex, this will happen, it will happen, be patient.' I'd got to hope in turn that the operational blokes were going to be patient along with the Yard bosses, something they are not always renowned for if there is no result in immediate sight. Sometimes the guv'nors will put a time limit on an operation – pull out at ten o'clock if nothing happens, or whatever – or they may say, 'Play it by ear, you make the decisions.' It depends on the day-to-day operational head, what he's like, and what he thinks of you and your abilities.

The onus was squarely on me, so I decided to let it run. We were in a pleasant, cool flat in Earl's Court on a hot summer's afternoon, we were eating take-away pizzas with extra pepperoni, Levi was rolling spliff after spliff, offering them to me. I was facing the archetypal problem – do I partake or don't I?

I said, 'Oh, I'm driving, I'll have a smoke later.'

On and on it went, comings and goings, frustrations mounting. It was agony for me, so I don't know what the blokes on the outside were like. 'Pissed off' is one phrase that sprang readily to mind. I had been able to give a quick update to my bosses on my mobile while the bad guys were out of the flat. I told them, 'Stick with it. Don't pull out yet, we're nearly there.'

At one stage, the villains said they'd be gone for an hour so I gave another call to say, 'Let the back-ups have a breather.' I knew some of the surveillance officers would be uncomfortable in their observation points by now and the attack teams in the hidden cars would be bursting for a piss.

After a whole day of waiting, Levi and his mates finally cobbled together about a kilo of heroin which they brought into the flat. Bingo. I tested it by burning some on silver foil. It was OK, so let's go with the trade. We all got up, ready to go, and moved to the door. Levi wanted the informant out on the street for the exchange, drugs for cash, cash for drugs, but I didn't. He wasn't going to be adept enough to escape from the attack team and I didn't want him there to be embroiled in the evidence.

Often, the subsequent prosecution case would parcel the evidence up to state only that at a certain time, date and place, 'I saw three men walking down the street. We approached and one ran off. We arrested the remaining two and we found ...' all done with a view to hiding the undercover nature of the operation and the identity of the informant and not requiring me to go to court. It didn't always work that way because some of the time I would have to supplement the evidence of other officers if there was a 'not guilty' plea, but ideally that's what we aimed for.

In the event, however, I managed to negotiate that the informant was surplus to requirements, saying I didn't need him, that we trusted each other, that I was willing to go out with Levi and his pal and I knew that was going to suit the troops outside. Once in the street, I'd give the signal and then, hopefully, the hit would go off. But things are never that simple...

Just as we were about to go, Levi started sort of adjusting his clothing, pulling at the waistband of his trousers. He motioned towards the toilet as if to indicate that he needed a pee. I didn't know what it was but at that second something clicked; I felt suspicious, uneasy. We'd said our OKs and our goodbyes and we were right on the point of strolling out. So what was he up to? It just concerned me that something was wrong, that something off the script was about to happen. So I grabbed the informant and motioned him to follow chummy into the toilet. He disturbed Levi still fiddling with his trousers. And it wasn't for a piss – we'd have been able to hear as we were just outside the door. Levi hurriedly came out, making out like he'd just had a wee, but we knew he hadn't. I was on maximum alert, but pretending to look nonchalant.

THE GANGBUSTER

We left the flat and walked into the street. I needed only to give the signal for the attack, a tug on my right ear, and the heavy mob would steam in. I couldn't communicate to the officers because I needed to get in a position to have it on my dancers and get the hell out of there when the action started. But I was worried about Levi and what was down his trousers. And I didn't mean whether or not he was endowed like Linford Christie.

As I was departing from the scene at a rapid rate of knots, I bolted round a corner to be confronted by the last person in the world I wanted to see on the plot, a lah-di-dah Chief Inspector out on his first-ever drugs bust. CID and uniformed branch had spread the senior officer authority between them on the Central Drugs Squad as part of the Yard's campaign to crack down on corruption. Now this awfully, awfully Chief Inspector, one of the uniformed chaps, full of 'what ho' and 'I say, old boy' (but a thoroughly decent cove for all that), had decided it would be a jolly nice bit of fun to get some of the action, have a bit of rough and tumble like the other troops, and he was there steaming in to arrest the baddies. Unfortunately, he was standing right in front of me as I was running full tilt to get out of the picture. I'm sorry, but he had to cop for it. It was fucking BANG as I crashed into him, called him a cunt, and sent him flying. He was none too pleased, but needs must ...

The hilarity lasted for days after the raid. 'I've never been called a cunt before,' said Chief Inspector Posh Bollocks.

'Don't suppose it'll be the last time,' one of my mates quipped, just out of earshot.

That indignity overcome on the raid, the attack team hit Levi and took out another geezer carrying the parcel of heroin. One of the uniformed guys had started to frisk Levi for weapons, not really taking the maximum precautions. He found a loaded Luger 9mm pistol stuck in the waistband of his trousers, hidden under a shirt and jacket. The PC's immortal quote, 'Fuck me, he's got a gun,' caused the odd wry smile when Levi stood trial and was given seven years inside for drug-dealing and firearms possession. His side-kick got three years. What exactly Levi had planned to do with the gun was never made clear. It was obvious from what he was doing in the toilet that he was trying to shift the gun from the back of his waistband to a more accessible place at the front, ready for action if need be. Whether that action was to take me out and run with the cash and the drugs, or to guard against himself being robbed, we'll never know. We had disturbed Levi in the nick of time because the gun was still in the back waistband when he was arrested. He'd not had the chance to move it to where he'd have a chance to whip it out and open fire. I wish I'd had an opportunity to tip off the raid party about my suspicions, but in the heat of the moment it hadn't been possible. Thank God he never had a chance to use the shooter; I'd hate the thought of a dead or injured copper on my conscience.

My bosses were delighted with the result. The Press were banging on daily about the new Yardie menace in London and here we had a West Indian drug-dealer nicked in possession of a loaded gun. It was grist to the mill and a positive indication that the police were hitting back at the Yardie gangs. Levi, or Keith Graham as he turned out to be, fitted the bill of the up-and-coming Yardie boss to the letter.

Although I met loads of West Indians involved in drug

trafficking and in firearms, no one ever said they were a Yardie. Nobody uttered the word. But their actions spoke louder than words. There were unexplained revenge shootings, often in front of other people, a sort of power thing, challenging anyone to grass them up. The word 'respect' echoed round the West Indian communities. Fear was close behind. There were arson attacks, and all sorts of vicious crimes linked to suspected Yardies. I suppose it was this sort of sinister unknown that made them so dreaded.

One tasty Yardie type who operated around the Lambeth council estates was with me in a car about to do a cocaine deal. There were squats, drug dens, spotters looking out for anyone suspicious, a typical run-down South London estate and I felt the spotlight was on me. But I had got to keep my cool, ignore what was going on around me, get on with the deal and get out.

We were in his car, driving to where the exchange was going to take place, and the small talk turned to our mutual hatred of the police. I had to go along with it, of course.

'I can't stand the bastards,' he said with venom. 'They've even put undercover Old Bill onto me twice. But I've sussed them out both times. You can smell 'em, can't you?'

'Oh yeah, fucking right you can,' I said.

Five minutes later, he was standing there with handcuffs on and three fucking great coppers dragging him off to a police car.

You didn't smell this one, matey, I thought. Even though he was nicked fair and square with two other dealers, he was acquitted at Inner London Crown Court, so for legal reasons we can't use his name. I was actually called on to give evidence in the case and was the first police witness. I stood in the witness box with the jury slap bang in front of me and, like you do after taking the oath, you start scanning along both rows. I mean, you need to look them in the face; it's them you are trying to convince, they are going to make the guilty or not guilty decision. It was a Monday morning and, as I was looking along the jurors, there was my mate's girlfriend in the back row with whom, less than thirty-six hours earlier, I'd been doing the boogaloo at a wedding reception. Her face was a picture. She didn't know what to do; I didn't know what to do. Do I declare it or do I stay *stumm*? I had to make a split-second decision. I turned round to the judge, who was pissed off enough already because it was an undercover job and he didn't like undercover policing, and said, 'Excuse me, Your Honour, before I start my evidence I need to say something in the absence of the jury.'

His look was priceless – who is this jumped-up fucking nobody? Anyway, when he'd ushered them out I explained the situation. He dismissed the whole jury and started again with a fresh one. The second jury was subsequently nobbled and all three defendants got off. I saw my mate's girlfriend a few days later and she said, 'It's a shame you said anything. Once we had heard the opening speeches and knew what the case was about we said, "Well, the Old Bill wouldn't go to all that trouble if they were innocent,"' so they had all started the trial with a guilty mind-set and we could have had three more bad bastards behind bars if I'd kept my mouth shut. But losing one here and there, even through jury nobbling, is something you have to take in your stride. You risk life and limb to get them nicked and the heavies go in to the juries with threats or bribes and they all walk out scot-free.

THE GANGBUSTER

We know for certain the second jury was got at because one of the women on it subsequently broke down and confessed. She was sobbing uncontrollably after the acquittal and asked to see the officer in the case. She said that on the second day of the trial, she had been followed from court and threatened that if she didn't acquit them, her kids and other members of her family would be hurt. Other jurors got the same treatment and at the end of the day were too scared to convict any of the accused. This gang were horrors. I really wanted to see them convicted; after all I'd bought the drugs off them so I knew they were at it. But you must never take it personally. We'll always be back. It's war out there on the streets and the police will use whatever methods they can to nick the bad guys, so we can't be surprised if the villains use everything they've got, including jury nobbling, to try to stay ahead of the game.

* * *

The technology in use by the police, both in undercover operations and more conventional investigations, gets more sophisticated year by year. Call it Big Brother if you like, but it gets results. I've been involved in several cases where micro-sized video cameras have been hidden in suspects' premises and monitored for hours, days or weeks in an attempt to obtain incriminating evidence. It's the most gutty job sitting and watching a video screen hour after hour but it can be great fun because you truly see people as they are, picking their noses, scratching their arses, taking drugs, whatever; it can be really quite entertaining. Coupled with that, an audio-visual insert can be used to great effect, picking off villains one by one without them having a clue where the information is coming from. 'Disruptive policing' they call it. You target people on the periphery of a criminal organisation and take them out one by one, thus disrupting the gang and throwing in a nice bucketful of confusion for them to stew in. You'd see them come in the next morning looking worried.

'Did you hear Freddie and Billy got nicked last night?'

'Yeah, but how the fuck did the Old Bill know? Everything was kosher, we knew everyone on the job was OK, yet suddenly Old Bill pops up in the middle of it.' They just couldn't figure out how the blokes were getting caught. We used this successfully time and time again, usually at business premises rather than at private flats or houses.

Bugging a business premises required the authority of an ACPO-ranked officer – above a superintendent – or a Deputy Assistant Commissioner. Each force throughout Britain has one senior officer set aside to make the decisions and he's kept busy.

Before planting a camera or listening device, you always had to recce the premises to see where the best location was. That could be very exciting. You always did it between 2.00am and 4.00am because that's when people are at their deepest sleep. You go in kitted out like the Cadbury's Milk Tray man in dark clothes and balaclava hat, you're briefed at 1.00am then you're cutting through fences and creeping under them, tying them up for your escape route, and you're negotiating quarries, woods or 6ft walls. Criminals put a lot of thought into these premises and they don't make infiltration easy. You take out the experts in locks and alarms to help you get in undetected. It's very James Bond. Then once you're in, you carefully insert your bug or miniature video camera where it's least likely to be detected but most likely to yield the sort of information you need. You could put them in the roof, the floor, the walls, anywhere the technical experts felt they could get the best response but leave no trace behind. The technical bods would always want you to do your recce first, and then they'd pitch in and insert the equipment accordingly and get out fast.

It was terrific once they were up and running because the villains often hadn't got a flying fuck's idea of where the leaks were coming from. They'd think they'd got a grass on the firm, they'd start going down blind alleys to see who it was, and it was very frustrating for them but very entertaining to watch.

Nicking villains was not the only way you could disrupt a criminal organisation. You could make them skint by taking out people on the periphery with whatever commodity they were dealing in – drugs, whatever – so it wasn't getting to the main players and they were not getting any money in to continue operations. You could see them losing tens of thousands of pounds, making them do more and more risky things, so that finally you could orchestrate them into a position where you could nab them absolutely red-handed, patience rewarded. Villains of long standing found themselves forced into doing things they normally wouldn't dream of because all their troops or parcels were being taken out, or their money was being lost. You could cause massive disruption to their lives and they just didn't know why or who was behind their demise.

Sometimes, it was considered prudent just to leave them be once they were on the ropes, feed off them via the bugs and see where they were going next, and maybe come back later and have another go at them. If you'd got their every move covered, you'd taken out their infrastructure, had all their money and made their lives an absolute misery, you might just as well leave them to sweat.

A mains-powered bug properly hidden can keep supplying you with all the inside gen for months. Obviously, you don't watch or listen day after day, but it's nice to be able to go back whenever you want to check up on progress, see if they've got any new scams on the go.

One very satisfying job I was on involved the bugging of a warehouse in St Albans after a tip off that very large quantities of smuggled cannabis were being distributed from there. We put in audio-visual equipment, sat back and waited.

Huge quantities of dope were coming into the UK in plastic-lined metal containers. It was a great operation because you'd see the shipment arrive at the warehouse, ready for dealers to pick up, and you could see the gang dancing about singing, 'We're in the money, we're in the money.'

We were sitting watching them on the monitor and we were saying, 'Uh oh, are you boys in for a real shock!'

Then the various dealers would arrive to collect their parcels, drive off a couple of miles down the road, we'd scoop them up and repeat it over and over. We got a lot of dealers from that, as well as the importers, so it was a very satisfying operation.

I remember another observation on a couple of likely lads who were real 'cor blimey' villains out of the East End. They had us in hysterics and even though their empire was slowly crumbling around their ears, they never lost their sense of humour. They turned up at their bugged offices one morning and one bloke turned to the other and said, 'You won't fucking believe what happened yesterday afternoon when I got home. My Rottweiler had dug a fucking hole under the neighbours' fence and got into their garden. He's back in mine when I get home and he's only got the next door's pet rabbit, tossing it around and playing with it. I belted the dog, got hold of the rabbit and it was stone fucking dead. It was covered in mud and shit and what have you. I knew it belonged to the little girl next door, so I panicked, shoved it in the washing machine on a short cycle, filled in the hole my dog had made and levelled it all out so nothing showed. Then I've bunked over the fence before the neighbours got back and laid the rabbit in its hutch, all clean and fluffy. I've washed me hands and waited. I'm having a cup of tea when I hear this God almighty scream from next door. I thought the woman was upset because she'd found the rabbit dead. So I run out to try and console her. I ask her what's wrong and she says, "It's the rabbit, it's the rabbit. It's dead in the hutch!" I said, "Oh, sorry to hear that, but calm down, it's not that bad." She says, "No, no, you don't understand. We buried it three days ago."'

We were rolling about when we heard the story, a real gem. Another incident that gave us a chuckle was when we fitted a tracking device to a villain's car because we needed to monitor his movements between the West End and Heathrow Airport. He sussed it out very quickly and sent it back to New Scotland Yard, all neatly packaged up, with a note saying, 'I believe this is yours. Thanks for the loan.' The police now have an armoury of hi-tech gadgets that would rival M's store room in the Bond films, and secret bugging operations have risen to almost 2,500 a year involving offices, homes, hotels and vehicles. The combination of trained police and skilled technicians makes a big dent in criminal activities and is growing more important all the time in the battle against the villains. They use technology, too, so we've got to keep ahead of the game. Until encrypted radio frequencies came in recently, the crooks all tuned in to police frequencies to hear what was going on, and whether they'd been sussed on a job. On a number of undercovers, I worked with blokes who habitually had an ear tuned to Scotland Yard frequencies to see what was happening on the police airwaves.

All this technology made a lot of villains paranoid about their phones being tapped. I knew one bloke who adapted a shoe box, put a nine-volt battery in it, taped it all up to look like a proper bit of electrical kit, added a red light indicator and a couple of crocodile clips, and he would go round to villains' houses and for £500 he would check their phones for bugs. He'd unscrew the bottom of their phone, attach the crocodile clips and up would come the red light, because it was the only light that ever came on, which indicated that your phone *was* being bugged. It was a brilliant scam because he could never say no in case they were and, of course, the villains were pleased as punch and recommended him to all their mates to test their phones at £500 a throw. We certainly didn't want to do anything about it. It was costing the villains £500 a time, so we left him to it.

Chapter Fifteen

PISS POUR

I knew this would be a tasty sort of job, in every sense of the word, the second I arrived at the restaurant. The glowering Nigerian doorman, standing casually on the basement steps, was packing a shooter. A 9mm pistol in a shoulder holster, unmistakable to the experienced eye of a Scotland Yard-trained marksman like myself. He wasn't making a lot of effort to conceal the tell-tale bulge either, and he looked mean enough to use it.

What had started out as a routine undercover operation to nail another cocaine ring – this time involving South Americans and Nigerians – had taken an unexpected twist that put me and my back-up team in immediate peril. Up to this point, there had been no hint of guns, or weapons of any kind. Now I was looking at a bloke a few feet away, armed and dangerous, as I strolled in to do a drugs deal under my regular guise of hard-nosed London trafficker with money to burn and drugs to buy.

THE GANGBUSTER

An informant had put me in touch with the middle man in the deal and we had set off by taxi to this restaurant in Bayswater, West London, to discuss business and meet the man controlling the gear.

Well, what a sumptuous place it was. I clocked the tooled-up bouncer within seconds and thought, fuck me, that's not in the script. But my game was all about thinking on your feet and staying cool. I showed no surprise that the bad guys would ever pick upon.

We walked down into the plush forty-seater restaurant with me trying to work out how I could get a message to my back-up team, hidden close by, to warn them that this might be a little trickier than we'd thought. I deliberately chose a table near the door and sat in a position where I could see the bouncer. I was trying to manipulate things without arousing suspicion. A million things were whizzing round my head – an armed bouncer ... I'm on enemy premises ... the threat of kidnap ... a possible shoot-out as the other cops come in – the permutations were endless. So I managed to sit with him in my sights pretty much all the time and drinks were ordered all round. I think I asked for a vodka and tonic.

I thought things couldn't get much worse. I needed to stay cool. Then I sneaked a look towards the bar and the waitress heading our way with our drinks, and to my horror I realised it was a Nigerian girl I had nicked a few years earlier for kiting – cheque card fraud – when I was attached to Kensington CID. I'm dreadful with names but I never forget a face. And that face was coming straight towards our table. I sort of slouched into my right shoulder and propped the other one up to try to hide part of my face, then pretended to scratch my face, then rubbed my eye in the hope that it wouldn't click with her where she'd seen me before. Then the drinks were on the table and she was moving away. I breathed a sigh of relief inwardly. It was the one and only time I came close to being compromised on an undercover job by someone I'd investigated before. And what a time to be sussed out with a tame bouncer kitted out with a 9mm lurking just a few feet away.

So now in my game plan I've got the gunman, a one-kilo cocaine deal is about to go down in this den of iniquity and then a waitress who knows I'm really a copper has popped up out of nowhere. The bloke is sitting there opposite me insisting and insisting that I bring the money into the restaurant to get the deal sewn up so we can all get on our way. I knew I couldn't do this. My bosses wouldn't let me do this. I'd got the £25,000 in the boot of the money car parked up the road with my colleague guarding it and that's where the deal had to go down. The car was staked out on all sides by back-up teams. We stayed chatting away in the restaurant and the bad guy was saying, 'You must bring the money here then we give you the drugs.' There was just no way I was going to take him the cash and walk out with the parcel and tell the boys, 'Look, I've bought it, didn't I do well.' No, this one had to go to plan. We wanted bodies in handcuffs. We then entered a period of fierce negotiations into what was going to happen, about why I was refusing to bring the money inside. I turned the geezer with the gun to my advantage. I said I was very much thinking of walking away from the trade because I'd seen that the bouncer had got a shooter on him and I was concerned about what might happen. 'Where did we ever say there were going to be shooters on the plot?' I said. The negotiations got even more heated. And for once in my life I refused a second drink, for the simple reason that I didn't want the waitress coming over and complicating the matter even further. Normally it's nice to have a drink at the height of negotiations to keep your whistle wet, but not that day. Waitress service was off the menu. I enjoy a good drink but I try never to get pissed when I'm working. I always let my company order their drinks first on whatever job I was doing, then I'd normally have what they were drinking. If they had soft drinks I would do the same. But if they were having a proper drink it would have displayed a lack of professionalism not to have joined them.

Anyway it took all my powers of persuasion to work out a solution with the supplier. We decided the go-between on the deal, who was with me, a crook not an informant, being my buddy, was going to earn his money on the deal and take hold of the parcel. He was now middling it where originally he had just intended to do the introductions and get out of it. We were having to think on the hoof again and he seemed the best bet to break the deadlock. He was getting paid handsomely for the introducer's fee so we all agreed he should earn his corn. He agreed because he could see his fee going out of the window if we reached a stalemate and neither side would budge. Up until now he'd taken a backseat role; now he could see his services were needed. Both sides were at a point where we were getting exasperated and ready to walk away from it. He could see the deal falling apart before his eyes so rather than lose out he said, 'OK, I take the drugs to the car for you. We must not waste any more time here.' That suited the guy supplying the drugs and that suited me because I could now orchestrate the arrest outside the premises away from the bouncer with the gun. At least that would prevent any of my police colleagues getting shot. I thought, 'Yeah, we can pull this off,' and in a split second it was all go. The middleman, one Hamid Moore, didn't know, of course, that by volunteering to be the courier on that short but crucial journey he was volunteering himself for six or eight years in prison.

I was moved to the front of the premises by the villains. The others went to the back somewhere to get the gear. There was a lot of mumbled talk in a foreign language. They made sure I didn't see where it was stashed or how much they'd got. I understood that but I knew we'd find it soon anyway. Hamid stuck the parcel under his coat and said, 'Come on, we're ready,' and off we went. We walked up the road towards the money car and, as soon as I knew we were in sight of the surveillance people, I gave the signal and waited until I saw the troops steaming in and had it off on my dancers. I jumped into the car as the police grabbed Hamid and the other geezer and screamed off at a rate of knots.

We got to the first set of traffic lights and found ourselves in a fucking traffic jam. Everything was stuck, we couldn't escape, couldn't go anywhere. We were sitting there embarrassingly jammed up and trying to look innocent as half a dozen burly Old Bill jumped on Hamid, pushed him to the ground and handcuffed him. He started kicking up like a loony, ranting and raging and there was soon a huge commotion going on. He was really putting up a fight, lashing out at the cops and trying to get away.

Whether it was a coincidence or not, a large Nigerian lady

appeared at a second-floor window of a block of flats above the commotion. She started screaming and shouting at the Old Bill and then grabbed a bowl of something and launched it out of the window over the coppers below. Most of them thought it was urine judging by the smell of it. It might have been washing-up water but there were a lot of blokes brushing themselves down shouting, 'She's thrown piss over me.' I don't think she had any connection with the Nigerians involved, or with Hamid, it had probably just been coincidence that she looked out and saw a black guy in trouble and thought she would put in her penny worth of piss.

In the middle of all this, I had to nip round the back of the premises and make contact with the arrest and search squads to warn them that when they hit the restaurant premises, they had to be careful because the doorman was armed with a shooter. I was conscious all the time that they would have seen us come out of the restaurant and, once they had floored Hamid, would say, 'That's where he came from, the deal must have happened there,' and hit the premises running. I had to tell them to watch out. The bouncer might mistake them for robbers and start giving them some.

I managed to get a word of warning to them in time and they stormed the premises without incident. They didn't find any more drugs down there, which was a disappointment, because we had thought our kilo parcel was one of many that had come out of a store, and that was possibly the premises for keeping a great deal more gear. But it wasn't; they just used it for individual transactions and a place for doing the negotiations. The doorman was nicked for illegal possession of a firearm and sent to prison. The drug-dealers also ended up inside. A good result that could so easily have turned very nasty.

* * *

Shooters were always a part of my life undercover, for good and for bad. Good when they were looking after my interests, bad when they were in the hands of dangerous villains. So when we had an informant go to the police at one North London nick with a tip about a geezer claiming to be part of a firm of gangland armourers, we were doubly interested and yours truly landed the job.

The informant said these hoodlums had access to unlimited weapons and could supply anything you wanted. So I got briefed up for a big, big weapons job with loads of armed cops on stand-by as back-up. So I went in as a dodgy arms buyer and met them to see what was on offer, thinking in my mind of Uzi machine pistols, AK47s, that sort of thing. Unfortunately, it quickly transpired that our informant had been more than a little imaginative in his description. Far from being international arms dealers to the underworld, they were a team of two-bit burglars who'd done a job and picked up a pump-action shotgun. Just the one gun.

I had to start thinking about what to do now about this big undercover operation that had been started in anticipation of a big result and was now tin pot. What should I do about this one and only gun on their 'for sale' list? I decided the best thing to do was to buy the poxy thing for £500 and get it off the streets. It was an on-the-spot decision and seemed the best solution all round. We probably wouldn't even prosecute them for it to preserve the undercover involvement and the informant, but the gun had to be binned.

First, I had to go through the whole rigmarole of testing it, chatting to the villains just to make sure there weren't any other shooters about, that sort of thing. As a registered shot I knew pistols but I wasn't all that familiar with sawn-off, pump-action shotguns. I needed to look proficient to kid even this ragged mob that I was a genuine gun expert. I knew you could blow your fingers off if you weren't really careful.

So I went to the police firearms unit and told them I was doing this undercover job and could they teach me how to load and unload a pump-action and how many types were there and what was the best way to use them. I needed to be seen to be proficient with them in front of villains. They were happy to help, so I went along to the armoury and they showed me how to load and unload, load and unload over and over until I was doing it like it was second nature. Then I let a few off to see what it was like, blasting shit out of some targets.

My next step was to go out with one of the burglars to the wilds of Hertfordshire to test the gun for real. He was only a kid, in his twenties, I suppose, and then we met up with one of his mates and went to this field which was littered with half a dozen derelict motors. Of course, I needed to know if the gun worked. He said indignantly, 'I'll show you if it fucking works.' He loaded it up and started pumping rounds into the cars. Doors were having fucking great holes blown in them, every window that was left, BANG, we'd have a pop at that. We'd been in the pub all afternoon and we were all a bit pissed.

'Do you want a go?'

'Bloody right.'

And there I was blowing holes in these fucking motors. Flying glass everywhere, Ford Escort shrapnel in the air. What was I going to do, say 'No'?

There were a few people I wouldn't have minded having a shot at! It was what the geezers would have expected me to do. And it was bloody good fun.

So I bought the gun, slung it in the back of my car, returned to base and said, 'Look, these are not really great armourers, they haven't got access to zillions of firearms, your informant has been prone to a bit of exaggeration, I'm afraid. I've bought the only one they'd got on offer and there's a £500 hole in the expenses.' I didn't mention the holes I'd made in the motors in the course of my enquiries. The gun was forensically tested to see if it could be linked with any unsolved crimes, but it was clean. Then it was destroyed. Off the streets for good.

* * *

If variety is the spice of life, then variety certainly spiced up my career as an undercover cop. You never knew what was coming up next. Although I became an acknowledged expert in drugs, I was happy to tackle any operation of any nature to the best of my ability. One of the longest I did involved me posing as the manager of a transport company warehouse in Thurrock, Essex, to nail a gang of cannabis smugglers. It was the nearest thing to a nine-to-five job I'd had. I'd drive there every day through the Dartford Tunnel and clock on like the rest of the staff. I was full-time undercover, lunch breaks and all. I had a sort of managerial post, in the office, but, of course, I had to muck in and help when necessary to keep my cover. We had all the props in there – trucks, forklifts, all that kind of stuff – it looked like a proper *bona fide* company. We were looking to arrest members of a cannabis ring bringing the gear into Britain in furniture lorries through the docks at Dover, so we needed someone to be at the warehouse full-time so they got to know the face. You never knew when members of the gang might pop in to suss things out. They wanted to use it as a transit station between imports of hash and a distribution network in this country. So it was important we had continuity at the premises, and that they'd see a face they could trust. The firm were bringing in large quantities of puff hidden in furniture and household goods so cleverly they were beating the Customs blokes at Dover on every run.

They would bring the stuff to the warehouse, unload, and I would look after it until their other transport arrived to move the goods onward to the dealer network. You would never know, looking at the furniture, that it was anything but innocent. The cannabis resin had been so carefully built into chairs, sofas, three-piece suites, washing machines and so on; a few kilos here, a few kilos there, but when it was all added up, it was a nice earner. They were bringing over the contents of people's houses who were moving to or returning to England, so there were all sorts of places for concealment of drugs. Of course, the owners never knew their precious property had been opened up and abused in that way.

The gang just thought I was a bent warehouse manager who would be paid handsomely to keep his mouth shut. What the villains didn't know, of course, was that the depot had been bugged to catch every movement in and out and every conversation. They'd come in and deposit each load and then disappear. I'd be told that so and so would be there to collect it in an hour. And that's when I started earning my money.

The premises were fully rigged up with video and audio equipment, but we still needed to know if there really were drugs inside the various items of furniture, and where they were stuffed. I'd have to open it all up, find the drugs and put them on show to photograph them for evidence for the eventual court case. The driver would play the innocent and say, 'I've only got some furniture on board, mate,' if he was pulled, so we needed to know that the drugs were definitely in there. I'd have an engineer available who would help me dismantle the settee or whatever, get the hash out, get a photographer in to take photos, and stick everything back exactly as it was. This took a great deal of skill. Our man needed to be able to replace everything in such a professional way that it wouldn't be noticed. He'd stick settees back in place, replace the backs on washing machines and other domestic appliances, and get it all sorted so it didn't look as though it had been tampered with. He'd have earned a fortune with MFI.

Once that was done and looking ship-shape, I'd sit and wait for the next lorries to arrive to move the stuff on. This was the beauty of it being a police job, and not a Customs job. Although technically it was an importation, we could keep it running and nick the entire network, not just the drivers bringing it through the docks. We knew it was going to keep on coming in and, if we acted half-blind about it, pretended we didn't know and Customs didn't happen to get lucky and make a seizure, it would enable us to take out a very big distribution network if left to our own devices.

When the mainland crooks came to pick it up and load it all back on another lorry, we'd have a chat, and I'd try to embroil the driver in a conversation in which he would implicate himself.

'Ooh, that's a heavy sofa, ha ha ha ...' I'd say, in the hope he might say something that would drop him in it, along the lines of, 'You'll never guess what's in there, mate.' Sometimes they couldn't resist telling you.

'What, wacky baccy? You're kidding.'

They'd also go to other premises where they'd start to dismantle the settees and other items themselves. We'd get these wired up as well and you'd hear them meet up with the gang chiefs and get excited about it all. They found it very difficult not to go and fawn over the drugs parcel, to be a part of it, to look at it. This was holiday money they were looking at – 'Hawaii, here we come.'

We started nicking members of the distribution ring over a hundred-mile radius after following various vehicles to various addresses and setting up observations in garages, warehouses, wherever the drop was. The Old Bill would steam in and scoop them up and the beauty was that, when it got to court, the evidence would start at the point of arrest: 'At such and such a time on such and such a day I was observing premises at ... this man turned up, I saw him unload ...' It was standalone evidence and once again we could preserve the overall undercover operation and our source of information. I would still be intact at the Thurrock warehouse waiting for the next lot to arrive. Nobody ever twigged.

I think, at the end of the day, about half a dozen people were nicked, there was some sort of family link among the gang, but some were left free to protect the operation. They didn't know it, but they were living on borrowed time. There was always tomorrow once we knew who they were. We'd be back.

The operation lasted about six months and I came out of it knowing a damn sight more about the transport system than when I started. I'd had to gen myself up on transport policy, lorries, HGVs, tachometers, fuel prices, motorway links, all that sort of stuff, because people would be coming in all day talking to you about it and you couldn't afford to look like some incompetent idiot. They'd soon become suspicious of you. It helped if you kept saying Norbert Detrassangle a lot!

I had a couple of mates with HGV licences and I picked their brains to get a quick lesson in the transport business. It was all playing roles, being an actor in a black comedy half the time, stopping yourself from getting killed by some nutter or other. Preparing your act properly and professionally was the art of the undercover business.

I had a legitimate pal at that time who ran a market stall. Sometimes, at weekends he couldn't make it so I would go in and do his stall for him. Just a favour for a mate. I'd go to work at Eltham Sunday market, set my stall up, get all the gear out and wait for the punters. I was a weekend stall-holder. Terrific, it was on-the-job training. Once I'd done that a few times, I knew what being a stall-holder was all about. And I used that cover quite often when I went out and met the bad guys. I'd been there, done it and got the T-shirt, so I knew what I was talking about. I knew who the 'Toby' was, the guy who collects the rents,

I knew the market jargon, how to haggle a deal, all the little bits and pieces you pick up. The only thing I would ever make up if I was using that cover was the fact that my mate was actually selling potpourri and potpourri oils. Now that wasn't exactly the hardest thing to have been doing if you were going out and buying heroin and cocaine, so I said I dealt in nicked antiques and bric-a-brac. You couldn't afford to look a bit of a poofter with some of the geezers I ended up dealing with.

But that, strangely, is where my undercover career all started. It was back in the early eighties, I was in CID at Kensington, and working with an informant who was gay. No problem. He put up some information about a gay antiques dealer in Fulham who was dealing in LSD. Now, officially, Fulham was part of a neighbouring manor and, going strictly by the book, we should have passed the job over to them. But there had been a lot of rivalry between different police stations and we were very loath to give this job away. We went out and obtained a search warrant to turn over his premises. He lived in a flat above his business premises. Our informant was insistent that the guy would only deal with other gays, and the code word to use to get drugs was 'stamps'.

The informant assured us we could set up a deal over the phone, using the code word, but said that the person who picked up the stuff must look obviously gay or there would be no deal. So I phoned up the fella, a very flamboyant member of the gay community, and said, 'Got any stamps?'

'Yes,' he said.

'Right, I'll be round this afternoon, about two o'clock.'

'Yes, see you then,' he lisped.

So there we were, a bunch of young, relatively inexperienced detectives flying by the seat of our pants and wondering where to go next, making it up as we went along. Who's going to do the buy? All eyes were on me. OK, I say, I'm game.

Now we were going to need some money for the transaction. Bearing in mind this was before the introduction of the undercover unit as we know it now and the capacity to draw police funds for such an operation, we turned to our own devices. We knew that a lot of LSD could be concealed in a very small space, such as on blotting paper, and we needed to buy a substantial amount to prove he was a dealer of some calibre. So we all went to our hole-in-the-wall bank cashpoints, got a few quid out and everybody lent it to me so that it looked as if I'd got a bit of a wad. Talk about Keystone Cops. But these were early days in my undercover career. It was my case, my informant, I was keen to do it, so it fell upon me to be the gay boy who did the buy. At the time, I was boxing for the police so I was as fit as a butcher's dog and didn't carry an ounce of fat. I put on my tightest pair of faded jeans, went to Marks & Spencer and bought a string vest, which was all the rage at the time, heavily slicked my hair back with gel, wore a couple of leather wrist bands I'd bought from Kensington market (again, *de rigeur*) and got dressed up in the bogs. When the CID lads saw me they just pissed themselves laughing. They were in hysterics. So I slipped a heavy coat on in the height of summer and slunk out of the back door of the nick to go about my business, hoping no one else would see me. I arrived at the geezer's flat in Fulham, by then rid of the coat, and as directed by him I hadn't gone into the shop but round the back way, if you'll pardon the expression, and crept up the metal steps outside the back of the flat. I got to the flat door and found it open. I rapped on the door. 'Hello?'

No answer.

I thought I might as well walk in. He knew I was coming. I was still calling out as I went inside.

I looked in one room, a bedroom, and there suspended from the ceiling was a full body harness. It was the sort of thing used for sadomasochistic games. I was thinking, uh oh, was this a very clever idea? Eventually, he heard me from the shop and he came tottering up the internal stairs. We met at the top of the stairs, he looked me up and down and said, 'Oh, my, you do work out, don't you?'

I said, 'Well, yeah, yeah, I do, but I've got a boyfriend and all that, so can we just get on with the business?'

He seemed a bit put out that I wasn't interested in a bit of hanky-panky but said, 'OK, then.' He disappeared off for a few minutes then came back with a huge sheet of LSD tabs. He lisped, 'And how many would you like?'

At that moment I pulled out my warrant card and said, 'All of 'em, 'cos you're nicked.'

With that, he threw his hands in the air and promptly collapsed on the sofa in a dead faint. I slapped him round the face a bit to bring him round and he went into a real drama queen number. 'Oh my God, I can't go to prison, I'd never survive.'

By then, the other lads were thumping their way up the stairs after I'd shouted, 'Come on, then,' and he was nicked and the flat searched. They found about 500 doses of LSD – a lot of trips which could have had horrific side-effects for the users. He went to court and pleaded guilty. There wasn't much else he could do in the circumstances. And lo and behold, when he was given a four-year stretch, we got the histrionics again and he fainted in the dock. In my book, another award-winning performance. But the operation gave me a taste for undercover work that was to last another ten years, a dress rehearsal for what became a life of professional deception.

Chapter Sixteen

SHADOW OF THE GODFATHER

He looked like a tourist enjoying the sights of London. But I knew he was here on more sinister business. And I knew who his bosses were back home in Italy ... the Mafia.

It was July 1991 and the police had been tipped off that a leading criminal figure, on the run from justice in Italy, had arrived in the UK with the specific intention of setting up a major drugs network, and was looking for buyers to handle large quantities of cocaine, heroin and other narcotics. He was known to be an organised-crime figure and to have a serious criminal record back home.

The job had been landed by one of the area drug squads but was considered too hot to handle in the light of the Mafia involvement. The call for specialist assistance came in to the Undercover Unit at the Yard. Drugs and Mafia? Step forward Detective Bleksley. I was dispatched to join the area squad with the aim of infiltrating this sinister Italian – known only to me as Bruno – and smashing his drugs operation before it got off the ground and before we found ourselves flooded with Mafia drugs and Mafia hoodlums.

I had first to be sure that the area squad was up to providing the sort of high-quality back-up that would obviously be needed in view of the quality target we were after. Fortunately, I knew a couple of the blokes on the squad and had worked with them before so I knew they had some pretty sharp operators up there, people with previous experience of undercover jobs with major targets. And once we'd had a couple of briefings to discuss our game plan, I knew they were more than capable of handling a job this size. In other circumstances, they might have been forced to hand the whole job over to a higher squad like Central Drugs, but with COG involved and some solid blokes on the home team, we were set to go.

I met up with the informant, usual old game, and I was told the Italian suspect I was about to meet didn't speak much English. I don't know one fucking word of Italian after 'spaghetti bolognaise' so I went back to the undercover unit and requested an Italian-speaking officer to be drafted in to help me. They searched through police personnel records and came up with a girl who could speak the lingo. This suited me fine because she could always pose as my girlfriend. She was pretty inexperienced in this sort of work but was mainly going to be there as a translator. With a little bit of coaching and a little bit of persuasion she agreed to be my side-kick.

She arrived looking every inch the part on the evening of Tuesday, 23 July and we set off for Shelley's Wine Bar in

Albemarle Street in the West End. We ordered a couple of drinks and I played the pinball machine while we waited for the informant and our Mafiosi mate to arrive.

Within ten minutes, they were there. The informant introduced me to Bruno, our target and a most unlikely-looking Mafia hood. He was about five feet nine inches tall, aged around forty-five, slim, with short grey hair, a distinctive lazy right eye and casually dressed in jeans, T-shirt and red cardigan. More like a favourite uncle enjoying a night out than a fugitive drug-runner. But I'd known too often in this game that appearances can be deceptive.

Bruno and the informant asked for drinks but were told the bar had closed. So we all went upstairs to Shelley's Pub, where the bar was still open, bought drinks all round and sat down. Like a lot of self-respecting villains Bruno didn't want to talk business in front of my 'girlfriend'. He didn't want to talk to her and didn't want her to be privy to any of our conversations. It was a case of 'Don't involve your women in your criminal activities,' a code which a lot of crooks abide by and which I have a lot of respect for. Consequently, she'd only been there a matter of minutes when she was banished to the ladies'.

When she came back, I said Bruno had asked that she shouldn't be present while we discussed business. She acted a bit put out, not too much but pouty enough to be convincing. She had a brief conversation with Bruno in Italian and as a result moved to another table ten feet away and out of earshot. I said, 'Right, if you're happy now, let's get down to business. I gather you've got some powder on offer. What have you got and what's the price?'

I had to get by as best I could on the language front. Luckily, his English wasn't that dire and I tried to keep my vocabulary as simple as possible so there wouldn't be any confusion. The informant knew some Italian and was able to translate if we hit a problem. He spoke to Bruno and the Italian said to me, 'Coke, forty-five thousand pounds a kilo, heroin same price.' That was way too high.

I said, 'Is this geezer real? What sort of mug does he think I am, or is he just taking the piss? Forty-five grand, no way.'

This sent the Mafia man and my informant into a heated debate for several minutes. Then the informant said, 'It has got to be that price because it is such high-quality merchandise and because this is a first-time deal.'

Bruno said the heroin was available immediately but the cocaine hadn't reached the UK yet. I had set my stall as a cocaine buyer and it would have looked a bit sussy if I'd changed my mind and said, 'Oh yeah, I'll have the heroin anyway.' If you started chopping and changing you could lose your credibility and he could start smelling a rat. I had to resist the chance of a big heroin seizure there and then and knock the deal back, albeit reluctantly. I said no thanks, I'd stick out for the cocaine, but I'd have a word with a bloke who could shift the heroin. But Bruno wasn't budging on his prices. If I had been a real drug-dealer, my profit margins would have been ridiculously small, even with cutting the gear. His prices were exorbitant even for top-grade gear. I said to the informant, 'You tell him he's in London now, not Rome or Milan or wherever. We do things our way over here. Either he gets sensible or the deal is off.'

I knew I was chancing my arm a bit, but I had to be realistic. At his price it worked out at £45 a gram and the street price then was only £60 a gram. There wasn't a dealer in town who would have touched it with those profit margins, even with Bruno's assurances that it was 90 per cent pure coke and each kilo could be cut to make a kilo and a half at street price. I think I must have taken a brave pill that morning because then I found myself getting Bolshie with a Mafia drug dealer and telling him how fucking pissed off I was with his prices.

Bruno seemed to have got a bit more grasp of English all of a sudden. 'I try to tell you story,' he said. 'Our operation have got stuff here. We not pay for it yet. So we have to charge high price to get more over. Will not get here unless we pay some money to them.'

I said, 'So how does that affect me? That's your problem not mine. If you've got the gear here, you can't expect to charge those prices to pay for your operation. You'll never sell it.'

Bruno replied, 'We have sell some. Only want two or three customers and then in six months everything OK and you can have ten, twenty, thirty, fifty, a hundred kilo a time of what you want.'

This was big-time stuff by any standards. We were talking millions of pounds here.

'Are you saying,' I asked Bruno, 'if I pay this high price now you will guarantee everything I want afterwards?'

He sure would, he said and went even further, promising to show us exactly how the drugs were brought into the country and how his operation worked.

'You will be very happy,' he said. He said that if I shifted some of the heroin for him he would share some of the profits with me.

I asked him why he didn't just bring down the price of his cocaine and share some of those profits with me. I was getting pretty pissed off so I said through the informant, 'Either he gets sensible or I'm out of here.' I was really calling his bluff.

I got up from the table, acting sort of humpy, and went and bought some more drinks. Then we had a chat about women, Italy, Italian football, and so on. Then Bruno cracked. The bluff had paid off. He agreed to a trial purchase of half a kilo of cocaine for £22,500 with regular supplies of two kilos a week at a much cheaper price to follow. Bruno wanted me to buy more but I said I wouldn't know what demand there was until I'd seen it, tried it and let my customers have some.

'I do for you any amount,' he said. 'All ninety per cent.'

He agreed to supply the trial package in a couple of weeks. And he was still keen to move his heroin. 'I do that now, you see,' he repeated for about the third time.

'Yes,' I said. 'I'm not deaf.'

We returned to more touristy lines of conversation like holidays, golf, racing, fucking and fighting and then said our goodbyes. The scene was set; the trap was laid. I beckoned my 'girlfriend' over and we strolled out into the night hand in hand. Her part was over.

Mine was now moving into top gear. I tried to persuade the management that this was a case that would justify buying the first consignment, without arresting Bruno, and setting him up for ten or twenty kilos or even more in the future. But they were always a bit suspicious of us, cops working undercover. There's got to be some sort of wheeze going on. They said no, that we'd have to take him first time up. They knew, of course, through Interpol, that he was high on the Italian wanted list and the sooner he was banged up and then deported, the better. I was keyed up and ready to go over the next few days expecting Bruno's call on my mobile to set a time and place for the hand-over. Nothing. It was a full two months before he surfaced again. Not unusual with professional criminals. It was often a waiting game.

It was on a Friday evening in late September when I met him again at Shelley's with our informant. I shook his hand, bought us drinks and said to him, 'I was wondering if I'd ever see you again.'

He said he'd had problems but it was all sorted now. 'You OK?' he asked.

'Yeah,' I said, 'I'm fine, but it's a good job I don't rely on you to make a living from or I'd be skint.'

It fell on stony ground and the informant had to translate the slang. Bruno declared that our cocaine was now on site and the trial half-kilo could be delivered the next day.

'How do you know I haven't found another source?' I asked a bit cheekily.

'But you here, must be good reason you want Bruno give you best coke,' he replied.

'I might just have a friend interested in the heroin,' I told him.

'Have you?' he said, spotting a chance to make a nice few quid from the smack.

'Let's deal with the coke first,' I said.

He wanted to arrange the hand-over next day but I said, 'That's no good, I'm busy.' I needed more time to set up the operation. So we agreed on the following day, a Sunday, to meet by the petrol station near the Kensington Hilton Hotel at 11.00am. Not a day of rest for drug-dealers or undercover cops! He said we would go to a safe house nearby for the exchange. He said he would bring a sample of the heroin he was so keen to get rid of to my supposed mate, free of charge. 'Very generous,' I said sarcastically as we parted.

I turned up at the Hilton Hotel sharp at 11.00am on the Sunday with £22,250 of the Commissioner's cash in a nearby car and a fellow undercover officer at the wheel. There was plenty of cover nearby from the back-up teams. They knew it was another roving plot and we might go anywhere. I saw Bruno waiting outside holding an umbrella. It was a dark, overcast day with frequent showers and we had both taken brollies. He said, 'Have you got the money?'

'Yes, nearby.'

Why hadn't I got it with me, he wanted to know.

''Cos I'm not taking my dough into some strange place and getting robbed, that's why. Bring me the parcel and I'll bring the money.'

He didn't look too happy as we walked into Russell Road, which consisted of a lot of big, old Victorian houses. He led me up some stairs to a communal front door, which he opened with a key, and we went up to flat number eight, right at the top. He unlocked that and we were in a bed-sitter. I had no idea what I might be walking into. All the time, I was looking for possible escape routes, a skylight or whatever; your bottle is screaming, taking chunks out of your underpants, and you are guarding your back without showing a glimmer of concern.

I saw another Italian standing there who looked like a Mafia hoodlum straight out of Central Casting – swarthy, black moustache, balding, slim, eyes darting everywhere. He produced a Boots carrier bag which he handed to Bruno, who put it down on the kitchen table. Then he took out two bags, heavily bound in masking tape, each containing a quarter kilo of cocaine, the archetypal packaging for powder.

'Now get the money,' he said.

'Hold up, behave yourself,' I said. 'Not 'til I've looked in one of them. Open one up.'

Bruno got some newspaper and laid it on the kitchen table. Bruno gave one of the packages to the other geezer and laid the other on top of the paper.

'Oh no, not that one, the other,' I said.

Bruno swapped them over and put my rejected one in the Boots bag. Then he took a knife from the other bloke and started cutting away at the masking tape. Now I was thinking about the other officers coming in afterwards looking for evidence and Bruno was playing nicely into our hands. Every time he ripped off a bit of tape, his fingerprints went on it and he slung it in the bin. When the police came in on a search later, which they would to cover my involvement, there would be perfectly legitimate evidence in the bin. I offered to help him to make sure my dabs would be on the tape as well as further corroboration if I was called to give evidence. If they said it was all fictitious and made up, then I could prove I was there. It was a matter of thinking on your feet all the time.

Once the masking tape was off, there was cling film to undo. This is how the dealers protect the powder: layers and layers of the stuff because you don't want bags bursting or losing the gear when someone makes a cut to sample it. As we were stripping the packaging away, some brown powder fell on the paper. I looked quizzical, though I had a shrewd notion what it was.

'Pepper, to put the dogs off the scent,' said Bruno. Yes, I'd guessed right.

Once all the cling film was off I saw a white plastic bag with 'Holland' marked on it, no doubt where this consignment was coming from. Bruno opened a final bag and showed me a lump of white powder. I knew instantly it was top quality. When it comes in a lump, it's always uncut and high grade. I smelt it and tasted it and knew it was the pukka gear. So now I had seen evidence galore piling up in the bin: tape, cling film, even the newspaper, all handled by both men. Slowly but surely I was nailing the bastards to the floor, and neither of them knew it.

I told them I wouldn't bother weighing the coke because if it was light I'd know exactly where to come for revenge. I could see the flat was lived in on a regular basis. The second Itie said, 'That won't happen. You'll see it's all there when you come to weigh it.'

I turned to him and said, 'Thank you, but I wasn't really talking to you.'

He said, 'It's OK, I promise.' The second geezer then proceeded to re-wrap the coke plus a sample of heroin which he thought would interest my other pals in the drug trade. Lovely, a bit of smack in with the Charlie, that'll go down well when it reaches court.

That was it, deal done, and Bruno and me walked down the stairs and into the street. As we strolled back towards the Hilton to pick up the cash to pay for the gear, Bruno was buzzing with enthusiasm for our new-found business relationship. 'Today we start great things, is so?' he said, in his broken English, beaming. You prat, I thought, the only great thing you've got to look forward to is seven years inside, minimum. And then I gave the pre-arranged signal for the hidden police team to break cover and move in for the kill. I shoved my rolled-up umbrella under my left arm, waited a few seconds and saw them swarming towards us from all directions. Hairy-arsed rozzers in black combat gear with Glock 9mm pistols descending from every which way. I was on my toes and away. Mr Mafia man never knew what hit him.

I was a bit worried that I'd had to leave the informant behind in the flat at Bruno's insistence. It was the Mafioso style of things. There was no choice. He stays here until we get the money, they insisted. Either that or no trade. But the risk assessment had been made at the start of the operation and my bosses considered that the snout must have needed his pay-off so desperately that he was happy to be on the plot when the job went down. His decision. He wasn't my problem at the end of the day. It was up to my superiors to deal with. You always tried to extract the informant when you could but this was one where it couldn't be done. If I'd kicked up a fuss about him coming with me it could have fucked it all up. These are on-the-hoof decisions you have to make while your brain is doused in adrenaline and you just hope you get it more right than wrong. When it's a case of ensuring your own escape from an ambush situation like that, to make it look like you really are a villain, you always have the upper hand. You know it's going to happen, so you're ready to exit stage left. The bad guy is taken completely by surprise. Most of the sensible back-up boys will make what appears to be a genuine effort to catch you but you either outrun them or disappear or whatever. On this occasion I was a bit pissed off because I'd taken my treasured golfing umbrella – I hadn't had it very long and it matched my golf bag and this, that and the other – and when the first of the pursuing coppers came at me I larrupped him with it and it went 'twang' and shredded in front of my eyes. I really loved that umbrella and I thought, now, why the fuck did you do that? Anyway they very kindly replaced the broken brolly ... with a lost property job that had been lying round the squad office for the last six months. Their resources didn't stretch to a new one.

But they were well happy with the result. Not only did we get the cocaine package, the search team found another six kilos of high-grade heroin worth about two hundred and twenty thousand pounds skilfully hidden in the flat. Bruno hadn't been kidding about his smack supplies. He got a lengthy jail sentence with a recommendation that he be returned to Italy to face a load of other serious charges there. The other geezer got a lighter sentence. It was another two scumbags off the streets, another bid to set up a multi-million-pound drug network foiled. There was no doubt at the end of the day that Bruno and his cronies had the capacity to flood Britain with the quantity of drugs they had talked about, according to highly-placed sources on the international drug scene, and what we'd seen was truly the tip of a very large iceberg.

These two were characteristic of the increasing Mafia involvement in the British drug scene, and other areas of organised crime. When I was with the Central Drug Squad we arrested a big leaguer called David Medin who was a known and very active Mafiosa member, in connection with thirty-three kilos of cocaine, then the largest land seizure of coke ever made in Britain. It was one of the most dramatic jobs I'd ever been on. I wasn't undercover but went along as one of the appointed firearms officers because we knew there was a big chance of the suspects being tooled up in view of the value of the gear. We had men up in a helicopter to intercept the villains' car on the M11 and we had police 'gunships', cars with armed officers aboard, placed along the motorway.

The swoop went off in the middle of the night with the helicopter flying low overhead illuminating the suspect car with huge searchlights from a height of just a few feet. The armed police vehicles boxed him in, slowing their speed all the time – 50mph, 40mph, 30mph, slower and slower running side by side, double-banked so he had absolutely nowhere to go. It was like Blackpool fucking illuminations, spectacular stuff.

Medin actually turned supergrass after his arrest, gave up his accomplices, confessed his Mafia connections then became a resident informant and was housed by the police in a secure unit. His output was phenomenal and, through him, the police got to know a lot about the operations of the Mafia in the UK and organised crime in general. The informant who had originally tipped us off about that job was Peter McNeil, who I mentioned earlier and who later got shot in a gangland execution.

We knew there were Mafia people operating here. It was considered a very lucrative market by the Mob. At that time in the early nineties, the Italian authorities were trying to hammer the Mafiosa at home and judges and politicians were all having their cars blown up. They were looking to move their activities elsewhere. There were a lot of suspicions about a lot of people here, such as Italians living in central London, or discreetly and apparently respectably in the suburbs with wives and families, who were turning over a lot of cash from invisible sources. The Yard intelligence boys were pretty certain it was the Mafia. Proving it was another thing.

They were also using ever more sophisticated ways of smuggling drugs into Britain. In the Medin case, for instance, the gear had been brought into the country hidden inside the metal arms of JCBs. They were cutting them open, stuffing them full of Colombian cocaine then welding them together again before shipping them into the UK from Argentina. They weigh tons anyway, so who's going to find the stuff in there? If we hadn't had a good informant on that job, the gang would still be doing it today and for donkey's years to come. I can't imagine some Customs officer deciding on a random check on a JCB arm and finding it stuffed with dope.

I think I've probably made it clear by now that the Customs and us didn't always see eye to eye on many things, even though our paths crossed a lot and we were basically supposed to be doing the same job, i.e. hitting the drug-dealers.

I remember on one occasion I had picked up, through an undercover operation, details of a clever scam for bringing in very large consignments of drugs. This gang had devised a special water-tight capsule which they were going to tow underwater behind their vessel on a wire. No drugs on the boat, nothing showing on the surface behind. If they were suddenly approached by a suspicious Customs cutter, they could just jettison the drug load and avoid detection. They had built-in, remotely-operated buoyancy aids, so if they had to ditch the load in an emergency they would record the spot – a good seaman can do that with pinpoint accuracy – then return when it was safe, trigger off the remote control to inflate the buoyancy aids, and retrieve the swag.

I thought it was ingenious, cutting-edge technology on the drug scene. I went to Customs because it was obviously a Customs job, a proposed importation, and told them all about it. I even took along a sketch of the submersible which I had asked one of the gang to draw for me. I'd told him I didn't really understand how it would work and needed him to do a quick picture for me. In truth, I was after evidence. I told Customs that the smugglers had all the technology for the capsules in place and all they were looking for was a boat and a crew. I was planning to go along as a crewman and lay on a good seizure for the Customs boys. We'd done that sort of thing before, such as Operation Dash in the Atlantic. But the Customs bosses wouldn't have anything to do with it. They told me to pull out and leave it alone.

You can imagine how I slammed the fucking door as I walked out of that meeting. I went back to the Yard, called Customs a bunch of wankers, went on the piss, and said I'd never work for them again. But, of course, I did because so many jobs were interlinked.

On one job, a close colleague and I were monitoring a bloke coming back to the UK from Colombia via France. We knew he had six kilos of cocaine body-packed on him tight as a drum. Another bloke in the same ring was also travelling but they weren't making any contact with each other. We had them under close surveillance from the moment they touched down at Charles de Gaulle airport in Paris. Again, because it was an importation, we thought we had better tell British Customs.

The following morning, the police met up for a 5.00am briefing at Heathrow before the arrival of the plane. Customs, the bastards, had met at 4.00am and had got out a rummage crew ready to search the suspect's plane before we could tag them. They just wanted to nick the bodies and the drugs. The police, on the other hand, had a major investigation under way to find out who was further down the chain of command here, and what the distribution network was, to follow it through to the dealers. Customs didn't give a fuck. But we knew where the guy with the drugs was going when he arrived back in England and we knew some of the people who were pushing his gear, so we had masses of Old Bill ready, dotted all over London, so that when he went off with his parcel and handed it on, we could scoop up loads of people and take out the entire network.

Well, we went fucking ballistic when Customs told us what they intended to do. It got very heated. So, after a word with my bosses, my mate and I sneaked out of the office, went to a phone box, rang a pal in France and said, 'Customs are trying to shaft us on this one. Get the French to nick 'em before they take off.' And they did. The French police got the seizure and British Customs got fuck all. Our squad claimed all the credit for it. 'We sold the job abroad ... so what?'

We walked out smiling but they were not amused. I'm afraid that was just an indication of how much conflict and lack of communal ambition there was between the two services. They are civil servants who are better dishing out the dole in my opinion.

I remember one particularly stroppy boss I had losing his rag with the Customs chiefs after one particularly onerous briefing and telling them, 'I think the best thing you lot can do is stand around the coastline of Britain and hold hands, form a chain around the coastline, it's about your best bet. You haven't got the brains for anything else.'

On another occasion a senior Customs official was trying to pull rank on the same DI. He said he wanted to remind him that his civil service grade was equivalent to that of a police superintendent. My boss turned round to him and said, 'I'd like to remind you that, in the police, people of your grade do my photocopying.'

Now rank never bothered me. I remained a detective constable all my working life and was happy with that. It was the job I loved, mixing it with real people, not climbing the ladder to the role of some pen-pusher-in-chief. People told me I should go for a higher rank but it meant taking a year off work, effectively, to study. As my school record shows, studying was not really my forte. I chose specialisation and never regretted it for a minute. I travelled the country, travelled the world – what the fuck did I want rank for? I had bundles of respect for what I did and that's what mattered to me.

Chapter Seventeen

POT LUCK

If there was action going on, I wanted a slice of it. As far as I was concerned, it was a war out there and I was ready to take up battle positions whenever and wherever I was required. For my part, it was an underworld theatre of war with me as an actor playing the starring role of villain with a supporting cast of villains playing themselves. Heart-thumping, sweat-making stuff a lot of the time. There were moments of the most intense drama, of ludicrous black comedy, and always the constant battle of wits against some of the most fearsome crooks in the world who would happily break your skull with an iron bar if they knew what you were really up to.

Some of our operations were stage-managed like major productions, with up to fifty officers, including yours truly, deployed against the enemy. I was in briefing rooms where the support units, surveillance, arrest squads, firearms and forensics were jammed in so tight you could barely get a decent lungful of air. It was important on every mission that everyone in the back-up squads knew exactly what I looked like. As the commanding officers briefed the assembled troops I would be shoved forward for all to see, a long-haired oik in jeans and T-shirt looking, hopefully, indistinguishable from the villains we were about to nick.

'This is our man on the inside. Whatever happens, don't shoot the fucker.' They'd all have a good look. Some would know me from old.

'Good luck, Blex.'

Some would be seeing you for the first time. You'd meet again months later and they would wonder why you hadn't remembered their name. 'You know, we met at the Clapham heroin bust briefing.'

'Oh yeah, I remember,' and you hadn't got a clue who they were. This was the work that I loved, in the spotlight using every bit of guile I possessed to infiltrate the big criminal gang. The undercover man became the linchpin of so many busts. The success or failure of the operations depended time and time again on the quality of our performance. My CV should have read: 'Professional liar, Metropolitan Police, treachery my speciality. Available for all kinds of undercover operations.' Perhaps it should have added, 'Prepared to sacrifice home life, domestic life, all friends and family and mingle freely with the dregs of society in the pursuit of duty.'

We'd only go in on undercovers if conventional methods of nicking the crooks had either failed or weren't practical. It meant we were up against the top echelons of the criminal underworld most of the time, tough, ruthless bastards most of them, who were going to become your mates, your pals, your drinking buddies, your drug-dealing cronies, as you systematically set them up for a bust at the hands of an awesome police raiding party storming out of the shadows. I don't want to blow my own trumpet but I do take great pride in the testimony of Deputy Assistant Commissioner Simon Crawshaw when he supported a recommendation for me to get the Commissioner's High Commendation, the Yard's top award, in 1990. He wrote, 'DC Bleksley, relying on his professional judgment, "entered the lions' den" placing himself at great risk should his expertise fail. Mr Bleksley, in addition to being a very fine officer, is also a realist, who is well aware of the serious consequences if he was to be discovered, yet has volunteered and used his expertise to obtain results which otherwise could not be achieved. We are indeed fortunate to have officers of the calibre of Detective Constable Bleksley to call on.'

I always hoped it would make my sons proud of what I did. All my eldest, Bradley, knew back then was that I did something a bit mysterious in the police force. I wore funny clothes and had long hair and stayed out a lot. I always wanted him to know about those fascinating years at the heart of crime fighting, and now he, along with my two younger sons, has the chance. I'll tell you how he happened against the odds, back in 1988.

It was a wet Wednesday in March when I picked up an emergency call on my car radio as I drove home from Scotland Yard through south-east London. It was an urgent request for help on a drugs bust. Another team from the Central Drugs Squad were about to smash their way into a flat in Plumstead and wanted to rip it apart in the search for a big cannabis haul. It was known to have been used by various members of a gang of marijuana dealers. Not strictly my patch, but drugs and villains just down the road, sounded like a piece of the action that was too good to miss. I spun the car round and my partner and I headed for the address. We were technically off duty by now but Plumstead wasn't too far off our route.

'ON WAY,' I yelled over the radio, 'with you in ten minutes.'

Then there was another panic call as we screamed towards the address. 'How far away are you now? We've got to go in right away.'

'We'll be there in five minutes,' I told them. We arrived to find that the raid team had already steamed in with backing from the local uniform section and police dogs. They'd done serious GBH in the process to the front door and windows to gain entry. It looked a decent job and worth staying around for. We'd put the pint we'd been looking forward to on hold.

My partner and I walked into the flat not knowing anything about the people who lived there or about the job. Nobody seemed to know very much. One team often didn't seem to know what the other was working on, for security purposes. Even so it didn't seem to be the best co-ordinated job in the world.

So I said to a pal of mine who was running it, 'What do you want us to do – search the bedroom?' Bedrooms were always the best places to search; you found plenty of evidence, got an idea of the occupant's private life and often found a good bit of humour at their expense.

'Yeah, crack on,' said my mate. My colleague and I went into the back bedroom and started rummaging about. Under the bed I found loads of letters written to a guy in prison and starting 'Dear Richard ...' I went up to the guv'nor in charge, showed him the letters and said, 'What's the name of the geezer who lives here?'

'It's Richard Rowbottom,' he said.

'Do you mean Rowbotham,' I said, emphasising the bit that sounded like Ian Botham.

'Yeah, that's him, do you know him?'

Did I know him? 'Oh, fuck,' I said, 'I certainly do.' This was none other than my then-girlfriend's elder brother. She'd warned me that he was a bit of scally, that he made loads of trips to Spain and had been a bit of a naughty boy in his younger days. I explained the situation to the guv'nor and he was as good as gold.

'Do you want to stay or do you want to fuck off home and not be part of it?' he said. I told him I'd started the search so I might as well carry on. I knew that any explanation to my girlfriend, Wendy, wasn't going to be easy. She'd never believe in a million years it was just a coincidence that I was involved in busting her brother's flat.

I went back into the bedroom to carry on with the search. Then my eye caught an unmistakable photo pinned on the wall. It was my girlfriend. I couldn't believe it. 'Fuck my luck,' I muttered as we rummaged through drawers and cupboards.

The search yielded twenty kilos of good-quality cannabis, a decent old haul by any standards and a fair pointer as to why Richard had taken so many trips to Spain every year. Not for a tan. I said point-blank, 'I'm not going to deal with him. Someone else will have to do the questioning.' So I helped deal with a couple of the other bodies arrested in the swoop. I did the necessary, got them on the charge sheet, then later that night I phoned Wendy. This I was dreading.

'We've got to meet up ... it's urgent. We've got to have a chat,' I told her. 'I don't want to talk about it over the phone.'

She said, 'It's Richard, isn't it?' She'd put two and two together and was spot on.

'Yeah, it is ... where shall we meet?'

We met up later and I explained the circumstances and how it had put me in such an invidious position. She was deeply upset, both for her brother and for us. She decided to go to court the following day when Richard and his cronies made their first appearance, charged with drugs offences. Of course, he'd not told anybody apart from his brief. All of a sudden, he saw his sister there.

'How the fuck did you know I was here?' he said.

She made up a cock-and-bull story, keeping my name well out of things, and he seemed happy with the explanation. Wendy and I agreed that she wouldn't let any alleged misdemeanours of her brother's spoil our relationship and that we would carry on seeing each other. I had to supply a confidential report detailing my involvement, which you had to do in any situation where you might be compromised. Wendy and I continued seeing each other right up to the date of his trial. I loved her and I didn't want the Richard problem to spoil our relationship.

I got up that morning, got dressed and went to court. She got up, got dressed and went to court via a different route. Then we were sitting outside the courtroom at Inner London Crown Court, together but apart, waiting for the case to start and expecting the worst. She'd already told him while he was on remand in prison that I'd been involved in the job leading to his arrest and he'd gone bananas. He believed that I had been using Wendy in an undercover operation to get at him.

As I walked into the courtroom to give evidence, I had to pass just a few feet away from him in the dock. There was a hiss like gas escaping then he muttered, 'You fucking bastard, you cunt, you dirtbag,' and a whole stream of other obscenities. It was very, very unpleasant.

I took the oath and stood there in the witness box to give evidence against one of the other defendants I had arrested. When I had finished I waited to be cross-examined by the defence counsel. The first question he asked was, 'Is it true you are the current boyfriend of the sister of the accused Richard Rowbotham?' I said, 'Yes,' at which point the judge's glasses nearly fell off the end of his nose, the jury suddenly woke up and you could see the look on their faces saying, 'Aye aye, this is going to be a bit lively.' There was a buzz round the court. People were staggered by what they had just heard. The defence lawyer was desperately trying to link my relationship with Wendy to the arrest of her brother. I told the court over and over that I had nothing to do with Richard's arrest or any kind of undercover operation. Although treachery was my profession I could say, hand on heart, that I hadn't cruelly used the one I loved simply to affect the arrest of her brother. 'This was just a million-to-one coincidence, a very unfortunate coincidence as it turned out,' I told court. I wished it had never happened. It had caused a lot of heartache to Wendy and a lot of heartache to me.

I got the biggest grilling imaginable from all three defence counsels representing all three defendants. They all got up one by one to have a pop. 'You *were* using your girlfriend to infiltrate Richard and his associates because you were so desperate to arrest them.'

'No, Sir, I wasn't.'

'You utilised your professional resources to go undercover to gain evidence against them?'

'No, Sir, that is untrue.'

All three of the lawyers knew within the world of the judiciary that I was a professional infiltrator. Word goes round the legal profession. It seemed to me that their technique was to paint me as a dirty sneaky bastard who would stoop to any level to get a conviction and persuade the jury to acquit. My evidence went on much longer than I had expected as they tried to nail the traitor tag on me. There were recesses, lunch breaks, adjournments. Each time I was recalled to the witness stand I had to pass within feet of the dock. Every time I left the court I had to do the same. Each time it was the hissing, the muttering, the barely audible death threats. Very uncomfortable, very unpleasant.

I'd booked a much-needed holiday to start after my evidence had finished. I couldn't wait to get some Spanish sun to clear my head. It was good, plenty of booze, pleasant company with a mate, and I returned two weeks later refreshed and ready to go, and anxious to see Wendy again. It was then I learned that Richard had been the only one of the three defendants to be convicted on the drugs charges and had got four years jail. The other two walked scot-free. That didn't help matters. Wendy had been called as a defence witness as the lawyers pursued the line that I might have deliberately used her to get to Richard, suggesting that our very first date was contrived to allow me to pursue an undercover operation. She was traumatised, her family were upset. Such was the impact of the case that we reluctantly decided to call an end to our relationship. She was torn between allegiance to her brother and her affection for me. 'OK, let's leave it,' I said. 'It can't work under those pressures.'

Wendy, who was a very attractive and bubbly barmaid, had worked in a pub in South London I used regularly. A pal of mine who was going out with a friend of hers fixed up a blind date. Not totally blind because I'd seen her working in the pub and knew she was no old dog. I didn't really know her, though, and she didn't know me even though she had served me a good few pints.

We went out and got on famously. We started to go out on a regular basis and over drinks one day she mentioned that she had a brother who was a bit of a scallywag. He'd been to Spain eighteen times in the last six months, had been in trouble as a youngster but despite that she still cared about him. I wasn't too bothered. It didn't matter whether her brother was a scally or not. It was us we were talking about. But I thought it wouldn't be a bad idea to pop into the local nick sometime when I was in the area and find out a bit about him. It was only a few days later that I picked up the assistance call and found out more than I ever needed to know. But I hadn't made any enquiries and I certainly hadn't put the cops onto him and definitely wasn't undercover to nail him. I could see how suspicious it looked from his point of view and Wendy's point of view. Now our romance had been killed stone dead simply because I was a cop doing my job. I'd answered a random call too many. A thousand other marriages and relationships, probably more, have been wrecked by the problems of being a policeman. Ours was another casualty.

That would probably have been the end of it. Then, one Friday night some months later, I was in the pub having a drink when in walked Wendy. I'd grown a beard by then as one of my ever-changing disguises for undercover purposes. I was forever growing beards, growing moustaches, growing long hair, cutting it short to vary my appearance. I thought, so, how's this going to be? She walked straight up to me with a big smile on her face, tugged my new whiskers and said, 'Hello, beardy.' That was it. The romance was re-ignited in a massive way. And just a few weeks later, she announced, 'Blex, I'm pregnant.'

She wrote to Richard in prison and told him she was expecting and, what was more, that I was the father. So now the man who hated my guts with a vengeance was about to become uncle to my baby. I could see more flak on the horizon.

Sure enough, Richard went ballistic. He hatched an escape plot from the Isle of Sheppey Prison where he had just been downgraded to a Category C inmate and was only a few steps from freedom. He intended to head on home to London to sort things out. He told the family, 'I can't believe this bastard Bleksley is back in my life and about to father my nephew.'

Fortunately, he only made it to the local railway station before he was apprehended. He lost remission and privileges, but none of his simmering hatred of me.

Brad was born in January 1988 three weeks prematurely weighing 5lb 13oz. And the first thing I said was that there was no way in the world that he was ever going to become a policeman if I had any say in the matter. As a boy he was a keen cricketer, footballer and rugby player, and a good pal to his dad. He's now twenty-eight and a fine young man. We love each other very much. My younger sons are fifteen and fourteen and find it difficult to believe that their middle-aged, slightly overweight and balding dad was once a fearless, long haired undercover cop.

But for Richard, even after Brad's birth, the hatred went on. I'd had Brad staying overnight when Wendy came to pick him up. I made her a cup of tea and put it down. Brad, who was just a toddler then, picked up the cup thinking it was a drink for him and spilt scalding tea all down his chin and his chest. I heard the most almighty scream and went rushing in. I rushed him to the cold shower hose and held him there for ages and ages 'til the pain eased. Then we rushed him up to the hospital for sedation and treatment, and fortunately the cold water had prevented any scarring. As we were driving home a couple of hours later with Brad safely curled up in my arms, I asked Wendy, 'Where do you want to go?' She said, 'Let's go to my mum's.' As we were pulling up outside she said, 'There's something I ought to tell you. Richard's coming out today and he's coming here.' I thought, how bad is this day going to get? We walked into her mum's house and Richard was already there. It was the first time I'd seen him since the Inner London Crown Court and been subjected to his tirade of abuse. Well, the atmosphere was unbelievable. I put Brad down and we exchanged small talk for a minute or two. Then Richard said, 'I think we'd better have a chat, don't you?' We walked out into the back garden. He was lean and fit. He'd done a lot of weights inside. You couldn't have fried an egg on him. I thought it was all going to kick off.

Then he turned round and said, 'Tell me, just tell me honestly, did you go out with Wendy to get at me?'

I said, 'Richard, you heard what I said in court, that was the truth. The answer is no. I'll tell you again now, it was just a dreadful coincidence. That is the top and bottom of it.'

Very magnanimously, and it can't have been easy for him, he shook my hand. The feuding was done.

Now, there's action with intent, in the line of duty. And then there's action you don't really expect or understand. Especially in sleepy Shrewsbury in Shropshire. I'd gone there with close friends who had returned from living on the West Coast of America. We'd enjoyed the heady days of California's Venice Beach together in the seventies when I stayed for extended holidays with them. We did the surfing, the smoking, the odd line of coke. It was an amazing insight into how the drug culture was sweeping through Middle America. And as time went by, an invaluable grounding for my career in the world of drugs investigations. But that was all behind them now and they were back in the UK looking to set up the archetypal small country hotel and bar in Shrewsbury. I'd spent a backbreaking day helping them move in one Sunday in January 1990. Come closing time we all sat down for a well-earned drink. We toasted their new life and wished them well. Then there was a load of noise outside, like the local yobbos on a night out. It passed. Then a guy came knocking on the door and asked, 'Is that your car out there?'

The VW Jetta belonged to one of my friends. 'Yes, it's mine,' he said.

'Well,' said the caller, 'a gang of local hooligans have just smashed it up.' We looked outside and there was glass everywhere.

POT LUCK

I was off duty, I was shagged out and I should have just dialled 999. But no. I went legging it up the road after the yobbos. I caught up with them, right lairy bastards, and said to one of them, 'Hey, I want a word with you.'

He sneered, 'Fuck off.'

Charmed I'm sure. So I walked right up to him and said, 'Did you just smash up my friend's car?' With that he threw a punch at me. I ducked. I thought, right, I'll have you for that. A full-scale punch-up started outside a church, spilled over into the graveyard and I was trading punches with all three of the yobs, a real bunch of scrotes. I was boxing at light heavyweight for the Met Police at the time so I treated it as a nice bit of practice. Wham, bam, it was fists everywhere. At one point I hit the lippy ringleader a stonking belt in the mouth and he went down on the deck with me after him. I told him I was a copper and was arresting him for assault and criminal damage. One of the others was yelling at me, 'Let him go, let him go.'

I said, 'No way.'

He stuck his hand in his pocket and repeated, 'Let him go. If you don't, I'll cut you.' With that he pulled out a knife. 'I'll fucking cut ya,' he said again. Then I saw my girlfriend and my friends from the hotel coming towards us.

'He's got a knife, get out of the way,' I shouted. I didn't want them involved with this bunch of shits. The guy with the knife decided not to stab me. Instead he ran at me and booted me right in the head. Then the others joined in a general kicking. I was stunned for a few seconds and the bloke on the ground got up and started to run off. With that the local police arrived in force and started to scoop up everybody they could lay their hands on. I staggered to my feet and I saw the fucker I'd had on the ground running off along the road. I was after him like a long dog and had my hands on him again after a chase. There wasn't so much resistance second time around and he was bundled off to the nick.

We all went back to the hotel with some of the local police to make our statements and what have you. Then the uniformed duty inspector strode in and said, 'Where's the man who took on the EBF?'

I thought, EBF – who the hell are they?

The EBF, he informed us, were the English Border Front, a gang of local toe-rags who had wreaked havoc in the town for years. 'If you knew how much trouble and disruption they caused in this town. This is a major success in our battle against the EBF.' He said the gang regularly went on raiding parties over the Welsh border and picked scraps with Welsh lads. In turn, the Welsh would retaliate with raids into Shrewsbury. On their home patch, the EBF had been responsible for thousands of pounds' worth of damage to cars and windows. My fleeting visit to Shrewsbury, said the local inspector, had cleared up the biggest gang of troublemakers they'd ever known. Not exactly big time on a global scale, but if the people of Shrewsbury can sleep easier, well worth the kicking.

Chapter Eighteen

CRACKING UP

I knew I'd become dangerously out of control the day I nearly killed a close pal with a bar stool. Ten years of undercover work among the scum of the earth had finally taken its toll. I'd flipped, lost it big time. I knew it and needed urgent help. But I was to wonder long and hard afterwards why nobody else had seen the warning signs and taken pre-emptive action.

My tangled home life coupled with the endless pressures of undercover work and the Zulu Cricket death threat from the Mafia had set me on the slippery slope that was to end the career I loved.

The crunch came one day in 1995 after I'd driven from Scotland Yard and headed south over the Thames towards Epsom in Surrey to be briefed on a new assignment, calling at the National Crime Squad headquarters in Spring Gardens, Vauxhall, to pick up my evidence book and one or two other bits and pieces. I needed petrol and pulled into the garage opposite Tintagel House, another Scotland Yard admin block, on the Embankment South Side, to top up. Out of nowhere, a youngish bloke suddenly came up to me on the forecourt and in a broad American accent said to me, 'Do you want to buy some speakers?'

I've been offered moody *schmutter* in the job and out but never by an American on a garage forecourt in South London.

'Er, no thanks, mate, I've just got a new music centre,' I said.

'It's the deal of a lifetime,' he replied.

'Well, thanks, pal, but I don't want to know.'

I walked into the petrol station to pay my bill when this voice boomed out right over my shoulder, 'Well, not in this lifetime then, eh?'

It was him again. All I could think to say was, 'Yeah, righto.'

Now it was becoming a bit unnerving. Was this just a quirky coincidence or was this the Mafia's threat to have me killed over the Zulu Cricket heroin bust at Gatwick Airport about to become reality? The bloke I'd had nicked, Alan Johnston, was safely away doing fifteen years but he had plenty of pals out there. My mind was working overtime. If the intention had been to unsettle me it was working. I thought, fuck this, and straight away threw all my anti-surveillance tricks into losing the bastard. I knew how to make him – or them – show out if they were really on my tail. I drove from Vauxhall to Epsom utilising every scrap of anti-surveillance knowledge at my disposal. On Clapham Common there is a big sweeping right turn going towards Tooting. I knew it well because I had lived in Clapham for a couple of years. I got there and I was not happy. I'd still got this distinct feeling I was being tailed. I did various back-doubles through Clapham and I was picking up motors behind me. I thought someone was definitely on me. There was a sure way to find out. I went up to the junction and did the most outrageous red-light jump you have ever seen. A real wrong 'un which only someone trying to commit suicide would follow me on. I wasn't doing it to jeopardise other road-users, but I was trained and I had the experience and knew what risks I could take. I pushed it right to the limit, screaming across the front of cars heading straight at me.

I saw someone had come with me, a little Ford Fiesta with two geezers in it. I made it by the skin of my teeth, and they had a real job avoiding a crash. They caught up with me a few hundred yards further on and pulled up alongside me. I thought, fuck me, this is right on top now. Both geezers were giving me the eyeball. I braked to let them pass. They stared back. I was expecting a shooter to appear and I was thinking it had to be a Mafia hit. The American in the petrol station, then someone tailing me, it was all slotting in.

I slammed on my brakes and they had to go ahead of me. I was behind where I could see them but they couldn't see me. Then at the next set of lights, they roared off.

Coincidence? I don't know. But the whole incident made me very, very jumpy. And that's how I had been for months. I didn't know it, but I'd become a bit of a monster to live with and work with. My girlfriend had even attempted suicide by drinking crushed paracetamol in a pint jug of wine because she couldn't bear the strain of my petulance and irritability.

Anyway, I continued on towards Epsom convinced that I'd

had a narrow escape from assassination. I then met the blokes from the operational squad who were going to brief me up about the new undercover job – I was to meet the informant, go out and get the lie of the land. They saw I was in a bit of a state by now. This wasn't the rough, tough, undercover cop with the red-hot reputation they'd been expecting. I rang the boss of the operation, who hadn't turned out for the preliminary briefing, and told him, 'I've had people on me, Guv. Don't know who, don't know why, but I'm not happy and I really don't want to go out and do this job tonight. There's something going on. I can't put my finger on it.'

The DI responded immediately. 'Right, no problem.'

He didn't ask questions. Such was my reputation at that stage that my word would not have been challenged.

'Are you all right? We'll get you out of Epsom in the back of a car and take you wherever you want to go.'

I was driven out, hiding under blankets like a fucking murderer and taken to my home. I said, 'Take me to the boozer, I need a fucking drink.'

I was totally hyped up and in a state of huge anxiety; my head felt like it might explode, and I foolishly thought a few pints would help.

I was sitting in the pub trying to fathom things out, like whether I was about to meet my maker, and what the fuck was going on. A drinking mate came up and started talking about another pal of mine who was going out with one of my ex-girlfriends. He said, 'When he took her out, you know, he did nothing but slag you off to her all night.'

Under normal circumstances I wouldn't have given a toss.

But with everything that had gone on that day and the fact that my mind was getting screwed up more and more by the day, it assumed an importance totally and utterly out of proportion. I finished my drink, put the glass down and walked straight across to the other side of the bar where my pal was sitting. With no further ado, I went BASH and gave him a fucking right-hander that knocked him flying right off his bar stool. It was a belter, the like of which had not been seen in that pub before.

He rolled over and over on the carpet and I then picked the bar stool up and raised it over my head. Now I was really going to do him. He was face down and I was going smash him on the back of his head. If I had, neither he nor I would be here to tell the story. He'd be dead and I'd be doing life. But literally in mid-swing, as I was bringing it down on him, someone shouted, 'NO ... NO.' At the very last second, I brought it smacking down into the middle of his back. That still hurt him a lot but, thankfully, it wasn't his bonce. People grabbed hold of me to pull me back. I was fired up and fighting them off. It wasn't me at all. I don't mind a good tear-up if it's part of the job or gloved-up in a ring, but I was never a pub brawler. I'd gone potty. At that moment in time, I was just a lunatic. I'd cracked and didn't know it. They managed to bundle me out of the back of the boozer and get me home out of harm's way.

I didn't sleep too well that night. There was too much going on in my head. Phantom assassins, untrustworthy friends, woman trouble. I woke up the next morning, took a long hard look at myself in the mirror and said, 'You need help ... you need fucking help ... urgent.'

I sent another pal round to see my mate I'd smashed up to say sorry, ask him not to call the police and to say I was straight off round to the doctor's for treatment.

Perhaps I should have seen it coming. Only a few months earlier, I had fucked up badly on a job in Manchester, a job that would normally have been a piece of cake.

I'd been called in by one of the out-of-town offices of the National Crime Squad, who had an informant giving them a lead into a gang of cocaine and cannabis dealers on Manchester's Moss Side, a district rife with gang warfare. The informant was totally different to the usual run of snouts I had dealt with, a bit of a country bumpkin, but that didn't make his information any the less valid.

I met up with him in turnip territory in Norfolk after he'd talked to the National Crime Squad and we got on OK. His info looked good and we set off for Moss Side ready to get stuck in. He was going to introduce me to a geezer who was ready to supply large quantities of cocaine or cannabis, whatever I wanted. We did the usual, got our background stories together, tested ourselves, checked each other. The five-hour journey up the motorway became a sort of classroom lesson on how to con a drugs gang and get out alive. I kept him on his toes, made sure he'd remembered what we'd rehearsed. Some of the informants were not the brightest people in the world and it was vital we'd got our act together. He was going to introduce me as a London drug-dealer, my tried and tested cover yet again, and we were going to do a £3,000 buy as a taster for bigger things in the future.

We arrived in Moss Side, inner-city decay at its worst, parked the car up, did the usual, but the geezer wasn't there so we were sent to the pub to wait. They left us for an hour, and came and spied on us a bit to see if they liked the look of us. Depending on your performance there, and it is a performance, you're summoned up to see the main man. We were led through the back of this pet shop, and talk about a run-down, shitty street in Moss Side – there were a couple of half-dead canaries and a moth-eaten parrot for sale but it was obviously a cover for drug-dealing. As I was taken out the back there were faces everywhere looking at me: they were all in on it. We really were in the heart of bandit territory. I went up the stairs at the back of the shop to a small office and there was a geezer sitting in a chair with a fucking 9mm pistol smack bang in front of him. I went through the door and he picked up the gun and pointed it first at me, 'Right, you sit there,' and then at the informant, 'You sit there.' I thought we were in trouble. I went right against all my better judgement. In all those years of being undercover, I should have known, should have turned round and said, 'Fuck you pal,' and walked away from it. I thought I knew my stuff. I should have said I wasn't dealing with some arsehole waving a gun. But no, I went ahead.

I analysed it time and time again afterwards. Now I know it was because I wasn't well, I wasn't myself, I had completely lost my sense of judgement.

Anyway, I didn't know then that I was cracking up. It's not something you ever want to consider. So I stupidly decided to carry on negotiating a drug deal with a gun-waving maniac. And he was a fucking nutter. Aged about fifty, local Manchester accent and built like a bulldog. And if we were talking mental illness at that stage, he would have left me standing. He would suddenly go off on long rambling statements in the middle of a conversation, about why we couldn't do the trade, this, that and the other. Not much of it made any sense. He was a horrible fucker, and I mean a really horrible fucker. Again, I had committed a cardinal sin in undercover work – I had taken a dislike to him. I'd let my personal emotions get in the way of the job. So now my motive to get him nicked was because I disliked him. That was wrong, and foolish. You've lost it when you do that.

We carried on with the deal despite my intense dislike of the man and agreed that the only way we could talk about him supplying big quantities of drugs, like hundreds of kilos of puff and kilo upon kilo of cocaine, was to start with a trial purchase, a tester. He offered me a kilo of puff. Well, he didn't exactly offer me, he told me exactly what was going down. Then he told me there would be an ounce of cocaine as well. The coke was about a grand and the puff about £1,800. The bastard was charging me street prices instead of wholesale prices. But I agreed to it and thought I could persuade the management to spend that amount of money to put him in the frame on bigger deals later on. This fucker did need nicking as far as I was concerned, and I wasn't too fussed how I did it. But the operation was becoming fatally flawed by now because I was riding a grudge.

We arranged to make a meet and do the trade a few days later at a service station on the M6 just outside Manchester. I pulled a colleague out from the squad to act as my driver. As we arrived, I could see the place was heaving with opposition. I could pick them out; I'd developed a technique over the years to spot the wrong 'uns. I'd just look around and see them immediately.

CRACKING UP

You weigh up the enemy before you start the trade. Again, I should have pulled out. The cards were stacked against us. We were horrendously outnumbered. The fuckers could have done what they liked to us. But still I went ahead. I went in and met nutty bollocks and he made a very distinct point of letting me know he still had the shooter on him. He was sitting there in the café area with this lunatic henchman of his beside him. These were not business people, they were thugs and robbers, men of violence. No fucking business acumen whatsoever. Lo and behold, against the odds, we did a transaction. He handed me an ounce of cocaine and kilo of cannabis. Only it wasn't. They'd dummied up some parcels to make it look like coke and puff. I just took them. I was so keen to get out of there I didn't test the gear in my usual way.

There was an underpass there and they followed us in; they had people plotted up at each end, and I became convinced we were going to be shot. I thought they were going to rob us for the three grand and leave us for dead. It seemed a lot of trouble for a miserly £3,000 in drug-deal terms, but the main man was so unpredictable and so frightening that I really wouldn't have put it past him. The atmosphere got increasingly threatening. I got hold of the parcels, gave them a quick feel and said, 'Yeah, seems OK,' and handed them the money my colleague had in the car plotted up close by. I couldn't wait to get out of there. I slung the parcels in the car and got in myself and told my driver to get the hell out of it. If I'd been myself I'd have carried out quick tests on the gear. Then, of course, I'd have been calling their bluff. And I honestly don't think I'd be here today to tell the tale.

'Look, mate, who are you trying to con?' wouldn't have gone down a bundle. Perhaps fate was on my side that day after all.

I opened up the parcels on the way back to the debriefing and said, 'We've been had. This isn't proper gear.' The young kid I had driving for me said, 'Oh shit, I hope this doesn't rub off on my undercover career.'

'Don't you worry,' I said, 'I've made the mistake. It's nothing to do with you.' I said it was one small slip in a ten-year career of undercover work in which I had seized drugs worth millions of pounds. I'd take it on the chin if there was a problem.

But I didn't reckon I'd be slaughtered over one cock-up, losing three grand, among my many successes. I explained to the operational bosses that we'd been had and suggested we just left it at that. We *had* to leave it at that. I couldn't go back into them for a second time. They'd know I was a patsy (stooge) and it wouldn't work. The Manchester mob was probably happy that they'd had a couple of Londoners over for three grand and would leave it at that. I supplied the local CID with all the intelligence I could and said the main man definitely did need looking at. With that I exited stage right and headed for home.

It was the last undercover operation of that nature I ever went out on. The storm clouds were gathering over the career I loved. The dreadful toll of my double life was beginning to manifest itself in bouts of irrational behaviour and marred perceptions about my own infallibility.

I was under a lot of strain, living full time under a moody name after the Mafia death threat, moving home for the same reason, negative equity as a result, love life falling apart, but I thought I could handle it all. I'd built up this reputation at work as the iron man who could handle anything and I'd ended up believing my own publicity. Realistically I was having to cope with it myself because the Old Bill had never done this with one of their own before – here's your new identity, live it. It was a ground-breaking development. They'd done it for witnesses and supergrasses under threat through the witness protection programme, but not for another copper. There wasn't a familiar procedure to go through. Now it was having serious detrimental effects on my work and my home life.

To give credit where it's due, my boss at SO10, Commander Roy Ramm, a greatly respected senior officer at Scotland Yard, was shrewd enough to notice there was a problem in the autumn of 1993, five months after my forced move.

'Bleksley is clearly showing signs of the strain of trying to resolve the situation,' he wrote in a confidential report which came into my hands. But the big white chiefs at the Yard did nothing. Anyone with half a brain would have said, 'What are we doing about it?' if they had read Roy Ramm's report. This invisible threat from the Mafia was doing my head in, and it was compounded by my workload and my domestic problems. It was all slowly churning away; my brain was doing overtime, my stress levels running on overdrive. By 1994, when I went back to my house and stuck the key in the door, I wasn't returning to a home. I was walking into living yet another life, swapping one false identity with another, an actor changing roles after the matinee performance. It wasn't like I was kicking my shoes off, putting on the telly and having a nice cup of tea, made up for the night, girlfriend on one arm and remote control in the other, resting up after a hard day's work. That's what I needed to get things straight in my head. It wasn't happening. I'd become very difficult to live with, I know that now. The strain I was under was taken out on the person nearest and dearest. I had become a horror to live with, a horror to be around.

It all came to a head when I came home one night, stuck my head round the kitchen door and saw my girlfriend downing the last of what I thought was red wine in a pint glass. I thought, what the fuck's she doing drinking pints of red wine? Then she slammed the glass down and I saw the residue of powder in the bottom. She'd got forty-eight paracetamol tablets, crushed them up and tried to kill herself with an overdose. I rang her sisters, who lived nearby, and they came over and rushed her into Bromley Hospital. I went along as well. My conscience was pricked even though I'd been such a monster to her.

They gave her a solution which made her vomit up the tablets and she was OK. But as I was waiting in there, feeling deeply chastened, nurses came up to me and said, 'Oh, who are you?'

'I'm the boyfriend,' I replied. You can imagine the reception. Everyone who walked past gave me that sort of stare that said I was little better than pond life. Her sisters took her home that night and I went back to my house with the song 'Things Can Only Get Better' blaring out of the radio. I stupidly thought to myself, perhaps they will now she's out of my hair, that's how arrogant I'd become, blaming her, not myself – but little did I know that things would only get a great deal worse. On the following Monday, I was back at work, the attempted suicide of my girlfriend adding to the pressures, but with me carrying on working with no apparent problems and still clocking up some notable successes. My performance level was not being affected, and I was still holding it together as far as the squad was concerned.

Then came the fatal trip to Manchester, followed by the unforgivable attack on my pal, which finally told me that it was all over in the world of undercover policing for Peter Bleksley. It was time to throw in the towel and seek medical help.

There were many dark days to come. Arrangements were made by the Yard to admit me to a private psychiatric hospital in Ticehurst in Sussex. I was referred to an eminent psychiatrist called Gordon Turnbull, famed for having debriefed the British pilots downed in the Gulf War and straightening their heads out. After the first consultation, he recommended that I should take a holiday from work. My symptoms were like the stressed-out Gulf pilots, he reckoned, and a nice golfing holiday in Scotland would soon put me on the road to recovery.

I enjoyed the golf; a couple of pals came up to stay with me, and we had a few drinks. But the demons were still there. I was signed off work for an indefinite period and Dr Turnbull agreed that it might be beneficial if I went to college. I signed on to do an access course at Greenwich University which would bring me up to entry standard and allow me to do a degree course afterwards, in psychology of all things. My employers were happy with this, and the eminent Dr Turnbull was happy as well.

Fucking psychology? I was off my trolley. I was fucking ill. I was a danger to other people. The runaway train was out of control. I should have been hospitalised by now, but that didn't happen.

So I signed on for college. I moved out of my home and began living as Peter Bleksley once again. The doctor agreed that

THE GANGBUSTER

I had been too many different people for too long and it was time to return to basics. I went from Peter Bleksley, undercover detective, to Peter Bleksley, mature student of psychology, and not surprisingly my health continued in a downward spiral to the detriment of all those who had the misfortune to be around me at the time. My behaviour became more and more unpredictable, irrational and anti-social. People began to distance themselves from me. Superman had broken down and there was nothing to fix him. No one knew what to do.

Finally, there was no alternative but to admit me to Ticehurst Hospital as an in-patient. I discharged myself after two days. I was still freaking out, so two mates took me to Greenwich District Hospital. I was in there for three and a half weeks and showed signs of improvement. The NHS doctors and nurses were fantastic, spending hours probing the deepest recesses of the mind and treating me with a marvellous drug called Stelazine which really worked. I knew I would never be able to resume my undercover career but now there was a light at the end of the tunnel.

I make no excuse for dealing with my illness in some depth because I feel it is important to the police service in general that much closer scrutiny is given to the health of all officers working in the more strenuous areas of the force.

It had been generally mooted before my breakdown that perhaps it would be a good idea if all undercover officers saw a psychiatrist or psychologist every six months to make sure they were handling the pressures. Lo and behold, overnight almost, the programme was brought into operation and remains there to this day. But it was too late for me. I felt the force had been negligent and that I deserved some compensation for this mental torture I had been through, and sought help from the Police Federation to sue the Met for damages. Substantial damages were being won for officers subjected to far less damaging conditions than mine, with some female officers winning huge sums for sexual harassment and what have you. The Federation solicitors told me in May 1996 that basically I didn't have a case. I was dumbfounded. Their arguments didn't stack up. I wasn't one for giving up, never had been, so I said 'Bollocks,' and went to a little old firm of local solicitors called Cattermoles in Welling, which had been recommended by a friend, sat down with one of the partners, Richard Lewis, to explain my position and he said, 'I feel confident you have a case. I'll be more than willing to take it on. But you need a barrister and it will be expensive,' he said.

Scotland Yard adopted their usual delaying tactics, a sort of economic Mexican stand-off until you crumble through lack of money, and Richard Lewis suggested I ask the Police Federation lawyers to reconsider. They got counsel's advice and were then told, 'Actually Mr Bleksley does have a case.' It was an amazing U–turn which left the Fed solicitors with egg on their faces but me feeling that at last I was on the road to getting justice.

The solicitor appointed to handle the case told me from the start that it was going to be a long, messy, tough fight. I said, 'OK, let's go for it. I believe in what I'm doing.'

I had been warned it wouldn't be easy and it wasn't. Months and months then years of paperwork, seeing this psychiatrist then that psychiatrist, and obtaining the opinions of employment consultants to calculate the potential loss of earnings which related to the size of the claim. It was extremely wearing, but I was determined to press on.

In August 1996, I returned to work, an office-bound job with shortened hours. Most of the squad were pleased to see me back. They'd known me in my heyday, respected me and no one gave me grief. I wasn't stigmatised, but there was plenty of piss-taking.

'Here comes the nutter,' and all that sort of thing, very light-hearted. A lot of the people there knew it could happen to them. I responded by acting a bit bonkers, feeding the birds with stale bread and talking to the trees. It was all a bit of a laugh and I was getting better all the time. I felt a bit guilty drawing a salary on the one hand and suing the Met on the other, but I felt it had to be done as much for me as for anyone who might find themselves in the same boat in later years.

* * *

I've thought long and hard about what I should say and what I shouldn't say in this book. I want it to be an accurate record of a remarkable chapter in my life. I don't want it to be a tirade against Scotland Yard, although there are areas of bitterness that will never diminish. I left, a sick man, after more than twenty years in the police, the vast majority of which was spent doing high-octane frighteningly dangerous work. All of this finally drained my mental resources. My reward: £10,000 in compensation. Less than six months' pay at the height of my prowess. I learned many secrets about Scotland Yard, and I learned of many shameful secrets of fellow officers.

I was once told of a plot to murder a detective and his

girlfriend over their involvement in the theft of £200,000 drugs money by other serving officers. I was never able to verify it and have consequently remained silent, though it troubles me from time to time. I was also told of a high-society drug-dealer allegedly supplying cocaine to a member of the Royal Family. A proposed undercover operation was abandoned in its very early stages. Because I cannot know whether such an allegation was true or simply one of the myriad unfounded pieces of information that are channelled into the police every day, I mention it only in passing.

In early 1999 I came to terms with the fact that the police force held no future for me in any capacity. It came to a head after I had been posted to Orpington police station. I was soon to be Mr Plod back in uniform, the glory days long gone and future prospects bleak. I thought I could fight back, but the sniping of my new so-called colleagues, the sniggering behind my back, finally made me decide enough was enough and I handed in my ticket. It was all over for Detective Constable Peter Bleksley, the undercover cop who got in too deep for his own good. The fight for damages continued for a full five years until April 2000 when it was finally settled out of court. Just £10,000. My lawyers had said to look forward to a six-figure sum. But it was an enormous relief all round in many ways.

* * *

I am well, and have now been married to my wonderful wife Sarah for nearly twenty years. My three sons are a source of continual joy. In recent years I have travelled the world providing security to the super rich and as a private investigator

THE GANGBUSTER

I have solved some very serious crimes. I've written for the BBC and worked as a consultant on many TV shows and films. You may have seen me recently as 'The Chief' on Channel 4's hit show *Hunted*, and you have almost certainly seen or heard me in the media commenting on crime and policing. I continue to explore new horizons and enjoy life as myself; no false identities, no disguises, just myself. The real Peter Bleksley.